THINGS FALL APART

THINGS FALL APART

Containing the Spillover
from an Iraqi Civil War

DANIEL L. BYMAN
KENNETH M. POLLACK

BROOKINGS INSTITUTION PRESS
Washington, D.C.

Copyright © 2007
THE BROOKINGS INSTITUTION
1775 Massachusetts Avenue, N.W., Washington, D.C. 20036
www.brookings.edu

A SABAN CENTER AT THE BROOKINGS INSTITUTION BOOK
Originally released as Analysis Paper 11, January 2007

Library of Congress Cataloging-in-Publication data
Byman, Daniel, 1967–
  Things fall apart : containing the spillover from an Iraqi civil war / Daniel L. Byman, Kenneth M. Pollack.
      p.   cm.
  "Originally released as Analysis Paper 11, January 2007"—T.p. verso.
  Summary: "Studies the history of recent civil wars to derive lessons regarding the impact of full-scale civil wars on the security, prosperity, and national interests of other states. Proposes recommendations for the United States as it confronts the possibility of a similar conflict in Iraq and its spillover into the region"—Provided by publisher.
  Includes bibliographical references and index.
  ISBN-13: 978-0-8157-1379-1 (pbk. : alk. paper)
  ISBN-10: 0-8157-1379-7 (pbk. : alk. paper)
  1. Iraq War, 2003– 2. Civil war—Iraq. 3. Civil war 4. Peace-building. I. Pollack, Kenneth M. (Kenneth Michael), 1966– II. Title.
  DS79.76.B96 2007
  303.6'4—dc22   2007012276

1 3 5 7 9 8 6 4 2

Printed on acid-free paper

Typeset in Minion

Composition by Peter Lindeman
Arlington, Virginia

Printed by Victor Graphics
Baltimore, Maryland

Contents

PREFACE

With each passing day, Iraq sinks deeper into the abyss of civil war. The history of such wars is that they are disastrous for all involved. Asking who won most civil wars is a bit like asking who "won" the San Francisco earthquake. Unfortunately, we may soon be forced to confront how best we can avoid "losing" an Iraqi civil war.

Starting to answer that question is the purpose of this study. We hope that the leaders of the United States and Iraq will find a way to stop what seems to be an irrevocable slide into an all-out civil war. Given their repeated failures to do so, and how badly the situation had deteriorated by the time this report went to press, however, we believe that the United States and its allies must begin thinking about how to deal with the consequences of massive failure in Iraq.

During the course of the research for this study, one ominous fact that loomed large from history was that in previous civil wars there seemed to be a "point of no return"—a moment when the psychological forces propelling civil war became irreversible—but that moment was never apparent to the participants themselves. Historians looking back on a conflict could often agree on when that point was reached, but at the time those caught up in the struggle typically believed that solutions and alternative paths were still available long after they had been overtaken by events. This should sober us to the possibility that it may already be too late to save Iraq. While we want to believe that an all-out civil war can still be averted, albeit if only through Herculean exertions on the part of Washington and Baghdad, the warnings of history suggest that perhaps we too are simply repeating the same mistakes of those caught up in past civil wars.

When we began this study in the spring of 2006, we made a list of indicators of when a state in civil strife passes such a point of no return. We watched with dismay as the situation in Iraq worsened and indicator after indicator went from our drawing board to Iraq's daily reality (these indicators are contained in Appendix F).

With this in mind, we set out to mine the history of recent similar internecine conflicts for lessons that might help the United States to devise a set of strategies to deal with the looming prospect of a full-scale Iraqi civil war. We scrutinized the history of civil wars in Lebanon in the 1970s and 1980s; Afghanistan, Bosnia, Chechnya, Croatia, Georgia, Kosovo, Macedonia, the Nagorno-Karabakh conflict, and Tajikistan during the 1990s; as well as the conflicts in Congo and Somalia that rage to this day (we present eight of these cases in five appendices to the paper to provide additional historical insight for readers wishing to delve deeper into this question themselves). From these wars we distilled a set of lessons regarding how civil wars can affect the interests of other countries, even distant ones like the United States, and then used those lessons to fashion a set of recommendations for how Washington might begin to develop a new strategy for an Iraq caught up in all-out civil war.

In doing so, we attempted to set aside our own feelings of sympathy and concern for the Iraqi people themselves. The only thing that the United States can do to help them is to *prevent* the descent into full-scale civil war. Once it has happened, the United States will have failed them; and this self-same history makes frighteningly clear that it is impossible for well-meaning outsiders to limit the humanitarian tragedies of an all-out civil war, unless they are willing to intervene massively to bring it to an end. We note that the commitments needed to end such a war are effectively the same resources the United States and its allies are unwilling to commit today to prevent its outbreak. Consequently, we felt that we had to look past the tragedy that will be visited upon the Iraqi people (for whose sake the United States nominally launched the invasion in 2003), and instead consider how such a civil war could affect U.S. interests and what the United States could do to minimize those effects.

Our conclusions are not encouraging. We found that much of what is considered "conventional wisdom" among Westerners about how to handle civil wars is probably mistaken. For instance, we found little to support the idea that the United States could easily walk away from an Iraqi civil war— that we could tell the Iraqis that we tried, that they failed, and that we were leaving them to their fates. We found that "spillover" is common in massive civil wars; that while its intensity can vary considerably, at its worst it can have truly catastrophic effects; and that Iraq has all the earmarks of creating quite severe spillover problems. By the same token, we also found that the commonly held belief that the best way to handle a civil war is to back one side to help it win was equally mistaken. We found few cases of an outside country successfully helping one side or another to victory, and the outside power usually suffered heavy costs in the process.

Nevertheless, because we fear that the United States will not have the option to avoid the problems that will be created for U.S. strategic interests by Iraq's descent into all-out civil war, we have presented a series of U.S. policy choices that Washington might employ to do so. They mostly amount to a reinforcing set of efforts designed to contain the likely spillover from this nightmare. Each flows from one or more aspects of our analysis of the patterns of spillover from civil wars. They suggest that if the United States is skillful, determined, patient, and lucky, it may be possible to limit the impact of an all-out Iraqi civil war. To be blunt, the same history suggests that it will be very, very difficult to do so. Few nations that tried to contain spillover from an all-out civil war were successful, and while they were all less powerful than the United States and did not attempt a systematic analysis of how to contain spillover from civil wars, the frequency of their failure should be foremost in our minds. It was arrogance in the face of history that led us to blithely assume we could invade without preparing for an occupation, and we would do well to show greater humility when assimilating its lessons about what we fear will be the next step in Iraq's tragic history.

ACKNOWLEDGMENTS

This study represents the culmination of considerable labor over the course of the past year, and as can only be the case there were many people whose assistance proved invaluable. We benefited from outstanding support for our research. Sara Moller, at Georgetown University, and Irena Sargsyan, at the Saban Center, served as our principal research assistants during this time and their efforts defy superlatives. We simply could not have completed this task without them. They, in turn, were assisted by Brad Humphries, Bilal Saab, and Blair Trimble at the Saban Center, all of whom took up their own pieces of our research with energy, enthusiasm, and efficiency.

A great many of our colleagues were willing to provide extremely useful comments on our work at various stages. Rochelle Davis of Georgetown; Bernard Harborne of the World Bank; Emile El-Hokayem of the Stimson Center; Ivo Daalder, Khalid Koser, Michael O'Hanlon, and Carlos Pascual of the Brookings Institution, and Martin S. Indyk, Bruce Riedel, and Tamara Cofman Wittes of the Saban Center, provided us with penetrating insights into our various case studies as well as trenchant criticisms of the study itself. In addition, we presented versions of this work to a range of experts in the U.S. military and intelligence communities at various times during 2006. While we cannot thank them all by name, their reactions, suggestions, and even disagreements were critical to us in refining our treatment of this subject.

Andrew Apostolou of the Saban Center did his usual superb job of editing this monster, and Chris Krupinski handled the layout of the original analysis paper with her usual style—and unusual speed—to ensure that it was produced in a timely fashion.

Abbreviations

ACR	Armored Cavalry Regiment
AMAL	Afwaj Al-Muqawama Al-Lubnaniya (Battalions of the Lebanese Resistance)
BCT	Brigade Combat Team
BOSNIA	Bosnia and Herzegovina
GCC	Gulf Cooperation Council
GDP	Gross Domestic Product
GIA	Groupe Islamique Armé (Armed Islamic Group)
IDP	Internally Displaced Person
IRA	Irish Republican Army
IRGC	Islamic Revolutionary Guards Corps
IRP	Islamic Renaissance Party
KDP	Kurdistan Democratic Party
KLA	Kosovo Liberation Army
LTTE	Liberation Tigers of Tamil Eelam
NATO	North Atlantic Treaty Organization
NGO	Nongovernmental Organization
NSC	National Security Council
OPEC	Organization of Petroleum Exporting Countries
PC	Principals Committee

PKK	Partiya Karkerên Kurdistan (Kurdistan Workers' Party)
PLA	Palestine Liberation Army
PLO	Palestine Liberation Organization
PUK	Patriotic Union of Kurdistan
RCT	Marine Regimental Combat Team
RPF	Rwandan Patriotic Front
SCIRI	The Supreme Council for the Islamic Revolution in Iraq
SLA	South Lebanon Army
UAE	United Arab Emirates
UNHCR	United Nations High Commissioner for Refugees
UNITA	União Nacional pela Independência Total de Angola (National Union for the Total Independence of Angola)
UNITAF	Unified Task Force
UNOSOM	United Nations Operation in Somalia
UNPROFOR	United Nations Protection Force
WFP	World Food Programme

THINGS FALL APART

1

INTRODUCTION

Iraq is rapidly descending into all-out civil war. Unfortunately, the United States probably will not be able to just walk away from the chaos. Even setting aside the humanitarian nightmare that will ensue, a full-scale civil war would likely consume more than Iraq: historically, such massive conflicts have often had highly deleterious effects on neighboring countries and other outside states. Spillover from an Iraqi civil war could be disastrous. America has too many strategic interests at stake in the Middle East to ignore the consequences. Thus, it is imperative that the United States develop a plan for containing an all-out Iraqi civil war.

As part of a containment approach, our new priority would have to become preventing the Iraqi conflict from spilling over and destabilizing neighboring states, an approach that requires deterring neighboring states from intervening, helping mitigate the risks associated with refugees, striking terrorist havens, and otherwise changing our policy to reflect the painful reality that the U.S. effort to bring peace and stability to Iraq has failed. Not planning now for containing the Iraqi civil war could lead its devastation to become even greater, engulfing not only Iraq but also much of the surrounding region and gravely threatening U.S. interests.

To that end, this study draws on the history of recent civil wars in Afghanistan, Bosnia, Chechnya, Congo, Croatia, Georgia, Kosovo, Lebanon, the Nagorno-Karabakh conflict, Somalia, and Tajikistan. It employs lessons derived from these cases regarding the impact of full-scale civil wars on the security, prosperity, and national interests of other states to derive recommendations for the United States as it confronts the possibility of a similar conflict in Iraq.

PATTERNS OF SPILLOVER

The United States will confront a range of problems stemming from the collapse of Iraq into all-out civil war. These will likely include the humanitarian tragedy of hundreds of thousands (or more) of Iraqis killed along with several times that number maimed and millions of refugees. American influence in the Middle East will be drastically diminished, as will our ability to promote economic and political reform there. The loss of Iraqi oil production could have a significant impact on global oil prices, and supply disruptions elsewhere in the region, particularly in Saudi Arabia, could be particularly devastating.

However, the greatest problems that the United States must be prepared to confront are the patterns of "spillover," by which civil wars in one state can deleteriously affect another, or in some cases destabilize a region or create global threats. Spillover is the tendency of civil wars to impose burdens, create instability, and even trigger civil wars in other, usually neighboring countries. In some cases, spillover can be as relatively mild as the economic hardships and the limited numbers of refugees that Hungary and Romania coped with during the various Yugoslav civil wars of the 1990s. At the other end of the spectrum, spillover can turn civil war into regional war—as Lebanon did in the 1970s and 1980s—and can cause other civil wars in neighboring countries—just as the civil war in Rwanda triggered the catastrophic civil war in next-door Congo. Unfortunately, Iraq appears to possess most, if not all, of the factors that would make spillover worse rather than better.

Historically, six patterns of spillover have been the most harmful in other cases of all-out civil war:

Refugees

In addition to the humanitarian considerations for innocent civilians fleeing civil war, refugees can create strategic problems. They represent large groupings of embittered people who serve as a ready recruiting pool for armed groups still waging the civil war. As a result, they frequently involve foreign countries in the civil war as the neighboring government attempts to prevent the refugee-based militias from attacking their country of origin, and/or the neighboring government must protect the refugees from attack by their civil war enemies. Moreover, large refugee flows can overstrain the economies and even change the demographic balances of small or weak neighboring states.

Terrorism

Terrorists often find a home in states in civil war, as al-Qaʻida did in Afghanistan. However, the civil wars themselves also frequently breed new terrorist groups—Hizballah, the Palestine Liberation Organization, Hamas, the Groupe Islamique Armé (Armed Islamic Group) of Algeria, and the Liberation Tigers of Tamil Eelam were all born of civil wars. Many of these groups start by focusing on local targets but then shift to international attacks—usually against those they believe are aiding their enemies in the civil war.

Radicalization of Neighboring Populations

Neighboring populations often become highly agitated and mobilized by developments in the civil war next door. Groups in one state may identify with co-religionists, co-ethnics, or other groups with similar identities in a state embroiled in civil war. A civil war may also encourage groups in neighboring states to demand, or even fight, for a reordering of their domestic political arrangements. Examples of this radicalization phenomenon include the anger felt by ethnic Albanians in the Balkans at the treatment of Kosovar Albanians by the Serbian regime during the Kosovo war—which might very well have pushed the Albanian government to intervene had NATO not done so instead—as well as the decision by Syria's Sunni Muslim Brotherhood to rise up against the ʻAlawi regime, which led to a Syrian civil war from 1976 to 1982.

Secession Breeds Secessionism

Some civil wars are caused by one group within a country seeking its independence, while in other cases the civil war leads one group or another to seek its independence as the solution to its problems. Frequently, other groups in similar circumstances (either in the country in civil war or in neighboring countries) may follow suit if the first group appears to have achieved some degree of success. Thus, Slovenia's secession from Yugoslavia started the first of those civil wars, but it also provoked Croatia to declare its independence, which forced Bosnia to follow suit, which later convinced Kosovar Albanian nationalists to try for the same, and eventually provoked a secessionist movement among Albanians in Macedonia.

Economic Losses

Civil wars can be costly to other countries, particularly neighbors. First, there are the direct costs of caring for refugees, fighting terrorism, and mounting major interventions, whether covert or overt. Beyond that, civil wars tend to scare off investment, impose security and insurance costs on trade, disrupt transportation networks and supplier arrangements, and increase a state's health care burden, to name but a few.

Neighborly Interventions

The problems created by these other forms of spillover often provoke neighboring states to intervene—to stop terrorism as Israel tried repeatedly in Lebanon, to halt the flow of refugees as the Europeans tried in Yugoslavia, or to end (or respond to) the radicalization of their own population as Syria did in Lebanon. These interventions usually end badly for all involved. Local groups typically turn out to be poor proxies and are often unable or unwilling to accomplish the objectives of their backers. This often provokes the intervening state to use its own military forces to do the job itself. The result is that many civil wars become regional wars because once one country invades, other states often do the same, if only to prevent the initial invader from conquering the state in civil war.

Iraq is already manifesting all of these patterns of spillover. This suggests that these factors may intensify as the civil war worsens, and argues that the United States should be bracing itself for particularly severe manifestations of spillover throughout the Persian Gulf region.

Options for Containing Spillover from an Iraqi Civil War

The historical record of states that attempted to minimize or contain spillover from all-out civil wars is poor. Nearly all of them failed to do so. Those that "succeeded" often paid such a high cost as to render their victories pyrrhic. In many cases, states failed so miserably to prevent spillover that they were eventually forced to mount massive invasions to attempt to end the civil war instead. Successful efforts to end civil wars generally required a peace agreement to bring the war to closure and then an international security intervention with a personnel-to-population ratio of 20 per thousand (or higher) to keep the peace, combined with a major injection of international resources. In Iraq (excluding Kurdistan), such a security deployment could equate to a deployment of roughly 450,000 troops.

Despite these odds, if Iraq does descend into an all-out civil war, the United States probably will have no choice but to try to contain it. Drawing on the patterns of spillover described above, we developed a baker's dozen of possible tactics that the United States might use, alone or in combination:

1. Don't try to pick winners

There will be an enormous temptation for the United States to aid one Iraqi faction against another in an effort to manage the Iraqi civil war from within. In theory, the United States could choose proxies and use them to secure its interests. However, proxies often fail in their assigned tasks or turn against their masters. As a result, such efforts rarely succeed, and in the specific circumstances of Iraq, such an effort appears particularly dubious.

It is extremely difficult to know which group will be able to prevail in a civil war. Civil wars are highly susceptible to the emergence of skillful military leaders who tend to start the war as unknowns and gain power only by proving their skills in battle, such as Afghanistan's Ahmed Shah Massoud. Numbers alone rarely prove decisive—Lebanon's Druze were a major force in their civil war despite the small size of their community, whereas Lebanon's Sunnis rarely wielded power commensurate with their demographic weight. This makes it difficult, if not impossible, to know which group could benefit from external assistance, and history is rife with states that poured arms and money into a civil war to back a faction that could not make use of it.

Moreover, Iraq is badly fragmented—especially within its ethnic and religious communities—making this approach even more difficult. There is no single "Shi'i" or "Sunni" faction to back. There are only dozens of small to medium-size militias, most of which hate one another with equal intensity regardless of ethnic or religious differences or similarities. Moreover, there is no manageable way for the United States to back one faction or another from a diplomatic and logistical perspective. The Shi'i groups are all tied in some way to Iran, and would have to be supplied through Iran because Iraq's other neighbors (except Syria, which has no border with Iraq's Shi'i Arab areas) are Sunni-dominated and would never allow American support to flow to Shi'i militias. The Kurds would be happy to have American assistance, but it is equally unlikely that we could convince any of Iraq's neighbors to support a Kurdish takeover of the country. Washington could certainly find regional support for backing the Sunnis, but most of their armed groups all seem to be closely tied to al-Qa'ida and other *salafi jihadists* (holy warriors), and their community represents only 18 to 20 percent of the population, making this a very difficult proposition. Indeed, the only Sunni warlord who effectively governed Iraq was Saddam Hussein, who had to build one of the worst totalitarian states in history to do so. Finally, as was the case in Lebanon, American backing of one side in the conflict could cause other states, particularly Iran, to ramp up their own interventions, rather than end them.

2. Avoid active support for partition. . . for now

Eventually, after years of bloody civil war, Iraq may be ready for a stable partition. However, a major U.S. effort to enact secession or partition today would be likely to trigger even more massacres and ethnic cleansing. Other than the Kurds, few Iraqis want their country divided, nor do they want to leave their homes. While many are doing so out of necessity, and some are even moving pre-emptively, this is not diminishing the impetus toward warfare. For the most part it is doing the opposite, causing many of those fleeing their homes to join vicious sectarian militias like Muqtada as-Sadr's Jaysh al-Mahdi (Army of the Mahdi) in hope of regaining their property or at least exacting revenge on whoever drove them out. Other than the Kurds, few of Iraq's leaders favor partition, instead wanting to control as much (or all) of it as they can. Nor is it clear that a move to partition would result in a neat division of Iraq into three smaller states. As noted above, the Sunnis and the Shi'ah are badly fragmented among dozens of different militias of widely varying sizes, but none of them are large enough to quickly or easily unite their community. Thus, far more likely than creating a new Sunni state and a new Shi'i state, Mesopotamian Iraq would splinter into chaotic warfare and warlordism.

Partition would be practical only if there were a political agreement to do so that was then enforced by adequate numbers of foreign forces. This would likely require at least 450,000 troops, the same concentration as was needed to enforce the Dayton Accords in Bosnia. Moreover, the situation would be worse in the near term because the Iraqis will see the United States as imposing a highly unpopular partition on them, as opposed to Dayton where the key parties accepted the peace agreement. In short, trying to partition Iraq as a way of containing or ending a civil war is unlikely to succeed absent years of slaughter, a peace agreement among the parties, and a much greater American military commitment.

3. Don't dump the problem on the United Nations

The United Nations can play a valuable role in helping legitimate international action in Iraq and providing technical expertise in certain humanitarian areas. The United States should seek UN assistance to provide aid, police camps, and otherwise help contain spillover. However, the United Nations suffers from numerous bureaucratic limits and should not be expected to provide security. In particular, Washington should not expect, or ask, the United Nations to police refugee camps, dissuade foreign intervention, or otherwise handle difficult security tasks for which it is ill-equipped. Likewise, UN administrative capacity is limited. Although the World Food Programme and United Nations High Commissioner for Refugees have many highly skilled professionals, the institutions as a whole move slowly in times of crisis. They often take months to fully establish themselves— months in which tens of thousands may die.

4. Pull back from Iraqi population centers

An all-out civil war in Iraq will be a humanitarian catastrophe, and there will be a strong humanitarian impulse to maintain American forces in Iraq's population centers to try to minimize the extent of the violence. Historically, the only solutions to this situation are either to prevent the outbreak of violence in the first place or to intervene decisively with the forces to end the war altogether—which in the case of Iraq would require the same commitment of roughly 450,000 troops. Half-hearted humanitarian interventions to diminish the violence tend to backfire badly, as the Multi-National Force in Lebanon in the 1980s and the misguided UN safe haven effort in Bosnia in the 1990s demonstrated.

While safe havens may prove to be an important element of a new American policy to deal with Iraq in civil war (see below), we should not assume that they can be easily created in the center of the country, in the midst of the combat, to protect Iraqi population centers. Limited forays are likely to do little more than cause American casualties and embroil the United States more deeply in the conflict while courting humiliating defeat. Consequently, when the United States decides that reconstruction has failed and that all-out civil war in Iraq has broken out, the only rational course of action, horrific though it will be, is to abandon Iraq's population centers and refocus American efforts from preventing civil war to containing it.

5. Provide support to Iraq's neighbors

Radicalization of neighboring populations is frequently the most dangerous form of spillover, but it is also the most ineffable, making it difficult to address. What appears to have prevented such radicalization in the past, against the odds, has been rising levels of socioeconomic prosperity and particularly high government capacity in the threatened neighboring states. This suggests that the United States can reduce the risk of radicalization in Iraq's neighbors by helping them to build government capacity and increase their ability to placate key segments of their populations. Wealthy countries like Saudi Arabia would not receive economic aid, but could instead be provided additional technical assistance to improve the country's overall strength in the face of various challenges. Aid also provides some leverage with these governments, making them more likely to hesitate before going against U.S. wishes. Generous aid packages can be explicitly provided with the proviso that they will be stopped (and sanctions possibly applied instead) if the recipient country intervenes in the Iraqi civil war.

6. Bolster regional stability

An all-out civil war in Iraq will increase instability throughout the region, possibly to disastrous levels, as a result of spillover. Consequently, it will be of considerable importance that the United States do whatever it can to remove other sources of instability in the region and otherwise increase its stability. Unfortunately, at this point a number of other problems are adding to the general instability of the region. Two that loom large include the ongoing deadlock in Lebanon and the worsening state of Israeli-Palestinian affairs.

These two problems will magnify the shockwaves coming from Iraq; therefore, the threat of spillover from an Iraqi civil war ought to add a strategic imperative to the diplomatic and humanitarian considerations pushing the United States to make a greater effort to stabilize Lebanon and revitalize a Middle East peace process. Moreover, the absence of a peace process between the Israelis and Palestinians bolsters radical forces in the Middle East and hurts the credibility of U.S. allies. Throughout the 1990s, the appearance of a vital peace process made it easier for the United States to deal with any number of ultimately unrelated problems in the Middle East, and a revival of that process would likely do so again, particularly with regard to coordinating regional efforts to contain spillover from a civil war in Iraq.

Saying that the United States should aggressively pursue an Arab-Israeli peace should not be seen as code for pressuring Israel; Washington must work tirelessly to broker a peace, but should not attempt to impose it on any party. Likewise, a peace process itself is not a panacea. However, it will help improve the U.S. image among many Arabs. Even more important, it will allow more moderate voices to move closer to Washington without being discredited. This will be vital for close, open, and continual cooperation with Iraq's Arab neighbors.

Similarly, the United States must make a more determined effort to build a capable Lebanese government able to provide its citizens with the security and basic services they often lack—and which among the Shi'ah has driven so many into the arms of Hizballah. Although Washington must also hold firm to its determination to see Hizballah disarmed, it should not hold the provision of aid to the Lebanese government and people hostage to this requirement. Doing so simply bolsters Hizballah's position both rhetorically and materially. Washington has made a number of good pledges since the Israel-Hizballah fighting of the summer of 2006; now it needs to live up to both their letter and spirit.

7. Dissuade foreign intervention

The United States will have to make a major effort to convince Iraq's neighbors not to intervene in an all-out civil war. Rewards for non-intervention should consist of the economic aid described above, as well as specific benefits tailored to the needs of the individual countries. On the negative side, the United States and its allies will have to make serious threats to Iraq's neighbors to try to keep them from intervening too brazenly. Multilateral sanctions packages could be imposed on any state that openly intervenes. At the very least, there should be a general embargo on the purchase of any Iraqi oil sold by anyone other than the Iraqi government or an Iraqi government-licensed entity.

8. Lay down "red lines" to Iran

As part of the negative incentives to prevent foreign intervention in Iraq, the United States may need to lay down "red lines" to Tehran which, if crossed, would provoke a direct American response, whether in the form of political, economic, or even military pressure. These "red lines" should include the entry of uniformed Iranian military units into Iraq, Iranian claims on Iraqi territory, or Iranian incitement of Iraqi secessionist groups. Possible punishments include additional economic sanctions, and, for egregious violations, the United States could employ punitive military operations.

9. Establish a Contact Group

The United States would do well to consider convening a formal, standing group consisting of Iraq's neighbors (and possibly the permanent five members of the UN Security Council) to consult and act collectively to help contain the spillover from Iraq. A Contact Group for Iraq could provide a forum in which the neighbors could air their concerns, address one another's fears, and discuss mutual problems. This alone might help allay suspicions about the activities of others, and so prevent the kinds of interventions that would add fuel to the fire of an Iraqi civil war. In addition, some problems like terrorism, refugees, and secessionist movements will benefit from being addressed multilaterally. For this reason, it will be particularly important to invite Iran and Syria to participate.

10. Prepare for oil supply disruptions

In its own planning exercises and as part of a multilateral effort, the United States should prepare for potential supply disruptions stemming from the Iraq conflict. Washington should consider further increasing the Strategic Petroleum Reserve in order to mitigate the impact of supply disruptions on the oil market. Washington should also encourage the International Energy Agency to develop contingency plans so that leading oil-consuming countries can collectively manage the risk of disruptions. Such efforts might even reduce terrorist incentives to attack oil production and transit facilities.

11. Manage the Kurds

Because of the ease with which secessionism can spread, it will probably be necessary for the United States to persuade the Iraqi Kurds not to declare their independence anytime soon. The United States could offer to help the Kurds deal with their own problems of spillover from the civil war in the rest of the country in return for their agreement not to declare independence or "intervene" in the rest of Iraq. That will mean helping them with their refugee problems, providing economic assistance to minimize the radicalization of their own population, and providing security guarantees—or even U.S. military forces—to deter Iran and Turkey from attacking the Kurds.

12. Strike at terrorist facilities

Should Iraq fall into an all-out civil war, Washington will have to recognize that terrorists will continue to find a home in Iraq and will use it as a base to conduct attacks outside it. Nevertheless, the United States should try to limit the ability of terrorists to use Iraq as a haven for attacks outside the country. This would likely require the retention of assets (air power, Special Operations Forces, and a major intelligence and reconnaissance effort) in the vicinity to identify and strike major terrorist facilities like training camps, bomb factories, and arms caches before they can pose a danger to other countries. Thus, the United States would continue to make intelligence collection in Iraq a high priority, and whenever such a facility is identified, Shi'i or Sunni, American forces would move quickly to destroy it.

13. Consider establishing safe havens or "catch basins" along Iraq's borders

One of the hardest aspects of containing the spillover from an all-out Iraqi civil war will be to limit, let alone halt, the flow of refugees, terrorists, and foreign agents (or invasion forces) across Iraq's borders. One potential option that deserves careful scrutiny would be to try to create a system of buffer zones with accompanying refugee collection points along Iraq's borders inside Iraqi territory, manned by U.S. and other Coalition personnel. The refugee collection points would be located on major roads, preferably near airstrips near the borders, and would be designed with support facilities to house, feed, and otherwise care for tens or even hundreds of thousands of refugees. The Coalition (principally the United States) would also provide military forces to defend the refugee camps against attack and to thoroughly pacify them (by disarming those entering the camps and then policing the camps). This option would require the extensive and continued use of U.S. forces.

Another key mission of Coalition military forces in this option would be to patrol large swathes of Iraqi territory along Iraq's borders beyond the refugee collection facilities themselves (though not near the Iranian border for political and logistical reasons). These patrols would aim to prevent both refugees and armed groups from skirting the refugee collection points and stealing across the border into a neighboring country. However, a second, but equally important goal would be to prevent military forces (and ideally, intelligence agents and their logistical support) of the neighboring country from moving into Iraq.

These buffer zones and their refugee collection points would thus serve as safe havens or "catch basins" for Iraqis fleeing the fighting, providing them with a secure place to stay within Iraq's borders while preventing them from burdening or destabilizing neighboring countries. At the same time, they would also serve as buffers between the fighting in Iraq and its neighbors by preventing some forms of spillover from Iraq into these states, and by preventing them from intervening overtly in Iraq (and hindering their ability to do so covertly).

Some or all of these tactics could be fashioned into a broader strategy for preventing an Iraqi civil war from destabilizing the entire region. Although all of them have advantages, none is a panacea, and many are half-measures at best. Some would require a continued large-scale U.S. military commitment (though less than current levels). A number have considerable costs and risks and would be difficult to implement. Nearly all could prove impossible for reasons of American domestic politics. Thus, no one approach is likely to solve the problem of spillover from Iraq, and even a strategy that saw the United States pursue all of them together with great skill and determination could still fail.

Be Wary of Half-Measures

To make matters worse, in the case of all-out civil wars, history has demonstrated that incremental steps and half-measures frequently prove disastrous. In Lebanon, both the Israelis and the Syrians tried half-measures—arming proxies, mounting limited interventions, striking at selected targets—to no avail. America's own determination to stabilize Iraq on the cheap and postpone making hard decisions has been a major element of the disasters that have unfolded there since 2003. The problems of spillover are likely to prove equally challenging—and we cannot afford to fail a second time.

If there is anything that should make us recognize the need to stay engaged in Iraq, it is the likely impact that such a war could have on the Persian Gulf region (if not the entire Middle East) and the enormous difficulties we will face in trying to contain that impact. If we cannot prevent such a full-scale civil war, then containment, as awful as it threatens to be, might still prove to be our least bad option.

PART I

PATTERNS OF CIVIL WARS
AND POLICY OPTIONS

2

CIVIL WARS AND SPILLOVER

B y any definition Iraq is already in a state of civil war. However, it is not yet at a Lebanese or Bosnian level of all-out
civil war violence and differences in degree matter. The turmoil
in Haiti, for instance, can be labeled a civil war, but relatively few
people have died or been driven from their homes. Moreover,
not all civil wars have the same strategic impact. Strife in Nepal
and Sudan has been bloody, but it has occurred in peripheral
regions and so does not affect U.S. and Western strategic interests directly, no matter how much it may tug at our heartstrings.
All civil wars are terrible, but the kind of all-out civil war that
Iraq appears headed for typically involves not only massive
bloodshed and even larger refugee flows, but also the collapse of
government institutions, the disintegration of the armed forces,
the spreading of sectarian and ethnic warfare to much of the
country, and an overall atmosphere of anarchy. The problem
with Iraq is that if the current conflict escalates to all-out civil
war, it may prove to be that rare combination of rampant violence in a strategically and economically crucial region.

   And the trends augur poorly. Inter- and intracommunal carnage claims more and more lives there with each passing month.

Anywhere from 50,000 to 150,000 (and perhaps more) Iraqis have already died as a result of violence since the U.S. occupation of Iraq began, including terrorist attacks, sectarian killings, and deaths from criminal activity.[1] The summer of 2006 has seen a surge in violence. According to the United Nations High Commissioner for Refugees (UNHCR), 1.8 million Iraqis had fled the country by November 2006, at least one million of them since April 2003.[2] While most still cling to the hope that their lives will improve, the numbers are diminishing. The sense of being an "Iraqi," as opposed to a member of a particular religious, ethnic, or tribal group, is declining too. Militias continue to proliferate as average Iraqis grow fearful of the multiplying reports of ethnic cleansing.[3]

The chaos and violence are discrediting moderate Iraqi leaders. In September 2006 the Shi'i leader Grand Ayatollah Ali al-Sistani declared he would focus exclusively on religious matters because he felt he could no longer restrain his followers or otherwise prevent Iraq from sliding into civil war.[4] Sistani has long been a voice of moderation in Iraq, and *New York Times* columnist Thomas Friedman dubbed him an "indispensable man" with regard to Iraq's future. As voices like Sistani's fall silent, ferocious rejectionists like Muqtada as-Sadr gain new adherents daily—not because Iraqis like what he stands for, but simply because he offers protection and basic services that the Americans and the Iraqi government have failed to provide.[5] Iraq has also proven a magnet for Sunni *jihadists* who admire Usama Bin Laden, and they have employed unprecedented numbers of suicide bombings with devastating effect. The wealthy, including those recently enriched by graft and organized crime, are sending their money out of the country as quickly as they can, along with their wives and children.

The only thing standing between Iraq and a descent into a Lebanon- or Bosnia-style maelstrom is 140,000 American troops, and even they are merely slowing the fall at this point. Unless the United States and the new government of Iraq take dramatic action to reverse the current trends, the internecine conflict there could easily worsen to the point where it spirals into a full-scale civil war that threatens not only Iraq, but also its neighbors throughout the oil-rich Persian Gulf.

This degeneration into all-out civil war may still not be inevitable (although if the point of no return has not already passed, it is doubtless drawing near), and we have laid out in considerable detail elsewhere our visions of alternative courses for the United States to pursue.[6] We desperately hope to see this scenario averted, and we are heartened by signs that some American and Iraqi officials, particularly in the U.S. military, recognize the grave problems we face in Iraq and are exploring options to change course. However, given how many mistakes the United States has already made, how much time we have already squandered, how difficult the task is, and how severe the deterioration has already been, we cannot be confident that even a major course correction from Washington and Baghdad will avert a full-blown Iraqi civil war.

If that comes to pass, our priority will have to become preventing the Iraqi conflict from spilling over and destabilizing neighboring states: an approach that requires preventing neighboring states from intervening, helping mitigate the risks associated with refugees, striking terrorist havens, and otherwise changing our policy to reflect the painful reality that the U.S. effort to bring peace and stability to Iraq will have failed. Not planning now for containing the Iraqi civil war could allow its devastation to grow far greater, to the point where it would threaten not only Iraq but also much of the surrounding region, as well as many vital U.S. interests.

The Humanitarian and Economic Consequences of a Civil War

A full-blown civil war in Iraq would have many disastrous repercussions. Without question, a wider Iraqi civil war would be a humanitarian nightmare. Based on the experiences of other recent major civil wars such as those in the former Yugoslavia, Lebanon, Somalia, Congo, Afghanistan, the Caucasus, and elsewhere, we should expect many hundreds of thousands or even millions of people to die, with three to four times that number wounded. The same experiences suggest that refugees, both internally and externally displaced, will probably number in the millions. The United States has *intervened* in other civil wars to stop tragedies on this scale.

Of course, an Iraqi civil war will be even more painful for Americans to bear because, if it happens, it will be our fault. We will have launched the invasion and then failed to secure the peace, a failure that will have produced a civil war. For years to come Iraqis, Americans, and indeed most of the world will point their fingers at the U.S. government.

Our efforts to promote democracy in the Middle East will be badly damaged. Americans may argue that what happened in Iraq was not a good test of democracy in the Arab world, but many Arabs are unlikely to see it that way. In particular, both the autocrats of the region and their Islamist political opponents will use a massive civil war in Iraq to argue that democratization is a recipe for disaster—ignoring all of the risks that democracy's more repressive alternatives may entail in terms of breeding more political instability in this troubled part of the world. Already in the popular mind in the Arab world the democratic gains in Iraq are being overwritten by the continuing violence and the sense that Iraqi governments are too subservient to the United States.

A full-blown civil war in Iraq could lead to the loss of most or all Iraqi oil production from the world market. Iraqi insurgents, militias, and organized crime rings are already wreaking havoc with Iraq's production and export infrastructure, generally keeping Iraqi production below prewar levels of about 2.2 million barrels per day (b/d), and far below Iraq's potential level of more than double this output. Larger and more widespread conflict would almost certainly drive down Iraq's oil export figures even further. Thus, an all-out civil war, even if it could be contained in Iraq, would put upward pressure on oil prices.

Spillover and Civil Wars

The above consequences are devastating morally and hurt U.S. influence in the region, but the greatest threat that the United States would face from an all-out civil war in Iraq is the problem of spillover—the tendency of civil wars to impose burdens, create instability, and even trigger civil wars in other, usually neighboring, countries.[7] If U.S. forces withdrew, a civil war that did nothing but consume Iraq for 5, 10, or even 15 years would be tragic and painful but not an actual threat to the security of the United States. But civil war in Iraq could drag down its neighbors as well. Saudi Arabia, Kuwait, and Iran are all major oil producers experiencing political and economic troubles. Jordan is equally fragile and in a critical location. We may not like the Syrian regime, but it too is in delicate circumstances and its collapse might not serve our interests either. Turkey is also coping with major societal transformations, and it is a NATO ally we have pledged to defend. In addition, civil war in Iraq could complicate several aspects of U.S. counterterrorism policy, both in the region and around the world.

As historians have noted since time immemorial, some degree of spillover from civil wars seems hard to avoid. Examples of the phenomenon can be found in works on politics from Thucydides to Machiavelli to Hobbes. However, both the frequency and intensity of spillover vary from conflict to conflict. At one extreme, spillover can mean something as simple and manageable as the loss of trade that Romania and Hungary experienced from the civil wars in the former Yugoslavia. This was unwelcome but hardly crippling. At the other extreme, spillover can create interlocking patterns of conflict, with one civil war in effect sparking others in neighboring states.

A good example of this latter phenomenon is the Israeli-Palestinian conflict that began in the 1920s between the Zionist movement and the Palestinians and continued even after formal hostilities between the newly created Israeli state and neighboring Arab states ended in 1948. The war produced many forms of spillover including masses of Palestinian refugees (augmented in 1967 by Israel's conquest of the West Bank and the Gaza Strip). These Palestinian refugees and their continued attacks on Israel contributed to the 1956 and 1967 Arab-Israeli wars and provoked a civil war in Jordan in 1970–71. Then when they were defeated and forced to flee to Lebanon, they triggered the Lebanese civil war of 1975–90. In turn, the Lebanese civil war galvanized internal unrest in Syria, which only ended its own civil war in 1982 by employing horrific levels of violence against its own people.

Frighteningly, such patterns of interlocking civil wars are not uncommon. Genocide and civil war in Rwanda triggered the Congolese civil war that has been raging since 1996, and that still continues, albeit in a more muted form. Civil war in Croatia in 1991 triggered the subsequent conflict in Bosnia, which in turn fed the 1998–99 Kosovo war, which gave rise to the guerrilla war in Macedonia in 2001. Likewise, in the Transcaucasus, the Nagorno-Karabakh conflict (a civil war within Azerbaijan that was at the heart of that country's conflict with Armenia) was an important spur to the fighting in Georgia, and both had an impact on (and were themselves affected by) the fighting in the Russian autonomous republic of Chechnya.

Unfortunately, Iraq appears to possess many of the conditions most conducive to spillover because there is a high degree of foreign "interest." Ethnic, tribal, and religious groups within Iraq are equally prevalent in neighboring countries, and they share many of the same grievances. Iraq has a history of violence with its neighbors, which has fostered desires for revenge and fomented constant clashes. Iraq also possesses resources that its neighbors covet—oil being the most obvious, but important religious shrines also figure in the mix. There is a high degree of commerce and communication between Iraq and its neighbors, and its borders are porous. All of this suggests that spillover from an Iraqi civil war would tend toward the more dangerous end of the spillover spectrum.

Consequently, if the United States is confronted with an all-out civil war in Iraq, its principal challenge will be to contain any spillover so that it does not destabilize the region. To do so, the United States needs to start thinking about how best to deal with the six most common and most dangerous forms of spillover.

Refugees as a Security Risk

Massive refugee flows are a hallmark of major civil wars. Afghanistan generated the largest refugee flow since the Second World War, with more than a third of the population fleeing. Conflicts in the Balkans and Somalia in the 1990s also generated millions of refugees and internally displaced persons (IDPs): in Kosovo, over two-thirds of Kosovar Albanians fled the country. Half of Bosnia's 4.4 million inhabitants were displaced, and 1 million of them fled the country altogether. Comparable figures for Iraq would mean roughly 13 million IDPs and over 6 million refugees running to Iraq's neighbors. Congo, Tajikistan, Lebanon, Somalia, and other civil wars also produced massive refugee flows that fundamentally changed the demographics of the country and the region.

The sheer logistical burden of handling the sudden inflow of so many traumatized, impoverished, and desperate people can strain even wealthy and developed economies. Countries in the developing world, which can barely provide basic services to their own people, may collapse under the strain. Providing water, food, shelter, medical care, and other necessities is often beyond them. Albania, for example, hosted over half of the 600,000 Kosovar refugees, amounting to roughly 13 percent of its total population— the equivalent of America suddenly taking in 38 million poor and brutalized people.[8]

When refugees flee the carnage of war, they bring with them a host of problems. Most important, refugees often continue the war from their new homes. At times, armed units and militias simply move from one side of the border to the other. The civil war in Tajikistan, for example, forced perhaps 5,000 fighters of the anti-government Islamic Renaissance Party (IRP) to organize and train from neighboring Afghanistan. Even more worrisome, the expulsion of refugees often swells the ranks of the fighters. Each round of new refugees brings with it stories of rape, murder, and pillage, generating new recruits for the militias.

The millions of Afghans who fled to Pakistan during the anti-Soviet struggle illustrate the potential for violent transformation. Stuck in the camps for years while war consumed their homeland, many refugees were easily persuaded to join radical Islamist organizations in Pakistan that supported various *mujahidin* (holy warrior) movements. When the Soviets departed, the refugees became the core of the Taliban, a movement nurtured by Pakistani intelligence and various Islamist political parties. Beginning in 1994, the Taliban steadily defeated their rivals and, as they did so, opened the door for Bin Laden to make Afghanistan al-Qa'ida's new base of operations.

The refugee camp, often under international protection, can become a sanctuary for militia groups, particularly if the state hosting the refugees is weak or supports the conflict. Militia leaders often become the new leaders of the refugee community. Because they have guns, they can offer protection to their kinsmen and impose their will on any rivals. In addition, many of the young men in the refugee camps become prime recruits for continuing the fight because they are angry and jobless, while tribal elders, peaceful politicians, or others who might oppose violence typically find themselves discredited and enfeebled by the flight and the loss of their traditional basis of power (typically control of land and jobs).

The presence of militias among the refugees tends to embroil the country hosting them in the civil war. From the camps, the militias launch raids back into their homelands, killing and destroying property. When confronted, they retreat back to their refugee camp, hiding behind their own civilian populations. Inevitably, this creates an incentive for their enemies to attack the camps to neutralize the militiamen—or even to attack the host government to try to force it to deal with the problem, a pattern Israel repeatedly used against Palestinian fighters in Lebanon. Host governments may also begin to use the refugees as tools to influence events back in the refugees' homeland, arming, training, and directing them, and thereby exacerbating the conflict.

Perhaps the most tragic example of the problems created by large numbers of refugees occurred in the wake of the Rwandan genocide in 1994. After the Hutu-led genocide unfolded and led to the death of 800,000 to one million Tutsis and moderate Hutus, the Tutsi-led Rwandan Patriotic Front (RPF), which had "invaded" the country in 1990 from neighboring Uganda, toppled the Hutu government. The RPF was drawn from the 500,000 or so Tutsis who had already fled Rwanda from past pogroms. As the RPF swept through Rwanda, almost one million Hutus fled to neighboring Congo, fearing that the evil they did unto others would be done unto them. Mixed in with many innocent Hutus were the *genocidaires.*

The international reaction to the genocide and RPF victory was muddled. Much of the world failed to recognize that the refugees were actually the perpetrators, rather than the victims, of the genocide. Thus, revolted by the Rwandan genocide, countries mistakenly gave humanitarian aid to the architects and implementers of that killing, many of whom had fled to neighboring Congo. For two years after 1994, Hutu bands continued to conduct raids into Rwanda and worked with Congolese dictator Mobutu Sese Seko, who used them for his own purposes to wreak havoc among the Banyamulenge, a Congolese Tutsi community that lived along the Rwanda-Congo border. Naturally, the new RPF government of Rwanda did not take this lying down: it attacked not only the Hutu militia camps, but also its much larger neighbor, bolstering a formerly obscure Congolese opposition leader named Laurent Kabila and installing him in power in Kinshasa after it fell to the Rwandan (Tutsi) Army. It was this move, coupled with subsequent machinations, that provoked the civil war in Congo in which perhaps four million people have died.

As the Congo experience makes clear, refugees can disrupt politics in their new host country with disastrous results. In this case, the refugees became the principal agents of spillover, spreading civil war from Rwanda to Congo.

This is a common consequence of large numbers of refugees from civil wars. The influx of hundreds of thousands (if not millions) of victims of strife often alarms and angers their kin and supporters in a different country. They may demand that their government take action against the perpetrators. They may directly aid refugee militias. Most worrisome, they may ally with the refugee militias and oppose their own government. Emboldened by the presence of thousands of potential fighters, disgruntled communities may believe they can challenge their own government.

This is particularly true in countries where there is a delicate demographic balance. In Lebanon, for example, the influx of tens of thousands of Palestinian fighters along with their families expelled from Jordan in 1970 changed the communal balance of power in the country and sparked the Lebanese civil war that began in 1975. The Palestinians were well armed and well organized, and they began to work with Lebanese Sunni Arab sympathizers. At first, this was simply to allow them to continue their cross-border attacks into Israel from Lebanon—something that had started well before the Palestinians were expelled from Jordan and increased after the 1969 Cairo Accords, in which the Lebanese government gave Palestinian militants de facto control over the Palestinian refugee camps. Over time, however, they came into conflict with the Maronites who dominated the government. The Palestinians wanted to attack Israel, a desire the Maronite-dominated government attempted to thwart out of fear of Israeli retaliation. In response, the Palestine Liberation Organization (PLO) increasingly opposed the government (including by force), created their own autonomous enclaves within Lebanon, and encouraged Lebanon's Muslim groups—particularly the Sunnis—to oppose the Maronites. Over time, the Palestinians focused more on Lebanon than on Israel. Because the Palestinians were heavily armed, this accelerated the Maronites' mobilization. It was no accident that the Lebanese civil war began with a series of attacks and counterattacks between the PLO and the Maronite militias. Other groups quickly mobilized in response to this violence, and the weak Lebanese government looked on helplessly. Thus, in Lebanon, the "external" problem of Palestinian refugees became a principal source of internal conflict.

The flow of refugees from Iraq could worsen instability in all of its neighbors. In particular, the potential for massive Shi'i and Sunni Arab refugee flows from Iraq could be devastating to Iran, Kuwait, Saudi Arabia, and Jordan. Kuwait, for example, has just over a million citizens, roughly one-third of whom are Shi'i. The influx of several hundred thousand Iraqi Shi'ah across the border would change the religious balance in the country overnight. Both these Iraqi refugees and the Kuwaiti Shi'ah might turn against the Sunni-dominated Kuwaiti government if it were to back Sunni groups in Iraq (as seems most likely). The influx of fighters from Iraq could also lead Kuwaiti Shi'ah to see violence as a way of ending the centuries of discrimination they have faced at the hands of Kuwait's Sunnis. Not surprisingly, the Kuwaiti government is highly concerned about refugees.

Numbers of displaced persons are already rising in Iraq, although they are nowhere near what they could be if the country slid into an all-out civil war. Altogether, as of November 2006, almost 2 million Iraqis have fled to neighboring states, and 1.6 million are displaced internally.[9] Roughly 100,000 Arabs are believed to have fled northern Iraq under pressure from Kurdish militias.[10] As many as 200,000 Sunni Arabs reportedly have been displaced by the fighting between Sunni Arab groups and the American-led Coalition in western Iraq.[11] In the past 18 months, 50,000–100,000 Shi'i Arabs have fled mixed-population cities in central Iraq for greater safety farther south.[12] Large numbers of Iraq's small Christian community are fleeing the country following attacks by a range of Iraq's various Muslim militias. They do not have the numbers to stay and effectively defend themselves, so they are increasingly just leaving.[13] In an eerie replay of Lebanon, the roughly 30,000–50,000 Palestinian refugees in Iraq are increasingly fleeing the country in response to threats and even attacks by Shi'i Arabs and Kurds, who see the Palestinians as former henchmen of Saddam and current allies of the Sunnis.[14] As of November 2006, the UNHCR found that 600,000 Iraqis had fled to Syria, 700,000 to Jordan, and 54,000 to Iran, among other locations. Perhaps 2,000 Iraqis a day were going to Syria, with another 1,000 going to Jordan.[15]

So far, in addition to the Palestinians and other foreigners, it is mostly the Iraqi upper and middle classes that are fleeing the country altogether. Many of them are moving to Jordan, Egypt, Lebanon, Syria, or the Arab Persian Gulf States, if they can afford it. As one indicator of the size of this flight, since 2004 the Ministry of Education has issued nearly 40,000 letters permitting parents to take their children's academic records abroad.[16] Similarly, in June 2006 the U.S. Committee on Refugees and Immigrants reported that the Iraqi government had issued two million passports (in a population of about 26 million) in the previous ten months.[17] To date, it has mostly been those with the resources to find a decent life in another country who have fled altogether. However, if the violence continues to escalate, those without the resources will soon be forced to do so out of sheer necessity and the only destination they will be able to afford will be vast refugee camps in the nearest neighboring country. Iran is particularly likely to receive an influx, given its historic ties to Iraq's Shi'i community and neighboring Sunni states' reluctance to take in too many Shi'i Arabs.

Terrorism

Another vexing problem of civil wars is their close association with the problem of terrorism. The worse the civil strife in Iraq becomes, the more countries there are that could be affected by terrorism from Iraq. Critics of the war in Iraq have argued, correctly, that it has proven a disaster for the struggle against Bin Laden and his allies. In Iraq, fighters are receiving training, building networks, and becoming further radicalized—and the U.S. occupation there is proving a dream recruiting tool for radicalizing young Muslims around the world. Michael Scheuer, a former senior CIA official and an expert on al-Qa'ida, acidly writes that the U.S. invasion of Iraq was a dream "Christmas present" for Bin Laden.[18] Peter Bergen, another al-Qa'ida expert, argues that the war in Iraq may prove more valuable to the *jihadist* movement than the anti-Soviet struggle in Afghanistan.[19]

Yet a closer look at Iraq and the problem of spillover suggests that a massive civil war there would also exacerbate many problems of terrorism and create new ones. Many civil wars have been breeding grounds for particularly noxious terrorist groups, while others have created hospitable sanctuaries for existing terrorist groups to train, recruit, and mount operations—at times against foes entirely unconnected to the civil war.

Internecine conflicts are frequently the most vicious conflicts of all, with many accepted constraints on behavior in warfare falling by the wayside. In part, this is derived from the fact that in many civil wars, there are no organized armies standing between a civilian population and an attacking army; both armies are generally drawn from, and therefore intermingled with, the civilians, which is why levels of civilian deaths and other atrocities are often proportionately higher in civil wars. This in turn tends to rapidly erode the moral prohibitions on killing civilians, and rewards those willing to do it. Thus inured, it is only a short step from killing large numbers of civilians in your own country in civil war, to killing large numbers of civilians in another country, especially one that you believe somehow aided your enemies in that war.

Examples of this phenomenon abound. The Liberation Tigers of Tamil Eelam (LTTE), the Groupe Islamique Armé (GIA, Armed Islamic Group), and the PLO were all born of civil wars. All eventually shifted from merely attacking their enemies in the territory in question (Sri Lanka, Algeria, and Mandatory Palestine, respectively) to mounting attacks elsewhere. The LTTE assassinated former Indian Prime Minister Rajiv Gandhi in 1991 because of his intervention in Sri Lanka. The GIA did the same in the mid-1990s, beginning with the hijacking of an Air France flight and moving on to bombings in metropolitan France. In the 1970s various Palestinian groups began launching terrorist attacks against Israelis wherever they could find them—including at the Munich Olympics, Athens airport, and Rome airport—and then went beyond that to mount attacks on Western civilians whose governments supported Israel.

Other terrorist groups that may have existed before a civil war broke out expanded their operations as violence at home intensified. As the "Troubles" persisted and led to a low-level civil war in Northern Ireland, the Irish Republican Army (IRA) decided that it had to take the conflict to the British people and so began a campaign of attacks on the British mainland (and against British targets in the Netherlands and Germany) beginning in the mid-1970s.

Over the past 25 years, however, the connection between terrorism and civil wars has become even more dangerous because of the rise of radical Islamist movements that have a strong anti-American agenda. The Lebanese civil war became a front in the war Shi'i extremists were waging to spread Ayatollah Khomeini's Islamic Revolution. Most famously, the Islamic Revolutionary Guards Corps (IRGC) helped create Hizballah to secure Shi'i goals in Lebanon and then turned it into an international terrorist organization that has attacked Americans, Israelis, and others on four continents. Hizballah and a number of smaller radical Shi'i groups found a cause, a sanctuary, and a recruiting center in the chaos of the Lebanese civil war.

In recent decades, civil wars involving Muslims have also been used by the Sunni *salafi jihadist* movement, inspiring young men to join the cause and serving as a place for them to arm, train, and organize. In Afghanistan, the

Balkans, Chechnya, Kashmir, and elsewhere, insurgencies that grew out of local civil conflicts steadily became enmeshed in a broader international movement whose figurehead is Bin Laden. Through skillful propaganda, Bin Laden's movement painted these struggles as instances of Western oppression of Muslims, inspiring young men to join the fight and other Muslims to give financially.

Although many local insurgencies and civil wars added fuel to the fire, nothing compared with Afghanistan in the 1980s and 1990s. The anti-Soviet struggle in the 1980s was a key incubator for the movement Bin Laden came to champion. The successful defeat of the Soviet superpower vindicated the *jihadists'* struggle. During the Afghanistan struggle, Bin Laden, his deputy 'Ayman al-Zawahiri, and many other senior officials and operators forged strong bonds that lasted after the battle with the Soviets ended in 1989. In addition, the Afghan war experience helped reorient *jihadist* ideology. Many young *mujahidin* went to Afghanistan with only the foggiest notion of what *jihad* ("struggle," often reduced to "holy war") was. They hated the Soviets, and they admired the *mujahidin* for fighting back, but they had few firm ideas beyond that. During the course of the fighting in Afghanistan, a frightening cross-fertilization occurred. Individuals adopted each other's grievances: the Saudi *jihadists* learned to hate the Egyptian government, and Chechens learned to hate Israel. Meanwhile, through intensive proselytizing, al-Qa'ida was able to convince them all that the United States was at the center of the Muslim world's problems—a view that almost no Sunni terrorist group had embraced before.

Civil wars such as in Afghanistan that involve terrorist groups can spawn new, previously unimaginable, forms of horror. Throughout the 1970s, Fatah (the main Palestinian group led by Yasir Arafat) and other PLO groups were often touted as the worst of the worst when it came to terrorism. Then the Lebanese civil war gave birth to Shi'i terrorist groups like Hizballah, which conducted mass casualty attacks on U.S. military and diplomatic facilities, and introduced the tactic of suicide bombing as well as aggressive hostage taking. Hizballah for many years wore the badge of "worst terrorist group" until, on 9/11, al-Qa'ida killed almost ten times as many Americans in one day as Hizballah had in its entire history. Iraq's civil war has already seen serial beheadings, mass kidnapping, and death by torture, including the use of drills, nails, acid, and electric shock.[20] The power of violence to shock often diminishes with familiarity, leading terrorists to seek new ways to impress and horrify.

Although locals may not share the terrorists' agenda, they may still seek their aid. Contestants in civil wars often cast about desperately for allies, regardless of how unsavory they are. Bosnian Muslims quietly invited *jihadists* from around the Muslim world to aid them: international censure of these groups meant little to the beleaguered Bosnians who welcomed allies who would fight.

The most worrisome terrorism-related problem should Iraq descend into all-out civil war is that Iraq could become a sanctuary for terrorist groups of all stripes, possibly even exceeding the problems of Lebanon in the 1980s or Afghanistan under the Taliban, especially if, as seems likely, a civil war were preceded or accompanied by a U.S. military withdrawal. Iraq would become an Afghanistan-like field of *jihad,* a place where radicals come to meet, train, fight, and forge bonds that last when they leave Iraq for the West or for other countries in the region. Although many Sunni *jihadists* travel to Iraq to fight today, the situation could easily get worse.

Right now, the U.S. military presence keeps a lid on the *jihadist* effort: although they are highly active, there is no equivalent to the massive training camps or above-ground existence that they enjoyed in Afghanistan. Likewise, Hizballah and other Shi'i terrorist groups have maintained a relatively low profile in Iraq so far, but the more embattled the Shi'ah feel, the more likely they will be to invite greater Hizballah involvement to teach them and even fight for them given Hizballah's demonstrated prowess in both guerrilla warfare and terrorism. Shi'i fighters might even strike the Sunni Arab backers of their adversaries in Iraq, such as Saudi Arabia and Kuwait, or incite their own Shi'i populations against them. In the fall of 2006, a new Shi'i terrorist leader emerged using the nom de guerre of Abu Deraa. While Abu Deraa has reportedly been responsible for many of the death squad attacks on Sunni Arabs in Baghdad, he has also been linked to the kidnapping of a U.S. Army translator, suggesting that he and his henchmen may have designs on more than just their immediate Iraqi adversaries.[21]

The Sunni *jihadists* would be particularly likely to go after Saudi Arabia given the long, lightly patrolled border between the two, as well as their long interest in overthrowing the al-Saud, who rule the heartland of Islam. Ties are tight: Sunni resistance groups in Iraq have at times turned to Saudi religious scholars to validate their activities.[22] Reuven Paz found that the bulk of the Arabs fighting in Iraq were Saudis. As he notes, "The Iraqi experience of these mainly Saudi volunteers may create a massive group of 'Iraqi alumni' that will threaten the fragile internal situation of the desert kingdom."[23] The turmoil in Iraq has also energized young Saudi Islamists, who see it as emblematic of broader problems facing the Muslim world. For now, many Saudi *jihadists* have decided to fight in Iraq, in part because doing so is a clearer "defensive *jihad*" than struggling with the al-Saud.[24] In the future, the balance might shift from Saudis helping Iraqi fighters against the Americans and Iraqi Shi'ah (and Kurds) to Iraqi fighters helping Saudi *jihadists* against the Saudi government with the Saudi oil infrastructure an obvious target. Indeed, in February 2006, *jihadists* launched a serious but unsuccessful attack on Saudi Arabia's key oil export node at Abqaiq. The attack failed but still caused oil prices to rise by $2 a barrel—a success would have led to a far higher jump.

The November 9, 2005 attacks on three hotels in Amman, Jordan, that killed 60 people may be a harbinger of a broader terrorism problem to come. The attacks were carried out by Sunni Arab Iraqis, though orchestrated by Abu Musab al-Zarqawi, a Jordanian. If the *jihadists* had even more freedom of action, the pace and scale of such attacks would certainly grow.

Although few Americans pay attention to the anti-Turkish Partiya Karkerên Kurdistan (PKK, Kurdistan Workers' Party, which also has gone by the names KADEK and Kongra-Gel), which has long fought to establish a Kurdish state in Turkey from bases in Iraq, it has been resurrected by the civil war in Iraq. PKK attacks had fallen off dramatically after the capture of the group's leader Abdullah Öcalan in 1999, and he subsequently endorsed a ceasefire. As a result of the growing violence in Iraq, the PKK has had a rebirth, conducting over 250 attacks on Turkish security forces during the first ten months of 2006 alone. In one week, they managed to kill 14 Turkish soldiers, a level of violence that Turkey has not seen since the PKK terrorist campaign of the 1980s and 1990s that resulted in the death of 37,000 people—from both PKK attacks and Turkish military reprisals.[25]

Radicalization of Populations

One of the most insidious problems of spillover created by civil wars is their tendency to inflame the passions of neighboring populations. At the most basic level, this is simply about proximity: chaos and slaughter 5,000 miles away rarely have the same emotional impact as massacres five miles down the road. It is far easier for people to identify and empathize with those they live near, even if they are on the other side of an imaginary boundary. When ethnic, religious, racial, or other groupings spill across those borders, the problem grows. Then the members of a group have a powerful tendency to identify with, take the side of, support, and even fight on behalf of the members of their group in the neighboring country. A sense of cross-border affinity, indeed kinship, is particularly strong in the Middle East. As one example, Arabs have embraced the Palestinian cause from Oran to Oman.

Frequently, people demand that their government intervene on behalf of their compatriots embroiled in a civil war. Alternatively, and especially if they perceive that their government will be reluctant to do so, they may begin to aid their co-religionists or co-ethnics on their own—including by taking in refugees, funneling money and guns, providing sanctuary, or furnishing information. The Albanian government came under heavy pressure from its people to support the Kosovar Albanians fighting for independence (or, at times, autonomy) from the Serbs. As a result, Tirana provided covert aid and overt diplomatic support to the Kosovo Liberation Army (KLA) in 1998–99, and threatened to intervene to prevent Serbia from crushing the Kosovars. Similarly, numerous Irish groups clandestinely supported the Irish Republican Army against the Ulster Protestants and the British, especially during the early days of the "Troubles." Irish Americans famously provided money, guns, and other supplies to the IRA and lobbied the U.S. government to intervene on their behalf against the British government. Indeed, the signature IRA weapon, the Armalite, was a civilian version of the U.S.-manufactured M-16.

Sometimes the radicalization works the other way around: rather than demanding intervention on behalf of their compatriots enmeshed in the civil war, neighboring populations can become radicalized and cause civil unrest and even conflict within these states. Often, the neighboring population feels the same or similar grievances as their compatriots across the border. Seeing them fighting to change their circumstances can provoke members of the same group in the neighboring country to take up arms, as Syria's experience during the Lebanese civil war demonstrates. Although Sunni Syrians had chafed under the minority 'Alawi dictatorship since the

1960s, members of the Muslim Brotherhood—the leading Sunni Syrian opposition group—were inspired to action by events in Lebanon. There they saw Lebanese Sunni Arabs fighting to wrest their fair share of political power from the minority Maronite-dominated government in Beirut. This spurred their own decision to begin a guerrilla struggle against Hafiz al-Asad's minority 'Alawi regime in Damascus. Unfortunately for the Muslim Brotherhood, Asad's regime was not as weak as the Maronite-dominated government in Lebanon, and at Hama in 1982 he infamously razed the center of the city, a major Muslim Brotherhood stronghold, killing 25,000–50,000 people and snuffing out the Muslim Brotherhood's revolt.

In still other cases, radicalization is manifested in a combination of the two phenomena: a desire to help compatriots mired in civil war leading to demands on the government, only to have the government refuse to act, which in turn provokes conflict with the government and its supporters. Many Lebanese Muslims staunchly supported the Palestinians against Israel and cheered the efforts by other Arab states to aid the Palestinians. After both the 1956 and 1967 Arab-Israeli wars, they were appalled that the Maronite-dominated government did nothing to help the Arab cause against Israel. This was part of the powder keg of animosity between Muslim and Christian Lebanese that the PLO detonated after it fled Jordan for Lebanon in the early 1970s.

Iraq's neighbors are vulnerable to this aspect of spillover. Iraq's own divisions are mirrored throughout the region: Saudi Arabia, Kuwait, and Bahrain all are Sunni-ruled states with sizable Shi'i communities. Kuwaiti officials are warning that the continued sectarian conflict in Iraq could spark similar problems in Kuwait, where 30 percent of the population is Shi'i.[26] In Saudi Arabia, the Shi'ah are only about 10 percent of the population, but they are heavily concentrated in its oil-rich Eastern Province. Bahrain's population is majority Shi'i, although the regime is Sunni. Likewise, Turkey, Iran, and Syria all have important Kurdish minorities, which are geographically concentrated adjacent to Iraqi Kurdistan. Jordan too has important societal cleavages (primarily between "East Bank" Jordanians and Palestinians), and factional conflict in Iraq could antagonize its internal relations as well.

Populations in some of the countries around Iraq are already showing disturbing signs of such radicalization. In Bahrain, organized confrontations between the Shi'ah and government security forces have become matters of real concern. In March 2006, after the Sunni *jihadist* bombing of the Shi'i Askariya Shrine in the northern Iraqi city of Samarra, over 100,000 Bahraini Shi'ah (along with a few sympathetic Sunnis) took to the streets in anger. In 2004, when U.S. forces were battling Sunni Arab insurgents in Fallujah, large numbers of Bahraini Sunnis likewise came out to protest. Bahrain's Shi'ah are simultaneously angry over the suffering of their co-religionists in Iraq and encouraged by the success of the Iraqi Shi'ah in gaining political power to seek the same for themselves. Naturally, Bahrain's Sunnis reject all of their demands and ascribe their unhappiness to Iranian machinations. The *New York Times* quoted one Bahraini Shi'i politician as saying, "It is only natural that we'd be affected by Iraq, but that effect has begun to hurt us. Whenever things in Iraq go haywire, it reflects here."[27]

Some Kurdish groups have called on their brothers in Iran to revolt against the Iranian regime.[28] There has been unrest in Iranian Kurdistan, prompting Iran to deploy troops to the border and even shell Iraqi Kurdish positions in Iraq. The Turks too have deployed additional forces to the Iraqi border to try to prevent the movement of Kurdish forces back and forth between the two countries.[29]

Most ominous of all, tensions are rising between Sunnis and Shi'ah in the oil-rich eastern province of Saudi Arabia, where a *Los Angeles Times* report quoted a senior Saudi Shi'i cleric as saying, "Saudi Sunnis are defending Iraqi Sunnis, and Saudi Shiites are defending Iraqi Shiites. There's a fear that it will cause a struggle."[30]

The horrors of sectarian war are only miles away. As in Bahrain, many of the Saudi Shi'ah saw the success of Iraq's Shi'ah as an example to follow and are now demanding better political and economic treatment for themselves. Initially, the government made a number of modest concessions, but now they are facing a backlash from the Kingdom's Sunnis, who accuse the Shi'ah of heresy and of being the puppets of Iran. Religious leaders on both sides have begun to warn of a coming *fitna*, a schism within Islam.[31]

Turmoil in Saudi Arabia would be disastrous for the world economy and could send the price of oil soaring. Widespread unrest that included attacks on pipelines and other facilities could easily send oil over $100 a barrel, but even limited strife is a problem for oil markets. The *Wall Street Journal* reports that oil has a "terror premium" because the fear of a supply disruption can often raise prices significantly even when the attacks do not occur.[32]

Secession Breeds Secessionism

Closely related to the phenomenon of radicalized populations is the tendency for one secessionist movement, especially a successful one, to spawn copycat attempts. Repressive regimes make this claim frequently to justify harsh actions against internal dissent, but there is historical precedent during instances of major civil war.

The mechanics are easy to understand. One oppressed group with a sense of national identity stakes a claim to independence and goes to war to achieve it. As long as they don't get crushed immediately, other groups with similar identities and aspirations can be inspired to do the same—it's often as simple as "if those guys can do it, so can we."[33] For that reason, foreign recognition and assistance to a breakaway republic are often crucial to whether secession spreads. If one group is awarded foreign assistance and recognition, other groups will feel that they should risk doing the same.

The various civil wars in the former Yugoslavia in the 1990s provide a good example of this form of spillover. Slovenia was determined to declare independence, which led the Croats to follow suit—even though they were nowhere near as prepared for it as the Slovenes. When the Serbs (first in Croatia, but quickly joined by the Belgrade government) opposed Croat secession from Yugoslavia by force, the first of the Yugoslav civil wars broke out. The German government then pushed the rest of the European Union into recognizing both Slovene and Croat independence in the mistaken belief that this would end the bloodshed. Not only did it not halt the Croat-Serb fighting, it placed Bosnia in a very tough spot. Many Bosnian Muslims wanted independence. When they saw both the Slovenes and Croats rewarded for their revolts, it encouraged them to pursue the same. By the same token, the new Bosnian government feared that if it did not declare independence, Serbia and Croatia would swallow the respective Serb- and Croat-inhabited parts of their country. Bosnian Muslims had been content in a multi-ethnic Yugoslavia, but the departure of the Slovenes and Croats meant that the rump state would be dominated by Serbs. As a result, Bosnia held a referendum on independence on March 1, 1992, that returned a 98 percent vote in favor of independence. The barricades went up all over Sarajevo the next day, kicking off the worst of the Balkan civil wars.

Nor did it stop there. The eventual success of the Bosnian Muslims was an important element of Kosovar Albanian thinking when they began to agitate against the Serbian government in 1997–98, for even though the Bosnians had suffered through four horrific years of war, the fact was that the international community led by the United States eventually came to their rescue, recognized their new state, and forced the Serbs to accede to their independence at Dayton in 1995. Serb repression sparked an escalation toward independence that ended in the 1999 Kosovo War between NATO and Serbia. Although Kosovo only won autonomy, it was a very independent form of autonomy, and in turn it inspired Albanians in Macedonia (aided by former members of the KLA) to launch a guerrilla war against the Skopje government with the hope of achieving the same or better.

Secession can engulf groups that seem too small or obscure to merit their own state. South Ossetia, a chunk of territory along the former Soviet Republic of Georgia's Russian border, objected to its inclusion in the new, independent Republic of Georgia and fought to secede. Seeing the South Ossetians' relative success, another small group, the Abkhaz, likewise proclaimed themselves independent, spreading the civil strife to the western end of the country. Both were inspired by Chechnya's struggle for independence against Russia and, not surprisingly, Chechen fighters reportedly assisted both groups in their struggle against the Georgian government.

In Iraq's case, the first candidate for secession is obvious: Kurdistan. The Kurds of Iraq are part of a distinct nation of 35 million people living in a geographically contiguous space with their own language, culture, and traditions. If any group on Earth deserves its own state, the Kurds surely do. However, if the Kurds do decide to go their own way, they might not be the last to do so. Smaller groups, like the Turkoman and the Assyro-Chaldean Christians, might try the same, believing that it will be too dangerous to remain a part of an Iraq that is descending into widespread ethnic cleansing. Even the Arabs could prove susceptible to the siren song of secession. Throughout the Ottoman period, Iraq was divided in three, creating a precedent for leaders to cite. Indeed, 'Abd al-Aziz al-Hakim, leader of the most powerful Shi'i party, the Supreme Council for the Islamic Revolution in Iraq (SCIRI), has been pushing for Iraq's nine southern provinces to form a regional bloc with all of the same rights and autonomy as Kurdistan. Although most of Iraq's other Shi'i leaders have strongly opposed SCIRI on this issue, Hakim's position is widely recognized as a first step toward secession for the south. Nor are the Sunnis immune. Sunni *jihadists* have declared the establishment of a Sunni emirate (that is, a Taliban-style state) in al-Anbar province.

Not only could declarations of independence by groups within Iraq spur other Iraqi groups to do the same, they could trigger secessionist movements (and civil conflicts) elsewhere around the region. Iraq's neighbors mirror many of Iraq's fractures. Should Iraq fragment, voices for secession could gain strength among Iraq's neighbors. Most obviously, if the Iraqi Kurds declare their independence and are recognized and protected by the international community for doing so, it is not hard to imagine Kurdish groups in Turkey and Iran following suit. Iran already has had problems with its Kurdish minority, and this might also encourage elements of Iran's Azeri, Arab, and Baluchi populations to do the same.[34] This alone could also have dangerous consequences for some of the Gulf States, but if Iraq's Shi'ah were to precede or follow the Kurds down the path of secession, it would raise a real threat of secessionist movements (and thus secessionist conflicts) arising among the Shi'ah of Saudi Arabia's eastern province. Nor should we exclude possibilities of surprise secessionist movements. Few outsiders knew enough about the thinking of the Abkhaz or South Ossetians to predict that they would seek self-rule: Iraq and its neighbors are also home to myriad communal groups that, while small, may decide that fighting for independence is better than being dominated by a hostile ethnic or religious group.

Neighborly Interventions

In part because of the four reasons enumerated above, another critical problem of civil wars is the tendency of neighboring states to intervene, turning civil war into regional war and often destabilizing the intervening states. Foreign governments may intervene to "stabilize" the country to shut down the masses of refugees pouring across their borders, as the European Union tried in the various Yugoslav wars of the 1990s. Neighboring states will intervene to eliminate terrorist groups setting up shop in the midst of the civil war, as Israel did repeatedly in Lebanon. They may intervene either in response to the radicalization of their populations (in other words, their populations are angry at the misfortune of compatriots embroiled in the civil war and their country is intervening to help those groups) or to end that radicalization by shutting down the civil war or to stop the inflow of "dangerous ideas" from abroad. Iran and Tajikistan both stayed involved in the Afghan civil war on behalf of co-religionists and co-ethnics suffering at the hands of the rabidly Sunni, rabidly Pashtun Taliban, just as the Syrian regime intervened in Lebanon for fear that the conflict there was radicalizing its own Sunni population. Governments afraid of secessionist movements in their country will often intervene to prevent groups across the border from successfully seceding. Pakistani governments repeatedly intervened in Afghanistan in part to forestall Pashtun irredentism that would claim parts of Pakistan. In virtually every case, these interventions brought only further grief both to the interventionists and to the parties to the civil war.

Of course, these are hardly the only reasons for foreign intervention in civil wars. At times, it happens for purely humanitarian reasons, although this tends to be half-hearted if there is no accompanying strategic motive. Thus, international action in Darfur has been motivated almost solely by humanitarian impulses, but for the same reason it has been rather feeble.

Opportunism is a more powerful motive. States often harbor designs on their neighbors' land and resources and will see in the chaos of civil war the opportunity to achieve long-frustrated ambitions. While Hafiz al-Asad clearly feared the impact of civil war in Lebanon on Syria's own internal stability, it also seems likely that he saw Lebanon as an illegitimate and artificial state wrested from Syria by Western imperialists in 1943, and that by invading Lebanon in 1976 he could re-establish Syria's dominance over its wayward province. Similarly, much as Franjo Tudjman and Slobodan Milosevic may have felt the need to intervene in the Bosnian civil war to protect their fellow Croats and Serbs, respectively, it seems clear that a more important motive for both was to carve up Bosnia between them.

Fear of a new, radical, or hostile government prevailing in a civil war can also trigger foreign interventions. Rwanda's repeated meddling in Congo after the fall of Mobutu led Angola and other neighbors of Congo to intervene to prevent the government from becoming Rwanda's pawn. A motley alliance of Iran, Russia, and several central Asian states banded together to intervene collectively in Afghanistan because all of them shared the same fear that a Taliban success would create problems for them. The fact that the Taliban were seen as Pakistan's creature was also a source of concern. An element of Israel's decision to invade Lebanon in 1982 was its fear that the Lebanese Muslims (with Syrian and Palestinian backing) would win the civil war and a new Muslim-dominated government would take a more active role in the Arab-Israeli conflict.

Intervention can also take many forms. Many states attempt only to influence the course of the conflict by providing money, weapons, and other support to one side or another in the civil war. In effect, they use their intelligence services to create "proxies" that can fight the war and secure their aims for them. Frequently though, these proxies prove too weak or too independent to achieve the backer's goals, which creates an incentive for the government to mount a more overt military intervention. Both Syria (1974–75) and Israel (1976–82) attempted to employ proxies in Lebanon but found them inadequate to the task, prompting their own invasions. Ethiopia has used proxies to fight Islamists and other anti-Ethiopian groups in Somalia from the 1990s to the present. In the Balkans, the United States provided some degree of assistance to the Croat Army, which was one reason for the wildly successful Croat-Bosnian offensive against the Serbs in 1995. However, by October 1995 the Croat offensive had shot its bolt and was in danger of being rolled back by Serb counterattacks had the Dayton Accords—and the deployment of 50,000 NATO troops, including a 20,000-person American division—not ended the war.

Interestingly, states typically opt for covert intervention to try to limit the potential blowback against them, but this rarely seems to work. The best example of this is the Pakistani intervention in Afghanistan. Pakistan is one of the few countries to have succeeded in using a proxy force, the Taliban, to secure its interests in a civil war. However, this "victory" came at a horrendous price. Pakistan's support of these radical Islamists affected its own social balance, encouraging the explosion of Islamic fundamentalism inside Pakistan, increasing the number of armed groups operating from Pakistan, creating networks for drugs and weapons to fuel the conflict, and threatening the cohesion of the state. Today, Pakistan is a basket case, and much of the reason for this state of affairs lies in its costly effort to prevail in the Afghan civil war.

Pakistan is an extreme example, but most of these interventions— successful or unsuccessful, covert or overt—tend to impose painful or even debilitating costs on the intervening countries. Israel's bitter experience in Lebanon from 1975 to 2000 illustrates the pitfalls that even a strong state faces when intervening in a civil war. Israel's interventions led to political scandal, the downfall of Prime Minister Menachem Begin, estrangement between the Israeli officer corps and its political leadership, and growing public animosity toward the government. From 1975 to 2000, nearly 1,500 Israeli soldiers were killed in Lebanon, the country's third deadliest conflict.[35] As every Israeli knows, Israel was attacked by the Arab states in its two deadliest wars—the War of Independence (1948–49) and the Yom Kippur (aka October) War (1973), while Lebanon was regarded as a war of choice, making its losses even harder to bear. The expense of Israel's 25-year involvement in Lebanon is ultimately unclear, but the 1982 invasion alone cost it roughly $2.5 billion, at a time when Israeli nominal Gross Domestic Product (GDP) was only $35 billion, and slowed growth to virtually zero while boosting foreign debt and inflation to record highs.[36] By the 1990s, Israelis called it "Israel's Vietnam." Israel, of course, is a wealthy country; the effects on the poor neighbors of Somalia, Congo, Tajikistan, and other conflicts were even more devastating.

Foreign intervention at the covert level is proceeding apace in Iraq. Iran has led the way and enjoyed the greatest advantage. American and Iraqi sources report that there are several thousand Iranian agents of all kinds already in Iraq. These personnel have simultaneously funneled money, guns, and other support to friendly Shi'i groups and established the infrastructure to wage a large-scale clandestine war should they ever need to do so. Iran has set up an extensive network of safe houses, arms caches, communications channels, agents of influence, and proxy fighters, and will be well positioned to pursue its interests if a full-blown civil war erupts.

Iran's calculus for intervention in Iraq is complex. On the one hand, Iran has numerous strategic interests in Iraq. Saddam's Iraq invaded Iran and sponsored various insurgent and terrorist groups against the clerical regime. The two powers have long been rivals for prestige and influence in the Gulf region, and the fall of Saddam gives Iran an unprecedented chance to become the dominant local power. Domestically, many Iranians have close personal and family ties to Shi'ah in Iraq, and the presence of Shi'i holy sites there makes the country of particular interest. Also, Iraqi Kurds have at times provided support and a haven for anti-regime Iranian Kurds seeking independence. The clerical regime has a particular interest in ensuring that Shi'ah, particularly pro-Tehran Shi'ah, are the dominant community in the country. Though Iran is particularly close to several Iraqi Shi'i groups, it has also tried to establish ties to groups throughout Iraq in order to protect its influence should power shift there. For instance, Muqtada as-Sadr's family has a history of enmity with the Islamic Republic and reportedly despises it himself. But this has not stopped Tehran from trying to curry favor with parts of the Jaysh al-Mahdi—nor has it stopped Jaysh al-Mahdi members from accepting Iranian support.

Although all of these factors have spurred Iran's deepening involvement in Iraqi affairs, Tehran also has an interest in avoiding chaos and massive refugee flows—factors that have also pushed Iran to try to mitigate the conflict in Iraq in various ways. In particular, Iran's encouragement to all of its Shi'i friends in Iraq that they should participate in the American-led process of political and economic reconstruction has been critical in allowing that program to make any progress at all. To some extent, Iran probably feels vindicated by that decision, since it appears to have been pleased with the results of the various elections in Iraq, which have left individuals with close ties to Tehran in positions of power.

Because of these multiple and at times conflicting goals, predicting Iran's response to the worsening chaos in Iraq is difficult. At the very least, Iran will seek to ensure its influence and work with different militias and local powers. The threat of instability may lead Iran to try to calm down violence in Iraq and cooperate with other neighbors, but it also might lead Tehran to try to intervene more decisively in order to "solve" the problem or ensure that its favorite militia "wins." Tehran could conceivably make a broader play for influence if it believes it has an opportunity to dominate the country with relative ease.

The Sunni powers of Saudi Arabia, Jordan, Kuwait, and Turkey are all frightened by Iran's growing influence and presence inside Iraq and have been scrambling to catch up. They have begun to create a network of informants and agents of influence commensurate with those of Iran, largely among Iraq's Sunni population. Nawaf Obaid, an advisor to the Saudi government, warned that an American departure from Iraq coupled with continued bloodshed there will lead to "massive Saudi intervention to stop Iranian-backed Shiite militias from butchering Iraqi Sunnis." Obaid notes that this intervention might lead to a regional war and grimly adds: "So be it: The consequences of inaction are far worse."[37]

Turkey may be the most likely country to intervene overtly. Turkish leaders fear both the spillover of Kurdish secessionism and the fact that Iraq is becoming a haven for the PKK. Turkey has massed troops on its southern border, shelled Kurdish positions in Iraq, and mounted raids into Iraqi territory, and its officials are already threatening much larger incursions. Fearful of the impact on their own restive Kurdish population, the Iranians have also reinforced their troops along the northern border with Iraq and have shelled a number of Kurdish villages.[38] Thus, it seems highly likely that there will be a considerable international component to any Iraqi civil war.

What's more, none of Iraq's neighbors believe that they can afford to have the country fall into the hands of the other side. Both Iran and the Sunni states would likely see victory for the other side in an Iraqi civil war as being an enormous boon to their rivals in terms of oil wealth and geographic position. The "victory" of one or more of the Iranian-backed Shi'i militias would put militant Shi'ah (perhaps even Iranian) forces in the heartland of the Arab world, bordering Jordan, Syria, Saudi Arabia, and Kuwait for the first time—several of these states poured tens of billions of dollars into Saddam's military to prevent just such an eventuality in the 1980s. Similarly, a Sunni Arab victory (backed by the Saudis, Kuwaitis, and Jordanians at the very least) would put radical Sunni fundamentalists on Iran's own doorstep—a nightmare for the Iranians because many *salafi jihadists* hate the Shi'ah more than they hate Americans. Add to this the tremendous incentive for each country to at least prevent any other from being able to capture all of Iraq's oil resources, and it argues that if these states are unable to achieve their goals through clandestine intervention, they will have a powerful incentive to launch a conventional invasion. The potential for civil war in Iraq escalating to a regional war is therefore considerable.

Economic Losses

Measuring the economic costs of spillover from civil wars is difficult, as the hidden or opportunity costs are often much higher than the direct losses. Nevertheless, direct economic costs can also be significant, as numerous historical cases attest. The cost of feeding and caring for hundreds of thousands or even millions of refugees; the cost of supporting proxy forces abroad; the costs of fighting terrorists emanating from the civil war–wracked country; and the potential costs of civil disturbances and overt military interventions can all be crippling for weak states and burdensome for strong ones. Moreover, the increased crime, drug trafficking, and other problems that often come with refugees and cross-border violence impose further costs.

There are also secondary, but often equally costly, effects on the economies of neighboring countries. Trade can decline, even plummet, if the country consumed by civil war was an important external trade partner for its neighbors. Likewise, increased violence in a region frightens away trade partners and investors.

As noted above, Israel's 25-year involvement in Lebanon was extremely costly to Israel in economic terms, as well as costly in terms of the more widely recognized political crises and casualties. The 1982 invasion of Lebanon cost Israel approximately 7 percent of its nominal GDP.[39]

The Syrian economy was also badly damaged by its even longer intervention in the Lebanese civil war. Some Syrians benefited as workers in Lebanon, while the Syrian officer class and élite engaged in smuggling and otherwise exploited the Lebanese economy. However, Damascus maintained 10–20 percent of the Syrian Army in Lebanon for nearly 30 years, which before 1982 was estimated to have cost Syria $1 million per day—a large amount for an economy whose annual nominal GDP was then only around $10 billion.[40] Moreover, at various points, Syrian actions in Lebanon cost it the generous subsidies received from Arab oil producers, including roughly $700 million per year from Saudi Arabia alone in the early 1980s. Syria also absorbed several hundred thousand Lebanese refugees, adding to its unemployment problems. Inflation accelerated as the government struggled to pay for the occupation with reduced income.[41] For example, as a result of the influx of Lebanese refugees and other demographic displacements arising from the civil war, Syrian housing costs soared by roughly 700 percent during the 1970s, and by a further 1,000 percent during the 1980s.[42]

The Yugoslav civil wars were devastating to all of the economies of the former Yugoslav republics, except for Slovenia, whose early and relatively painless secession diminished the impact on its economy. NATO's intervention in the Yugoslav wars proved fairly successful, however, in mitigating the economic costs inflicted on states neighboring the old Yugoslavia. Nevertheless, even in this instance of "successfully" mitigating the spillover, the effects were still significant. In Bulgaria, reduced exports, tourism, and foreign direct investment caused a corresponding slowdown in growth by 2½ percentage points while the current account deficit and inflation rose slightly.[43] For Romania, lost trade and higher transportation costs during the 1999 NATO air war with Serbia, which destroyed the bridges over the Danube, cost the country $30 million-$50 million per week at its height, while foreign direct investment dried up.[44]

Although Macedonia escaped a full-blown war unlike Croatia, Bosnia, or Kosovo, its economy was hammered, especially by the Kosovo war, which led to the loss of many of Macedonia's most important markets, gutted its exports, and boosted unemployment to as high as 40–50 percent.[45] Countries around the former Yugoslavia, such as Austria, Hungary, Italy, Greece, Moldova, and Ukraine, also suffered significant economic costs from loss of tourism, loss of trade, and refugees.[46] An International Monetary Fund study of the impact of the Kosovo war on six regional economies found an average decline in real GDP growth of 1 percent, coupled with a decline in output of about 2 percent, as well as "significantly" increased fiscal and current account deficits.[47]

In many ways, Pakistan's economy appears to have done well during its involvement in Afghanistan, another way in which Pakistan seems to be exceptional in terms of the impact of spillover. However, a deeper look reveals a less favorable picture. Pakistan's involvement in Afghanistan paved the way for the Pakistani military to dominate (and then take over) the government, which Stephen Cohen, one of the foremost authorities on South Asia, notes "has had a deleterious impact on Pakistan's economy" because Pakistan's military leaders have little understanding of, or interest in, economic policy.[48] Another effect of intervention has been the enormous growth of corruption, which had not been minor beforehand. By 1996, Pakistan's underground economy accounted for 51 percent of its overall economy.[49] There were many other effects of corruption. For instance, the Pakistani Army's National Logistics Cell became involved in running weapons to the Afghan *mujahidin* and is now Pakistan's largest freight company.[50] In the 1990s, Islamabad used scarce hard currency reserves to pay Taliban salaries.[51] Pakistan also lost customs revenue as smuggling exploded, to the point where in 1997–98, the government was losing roughly $600 million per year.[52] Narcotics trafficking from Afghanistan has engulfed Pakistan, with a variety of political, economic, and social ramifications; this, coupled with the instability, violence, and terrorism spilling over from Afghanistan, caused foreign direct investment largely to evaporate.

The economic losses stemming from the spillover of an Iraqi civil war are likely to be mixed. On the one hand, decreased Iraqi oil production might put significant upward pressure on oil prices, thereby benefiting Iran, Kuwait, and particularly Saudi Arabia, as well as Syria to a lesser degree. Of course, higher oil prices are a mixed blessing: they tend to allow governments to avoid making much-needed structural changes, can cause economic overheating and rampant inflation, and create massive disparities between rich and poor. It is worth remembering that Iran's sudden fourfold increase in oil revenues after the Organization of Petroleum Exporting Countries' (OPEC) price hikes in 1973 was a proximate cause of the Iranian revolution. On the other hand, the spread of violence would greatly hinder investment in Iraq's neighbors, most of which already suffer from capital flight and face difficulties attracting foreign investment. In Syria in particular, military spending is already an unhealthily large share of government spending, but this might increase in response to spillover from an all-out civil war in Iraq. The burdens of refugees, counterterrorism measures, and providing assistance to proxy groups inside Iraq (or even funding overt interventions there) would further encumber these economies. For instance, Saudi Arabia is planning to spend roughly $7 billion on a fence along its 500-mile border with Iraq to try to prevent refugees, militias, and terrorists from civil war in Iraq from spilling over into the Kingdom. Even for Saudi Arabia $7 billion is a considerable sum, especially for a project that may not work.[53]

Responses to Spillover by Neighboring States

States have tried a variety of means to manage spillover from a neighboring civil war when they cannot, or choose not to, end the violence directly. Although there have been a few notable successes, far more attempts have failed or exacerbated the problem.

Kingmaker

One of the most common methods that external powers employ to try to contain spillover is to back one side or another (usually a group with ties to the external power or perceived common interests) in the hope that it will gain complete political control. This is a policy of trying to create stability through victory. Proxies, however, are rarely able to defeat their rivals and, when they do, are often ungrateful to their foreign backers. Consequently, it is rare that a proxy actually succeeds in defeating its rivals, and on those rare occasions success often comes with a heavy price for the external backer.

This strategy often fails because other external powers prove equally willing and able to support their own proxies in thwarting such a bid. Indeed, in civil wars it is invariably much easier to play the spoiler than the kingmaker. Israel learned this lesson in Lebanon as part of its 1982 invasion. Not only did Israel push out Palestinians militants, but it also helped put in place a right-wing Christian-dominated government whose leaders agreed to a peace settlement with Israel. This government, however, quickly collapsed as rival factions rejected its hegemony and the deal with Israel—a rejection that Iran and Syria, Israel's rivals for influence, strongly backed. Through assassinations and continued civil war, the anti-Israeli forces and their Syrian and Iranian backers defeated the Christian-dominated, Israeli-backed government.

A related reason that playing kingmaker often fails is that the local forces can prove more formidable than originally thought in opposing the would-be leader. Syria's interventions in Lebanon (1975–76) were blunted by fierce resistance from various Lebanese and Palestinian factions. Originally, the Syrians tried to intervene minimally, employing only their minions in the Palestine Liberation Army (PLA), a Syrian-trained and -equipped force, not to be confused with the rival PLO. However, the Lebanese Muslim groups and the PLO proved too strong for the PLA and the Maronite Christians, the groups that Syria initially supported. This forced the Syrians to invade on their own, but this too turned into a humiliating series of defeats for Syria when the Muslim militias and PLO repeatedly blocked and bloodied Syrian armored columns driving into the country.

Moreover, the iron law of civil wars is that they are inherently unpredictable and it is difficult, if not impossible, to determine a priori who will prevail. Interestingly, the "victor" is often not a key player, or even a known commodity, in the country beforehand. Hizballah did not exist in Lebanon at the start of the civil war there, nor did the Taliban in Afghanistan.

At times, playing kingmaker can work. In the early 1990s, Russia worked with former Communists in Tajikistan to defeat the IRP and its allies in Tajikistan. Russia's far more skilled and organized forces turned the local power balance in favor of the former Communists. At their height, Russian troops in Tajikistan numbered between 20,000 and 25,000, a large force given Tajikistan's population of only 6.5 million. A senior Russian officer—General Alexander Shishliannikov—served as defense minister of Tajikistan during the war.[54] Similarly, Russian aid helped both the Abkhaz and South Ossetians to stalemate the Georgian government at various times, preserving their autonomy, although it did not win them outright independence.

However, these successes tend to be more limited than the external powers care to admit. For instance, U.S. support to Croatia during the Bosnian war is typically cited as a case of an external power helping one side "win" the civil war. However, at the time of the Dayton Peace Accords of 1995, the U.S. military believed that the Croats were at the maximum extent of their military success and were in serious danger of being thrown back by Serbian counterattacks.[55] The Croats had already been checked before they could take the main Serb city of Banja Luka, as well as several other key towns.[56] Moreover, Croat ground victories were only one element of success at Dayton: NATO air strikes on Serb troops in Bosnia, along with the crippling of Serbia's economy from the twin burdens of hundreds of thousand of refugees coupled with multilateral economic sanctions, convinced Milosevic to end the fighting and prompted him to force the Bosnian Serbs to lay down their arms.[57]

Moreover, at times even success has its drawbacks: the cost of engineering such a victory can be prohibitive, and the servant often turns on the master. In Congo, Kabila rode to power on the back of Rwandan army troops. Shortly after taking power, however, Kabila turned on his backers and began to work with Rwanda's arch-enemies, the murderous Hutu militias that were launching attacks into Rwanda from eastern Congo. Pakistan today is an economic, political, and social basket case, in part because of its sponsorship of the Taliban and its war to conquer Afghanistan. Although the Taliban at least showed more gratitude to Islamabad for the military and financial support they received than Kabila demonstrated to Kigali, they too repeatedly showed their independence from their backers. The Taliban worked with various Islamist factions in Pakistan, many of whom were not friendly toward the Pakistani government. The Taliban also resurrected a long-standing Afghan-Pakistani border dispute. Most important of all, the Taliban supported al-Qa'ida even when the terrorist group's activities threatened Pakistan's relationship with the United States.

Limited Meddling

A lesser variant of the kingmaker tactic is to work with one or several factions to help them increase their power, or at least survive. This may range from establishing ties to groups along a state's border to attempting to work with one sect or ethnicity of particular interest. The goal of this strategy is to satisfy a state's more minimal needs, such as ending terrorist attacks or staunching the flow of refugees at a tolerable cost.

Iran attempted such limited meddling in the 1980s and 1990s when it worked with various Shi'i Muslim groups in Afghanistan. The Hazaras of Afghanistan, the country's main Shi'i group, had long suffered tremendous discrimination. Even when they joined the anti-Soviet fight they often faced the hatred of many Sunnis, who saw them as apostates, or at least as a group that should be subservient. Iran worked with various Shi'i factions and tried to unite them in the Hezb-e Wahdat-e Islami Afghanistan (Islamic Unity Party of Afghanistan), an umbrella organization. Tehran hoped both to use the Afghan Shi'ah as a way to ensure some influence on its neighbor and to protect them from the depredations of other Afghan groups and the Soviets. After the Taliban began consolidating power in the late 1990s and massacring Shi'ah (and supporting anti-Iranian opposition movements), Iran also joined with Russia and Uzbekistan to back the anti-Taliban National Islamic United Front for the Salvation of Afghanistan (aka the Northern Alliance).

During the Lebanese and Congolese civil wars, many of these states' neighbors provided at least some support to one or more factions. Rwanda began the war by backing Kabila, but then sided with Kabila's foes when he turned against his erstwhile backers. At times, this put the Rwandans on the same side as Uganda and at other times left them rivals. The considerable role that both these states played often led other neighbors to intervene to prevent either of them from dominating Congo, which in turn led still other states to get involved to prevent any of them from making excessive gains in Congo. Thus, Zimbabwe, Namibia, Chad, and especially Angola all intervened in the Congolese fracas for these motives. Over time, the constant interventions and counterinterventions led Rwanda and Uganda to give up hope of playing kingmaker and having their proxies control the entire country. Instead, they settled for exerting influence along their borders, where they both hoped to destroy resistance groups using those areas as bases for cross-border attacks and to extract mineral resources.

In Lebanon, Saddam's Iraq backed Christian militias as a way of hurting its Ba'thist rival regime in Syria, and various Arab states provided financial support to Sunni Muslim groups out of a sense of religious solidarity. After Israel failed to impose a Christian-led government on Lebanon, it created the South Lebanon Army (SLA) to perform the lesser function of merely policing the Israeli border to prevent Palestinian, and later Hizballah, terrorists from launching attacks into Israel. Throughout the fighting in Lebanon, the Syrians tried to employ a variety of Lebanese proxies to secure their interests. At times, Damascus tried to play kingmaker and take over the country. Yet, at other times the Syrian regime was content to use its allies in Lebanon to try to keep the chaos in Lebanon from spilling over into Syria and to prevent Israel from invading—neither of which succeeded. In Somalia after 9/11, the United States has worked with various clans against the Islamic Courts Union in an attempt to weaken a movement thought to be sympathetic to al-Qa'ida.

Of course, such efforts were not complete failures. Although one SLA member described their role as "sandbags for an Israeli bunker," they did help Israel limit losses among its own forces. Various factions backed by Rwanda have helped contain Hutu fighters and ensured that Congo as a whole does not directly oppose Rwanda. Particularly successful were efforts to offset the dominance of another power. It is possible that one faction backed by a foreign power would have emerged victorious in Congo, Lebanon, Bosnia, or Afghanistan if foreign backing had not materialized to help their foes.

However, to achieve even these modest results, the costs typically have been high. The aid provided by the external powers to their proxies has generally exacerbated the fighting. Indeed, there is a path of escalation: typically one country's provision of weaponry and supplies to a group in a civil war provokes other states to provide similar assistance to rival groups. The result is that the fighting becomes more deadly, but the balance of power does not fundamentally change. The lines on the battlefield remain largely unaltered even as the body count soars. As a result, conflicts have gone from killing thousands to killing tens or hundreds of thousands (or, in Congo, millions). Frequently, the proxies also proved to be poor clients: they always took the money and weapons, but they did not always fight on their backers' behalf. When they did, their effort was often half-hearted or poorly crafted. In addition, the foreign backing decreased their luster, as the population saw them as foreign agents.

Divide the Opposition

The opposite strategy to strengthening a favored faction is to weaken those that oppose you. This enables the external power to maintain its influence and weaken those groups that pose the greatest threat to it. As noted above, it is much easier to play the spoiler than the kingmaker. Factions in civil wars are often highly vulnerable to division, with differences in leadership, region, ethnicity, tribe, and ideology all providing potential fracture points. At the same time, however, such divisions often exacerbate the bloodshed in a country and make it even more ungovernable.

Syria did this masterfully in Lebanon, turning groups against one another to forestall the emergence of an anti-Syrian leadership. To weaken the power of Yasir Arafat, Syria engineered a split within the Palestinian movement that led to a bloody competition for power within Lebanon. Damascus also selectively worked with different Christian groups, pitting one against another, always making sure that they remained divided. In the 1980s, Iran and Syria worked together to help form Hizballah to weaken the Shi'i militia Amal, because Amal was cooperating with the Israeli-imposed Gemayel government in Lebanon. In the 1990s, Syria helped prop up Amal against Hizballah, even though the former was increasingly viewed as corrupt and inept. The result was a division within the Lebanese Shi'ah that made Damascus's influence all the greater. Of course, none of this actually brought the civil war to an end or helped to stabilize Lebanon.

Humanitarian Missions to Alleviate Suffering

At times the international community, often with U.S. support, engages in a humanitarian mission to try to feed the hungry and take care of the refugees. Often this is done through various UN agencies, particularly the World Food Programme (WFP) and the UNHCR, which work with various nongovernmental organizations (NGOs). The goal is to take care of one of the most tragic aspects of war while recognizing that the conflict will go on regardless. On some occasions, these efforts include providing military forces to protect UN personnel, to protect civilians, or even to quell the fighting. The UN's Unified Task Force (UNITAF) mission in Somalia, which preceded the broader, second United Nations Operation in Somalia (UNO-SOM II) mandate that focused on a more comprehensive effort, was one such humanitarian mission.

Unfortunately, good intentions do not substitute for effective capabilities and the will to use them. The absence of real capabilities frequently undermines large-scale humanitarian missions, causing them to fail outright or, at best, make limited progress. Most often, humanitarian missions fail in all-out civil wars because the suffering is caused by security problems and cannot be alleviated without addressing that fundamental consideration. For example, UNITAF made only limited progress in stopping massive starvation in Somalia because warlords stole the food and refused to allow it to be delivered to areas outside their control. When UN agencies tried to work with the warlords to ensure safe passage, they merely strengthened the killers' control and legitimacy.

Even international efforts to care for refugees can sometimes make matters worse. When the Rwandan Hutu *genocidaires* fled to neighboring Congo, the international community initially saw them as victims of the mass killing and civil war and ignorantly strove to help them. As a result, international aid groups built and supplied refugee camps for the Hutus, but lacking major military forces these aid groups did nothing to secure those facilities. Unsurprisingly, various Hutu militia leaders used these camps to perpetuate their war against the Tutsis, and they used their control of weapons to strengthen their hold over the refugees. After two years of cross-border raids, Rwanda eventually invaded Congo and toppled the government there to end the problem, thereby precipitating the catastrophic Congolese civil war.

Even when the result is less disastrous, it can still increase the conflict by allowing militants new bases from which to act. Palestinians used refugee camps in Lebanon and Jordan to organize terrorist strikes against Israel and to foment unrest against their hosts. This, in turn, contributed to several Arab-Israeli wars, the Jordanian civil war of 1970–71, the Lebanese civil war of 1975, the 1975–76 Syrian intervention in Lebanon, and the 1982 Israeli invasion of Lebanon.

The Impartial Military Intervention

Seeking to rectify the weakness of purely humanitarian missions, the international community at times has intervened with force to protect aid workers and ensure the distribution of food. The goal is to avoid theft and force local warlords to allow humanitarian relief to reach the population. Perhaps the most famous example is UNOSOM II, which attempted to make up for the shortcomings of UNITAF by providing security for the relief effort.

The challenge is that local fighters do not perceive such an intervention as truly impartial and humanitarian. As Richard Betts has argued, food, medicine, and other supplies are forms of power—leaders who control access to them increase their influence, while those who do not suffer.[58] Somali warlord Mohammad Farah Aideed felt, correctly, that UNOSOM II's effort to feed the starving in areas he did not control was an attempt to weaken his power vis-à-vis his rivals. Even in parts of Mogadishu that he controlled, he feared that the aid would be distributed in channels outside his control because the United Nations and United States did not want to bolster warlords. Unsurprisingly, he turned his guns on UN forces.

Even if they can force warlords to cooperate, the task facing the interventionist powers is often massive and unending. Because they are in essence taking over the functions of the state—providing security and ensuring that people are fed—there is no easy exit from the conflict. Setting up state structures in a conflict-ridden land can take a generation, and there is no simple recipe. Thus, even if the intervention succeeds in the short term, its long-term impact is questionable.

How All-Out Civil Wars End

The problems generated by all-out civil wars are often so formidable, and the challenges in managing them so difficult, that they rarely end simply or easily. The average duration of modern civil wars is over a decade.[59] It is worth pointing out that many civil wars linger in various forms for years, if not decades: fighting persists in Afghanistan, Congo, and particularly Somalia, while the stability of Tajikistan remains precarious. Lebanon remains in limbo, with renewed fighting between Israel and Hizballah in 2006 conjuring fears that the embers of civil war will be stoked to flame again. In many of these and other cases the form of the conflict has changed. For instance, spillover from Afghanistan's civil war in the form of al-Qa'ida terrorism sucked in the United States, transforming it from the war of all against all that predominated in the early 1990s to an insurgency against U.S. forces and their NATO allies. Nevertheless, although the form of the fighting has changed, the conflict itself persists. To an unfortunate extent, most civil wars only ever truly end when one of the sides wins a decisive victory over the other (or others in a multisided conflict), or an external power intervenes massively and occupies the country until the original political order that gave rise to the civil war has been revamped (for good or ill) to the point that it cannot do so again.

Some wars decline in ferocity or end because one faction consolidates control or wins outright.[60] The Armenians of Nagorno-Karabakh defeated the Azerbaijanis. Similarly, the war in Tajikistan declined in scale even though low-level violence persisted because the Moscow-backed Tajik government won. Afghanistan, to return to that example, became far less bloody as the Taliban consolidated power in the years before 9/11. Even though Taliban rule was brutal and the organization supported al-Qaʻida, many Afghans backed it because it brought peace and stability to a country that had known only violence for a generation. Of course, the Taliban's gains did not end the spillover—refugees largely remained refugees, al-Qaʻida had greater freedom to launch attacks outside Afghanistan, the radicalization of neighboring populations (particularly in Pakistan) worsened, and Afghanistan's neighbors increased their involvement in its civil war as they became more desperate to stop the Taliban.

Another reason for wars to decline in scale and violence is a decrease in the meddling of outside powers. The war in Congo persists to this day, particularly in the eastern part of the country. However, most of Congo's neighbors no longer back one faction to undercut the power of their rivals. Nearly all of them suffered enough from their involvement in Congo that they eventually decided that "holding their noses" and remaining aloof was the least bad option. As a result, parts of the country have stabilized as different warlords have consolidated power locally—the exception that proves the rule is the ongoing fighting in the eastern part of the country where Uganda and particularly Rwanda are active. When warlords consolidate power, governance is limited and poor, and low-level strife often continues as the leaders battle for resources or pride. Still, the scale is often far less bloody than when the entire country is an international battlefield.

Civil wars can also be brought to an end by massive outside intervention. In both the Balkans and Lebanon, outside intervention on a large scale forced local combatants to make peace or, if they did not, risk being destroyed. The Ta'if Agreement was enforced by Syrian bayonets in 1990, and the NATO intervention in the Balkans was a critical element in forcing Serbia to accept the Dayton Accords—and then in enforcing them. In both cases, numerous attempts had been made to negotiate a settlement, but it took a massive intervention to convince local actors to drop their opposition to a deal.

Ending an all-out civil war typically requires the deployment of overwhelming military power to nail down a political settlement, along the lines that the United States should have employed during and after the invasion of Iraq in 2003. It took 45,000 Syrian troops to bring the Lebanese civil war to an end, 50,000 NATO troops to end the Bosnian civil war, and 60,000 to do the job in Kosovo. Scaling up for Iraq's much larger population, it would likely require 450,000 troops to extinguish an all-out civil war there. (Similarly, there are currently 35,000 U.S. and other NATO troops in Afghanistan, but they have not succeeded in bringing that civil war to an end—although Operation Enduring Freedom did succeed in ousting the Taliban from power.)[61]

Ending a civil war in this manner also requires a commitment to running the country for years, if not decades. Over ten years later, foreign troops are still in the Balkans, with no prospect of departure. Syrian troops stayed in Lebanon for 29 years (1976–2005). In both cases local institutions were weak or discredited and the potential for violence flaring again was considerable.

A few wars have ended in a partition, whether de jure or de facto.[62] The former Yugoslavia was "stabilized" in 1995 by breaking it into Slovenia, Croatia, and a further subdivided Bosnia, which were distinct from the rump state composed of Serbia and Montenegro. Even this partition did not hold, and four years later Serbia was further de facto partitioned, with Kosovo broken off. In both these instances, huge numbers of foreign troops were necessary to midwife the birth of the new states.

INDICATIONS AND WARNING OF
ALL-OUT CIVIL WAR

The worse the violence gets in Iraq, the worse the spillover is likely to become, which is why a clear warning that the violence is worsening (and that an increase in the intensity of spillover should be expected) would be of great value to policymakers on both sides of the Atlantic. Unfortunately, civil wars defy easy forecasts regarding escalation. They are, by nature, extremely unpredictable, being driven by collective perceptions and emotions. Events which appear beforehand to be merely "more of the same" often prove instead to be "the straw that broke the camel's back," causing a conflict to escalate dramatically. The signal for full-scale civil war to commence often seems clear to historians after the event, but rarely to analysts attempting to predict them ahead of time.

Nevertheless, during the course of our research a number of types of developments did strike us as good indicators that a civil conflict had escalated to the level of all-out civil war. We provide them here as merely an imperfect starting point for those hoping to track the descent of Iraq. We note that a great many of these warning lights are already shining brightly in the case of Iraq.*

IDENTITY

—The strength of state identity.† Do society's members consider themselves first and foremost to be members of the nation championed by the state? Are there rival cultural élites that do not accept the national identity (and are there national cultural élites that disparage other identities)? Do all members of society believe they have a shared history? Using similar measures, what are the strengths of rival identities, such as tribe, ethnicity, and religion?

—Do attacks (criminal, political, etc.) on one member of the population provoke outrage from individuals of different tribes, religious communities, or ethnic groups that do not know the person?

—Does the state fully control generators of identity? Who controls schooling? What are the language policies in the country in question?

RIVAL GROUP COMPOSITION AND STRENGTH

—*Personnel allegiance.* How many full-time cadre, part-time cadre, active supporters, and potential supporters are there of warlords, insurgents, and other armed groups opposed to the state? How many people are joining militia groups on a daily basis? Is the rate increasing, and has the rate increased significantly?

—*Weapons and matériel.* How large are the weapons and matériel caches of the rival groups? Are they able to replace lost weapons? How sophisticated are the weapons?

—*Breakdown in state control.* Is the group able to establish a social services network to extend its reach and popularity? Are non-state groups able to "tax" parts of the population? How much of this taxation is voluntary? How much is involuntary? (Both are useful, as the insurgent or militia must be able to use suasion and fear—but if individuals are giving despite their preferences, it suggests a high degree of militia/insurgent strength.)

THE USE OF VIOLENCE AND THE RESPONSE

—What is the rate of attacks on government forces? On the civilian population? Is the group able to attack guarded or other "hard" targets?

—How many civilians are dying on a daily or monthly basis? Has the civilian death rate increased markedly in the recent past?

—How wide is the armed group's area of operations?

—Are armed fighters able to show themselves openly? If so, in how wide an area?

—Is there violence against diplomats or other key figures overseas?

—How disciplined are the fighters? Do they conserve ammunition, target specific personnel, and obey a chain of command?

—Are cycles of violence developing? Are reprisals getting worse and more common for acts of violence?

GOVERNMENT MILITARY CAPABILITIES

—Are the armed forces still cohesive and professional, and committed to defending the nation as a whole? What is the desertion rate? Have desertions increased markedly? Do members of the armed forces see themselves as guardians of one particular internal group's interests over those of another?

—Are many key units penetrated by insurgents or warlords?

—Do local troops show loyalty to local warlords rather than the central government?

—Does the military plot against the government?

—Is the government negotiating with rebels it previously shunned without a change of agenda on the part of the rebels?

POPULAR ATTITUDES

—How many internally displaced persons are there? How many are fleeing the country altogether?

—To what extent are individuals living in demographically mixed areas fleeing (either under specific threat of force or a more generalized fear of it)?

—How much faith do the people have in the government, the police, and the armed forces to maintain order, provide them with security, and ensure that they have the necessities of life?

ÉLITES

—Are moderate leaders losing authority to radical ones?

—Are rising politicians engaging in communal "outbidding" (appealing to their own tribal/ethnic/religious constituencies with ever increasing rhetoric) rather than attempting to bridge differences?

—Are members of the moderate movement joining the radical wing? Are leaders moving from one camp to another? Are leaders hedging their bets with violent groups (that is, not remaining true to their personal convictions so as not to offend insurgent and militia groups either for fear of attack or in expectation that they will need protection from that group in the near future)?

Sanctuary Measures

—Are parts of the country a "no-go" zone for police and security forces due to violence, ethnic antipathy, militia control, or insurgent activity? What is the size of these zones and how are they changing?

—Are militias and/or insurgents able to sleep or rest in towns and villages outside the sanctuary area?

External State Support Effectiveness Measures

—Is the scale of international support increasing overall? Are outside states doing this out of necessity (because a group controls a key region) or out of conviction?

—What is the type and scale of support provided? Is the group receiving assistance in operational security? Operational planning? Logistics? Financial support? Do large numbers of group members travel to receive such assistance?

—Can the group draw on Diaspora support? How much is provided and what is the overall potential for support?

—Do group members in different foreign sanctuaries work together well, or do the different powers try to use them as proxies against other external backers?

—How many constraints does an external sponsor impose? Is the external sponsor limiting the type and nature of the group attacks or other activities for reasons that are tied to the sponsor's concerns (as opposed to helping the group make better decisions)?

—Is the external sponsor seeking to control the overall movement? Does the external sponsor divide the movement into smaller groups in order to better assure its own control?

—Is state support a substitute for local strength? Does the group have local networks that foreign support augments?

*For valuable indicators, see Central Intelligence Agency, *Guide to the Analysis of Insurgency* (Washington, DC: n.d.) and Daniel Byman, *Understanding Proto-Insurgencies* (Santa Monica, CA: RAND, forthcoming). These efforts focus primarily on the outbreak of an insurgency and its initial growth rather than the transition of a war from significant to massive.

†It is important to bear in mind that identity is never fixed, as it is influenced largely by the immediate and broader circumstances of the individual at the time. At one point, a group of people might declare themselves to be Yugoslavs first and foremost, for example, but under the strains of civil war, they will find themselves feeling more Serb, Croat, or Bosnian Muslim than they once had. This was the historical pattern in the former Yugoslavia, and it is occurring now in Iraq.

3

POLICY OPTIONS FOR CONTAINING SPILLOVER

If Iraq spirals into an all-out civil war, the United States will have its work cut out attempting to prevent spillover from destabilizing the Middle East and threatening key governments, particularly Saudi Arabia. Washington will have to devise strategies toward Iraq and its neighbors that can deal with the problems of refugees, minimize terrorist attacks emanating from Iraq, dampen the anger in neighboring populations caused by the conflict, prevent an outbreak of secession fever, keep Iraq's neighbors from intervening, and help ameliorate economic problems that could breed further political or security concerns.

This will not be easy. In fact, the history of states trying to contain the spillover from civil wars suggests that it is most likely that the United States will be unable to do so. But if Iraq does descend into an all-out civil war, America will have to try. With this in mind, below are a number of policy options and broader observations on containing spillover. At best these options are likely to solve only part of the problem. Moreover, all are difficult, and some are costly and require a large U.S. military commitment.

But planning now is essential. Iraq is descending into the abyss, and it risks taking its neighbors with it. Planning now, even while the Bush Administration struggles to prevent such a deterioration, will enable the United States to better limit the overall scale of the spillover and mitigate its effects on key U.S. allies if worse does ever come to worst. A failure to begin planning, on the other hand, will lead to an ad hoc approach that would almost certainly result in many avoidable mistakes and missed opportunities.

Don't try to Pick Winners

There will be an enormous temptation for the United States to try to aid one Iraqi faction against another in an effort to manage the Iraqi civil war from within. In theory, the United States could choose proxies and use them to secure its interests. James Kurth, for example, argues that the United States should "crush the Sunnis" and split Iraq between the Shi'i Arabs and the Kurds.[63] However, as noted above, proxies often fail in their assigned tasks or turn against their masters. As a result, such efforts rarely succeed, and in the specific circumstances of Iraq, such an effort appears particularly dubious.

Once an internal conflict has metastasized into an all-out civil war, military leadership proves to be a crucial variable in determining which faction prevails (sooner or later). In Afghanistan, Ahmed Shah Massoud's generalship was the key to the Northern Alliance's ability to hold out against the Taliban, and it is unclear whether it could have survived had the United States not crushed the Taliban a month after his assassination by al-Qa'ida on September 9, 2001. However, it is extremely difficult to know a priori who the great military commanders are because this can be demonstrated only by the "audit of battle." At the start of civil wars, it is the political leadership that is well-known, and this rarely equates to military capacity. Lebanon is the best example of this, where the highest profile political leaders of the Maronite camp at the start of the civil war (the Chamouns, Franjiyehs, and even the Gemayels) were displaced by military commanders like Samir Ga'ga' and Michel 'Aoun—who were unknown at the start of the war but emerged as the key leaders because of their battlefield skills.

In Iraq, as in most civil wars, it is not clear which proxy would be the most effective militarily. In Iraq, most observers know about Muqtada as-Sadr and Hakim but know very little about the field commanders of either the

Jaysh al-Mahdi or the Badr Organization—and none of them has yet been tested in combat. It may be that over time, if competent field commanders do not emerge in these militias, they will be defeated, taken over, disbanded, or co-opted into other militias led by those with real combat skill. To back a group now, without any proof that it can survive in a civil war, would be risky at best, and possibly counterproductive if it further alienates other Iraqi groups (including the ultimate victor in such a war) from the United States.

Likewise, numbers seldom tell the whole tale. For decades, Lebanon's Druze have been one of the country's most important military factions despite constituting a small fraction of the population. Moreover, many communities are divided, fighting against one another more than against their supposed enemies. Thus, Iraq's Shi'ah may go the way of the Palestinians or the various Lebanese factions, who generally killed more of their own than they killed of their declared enemies.

In addition to the historical problems of playing kingmaker and picking winners in civil wars, as a practical matter, the idea of backing one side to enable it to "win" in an Iraqi civil war seems particularly misguided.

First, at present there are no "sides" in Iraq's civil war.[64] Commentators often speak of "the Shi'ah" or "the Sunnis" as if they were discussing the Confederates or Yankees, Cavaliers or Roundheads. In fact, Iraq's Shi'ah (who are mostly but not exclusively Arab) are fragmented among dozens of militias, many of which hate and fight one another as much as they hate and fight the Sunni Arabs. While internecine violence within the Shi'i and Sunni Arab communities is less frequently reported by the Western press, it is an important element in the chaos of the country today and is attested to by recent battles in al-Amarah and ad-Diwaniyah, as well as the nightly bloodshed in Basra—all of which is Shi'i Arab on Shi'i Arab.[65] Jaysh al-Mahdi, SCIRI, and the Fadhila (Virtue) Party represent the largest of the Shi'i militias, but none is large or powerful enough to quickly or easily conquer or assimilate the others. Even speaking of these groups as coherent may be an overstatement. There is considerable evidence that many Badr Organization field commanders are not entirely under the control of Hakim and the SCIRI central leadership. The Jaysh al-Mahdi is even more fractured, representing less a hierarchic organization than a movement led by the titular figure of Muqtada as-Sadr, whose regional commanders largely conduct operations on their own—and often without any effort to coordinate with other Jaysh al-Mahdi elements, let alone the movement's leadership. What applies for the Shi'ah applies even more for the Sunnis, who are further divided by tribal, geographic, ideological, and personality splits within the leadership. The Kurds are more united, but even this community has two major political groups, as well as several other minor ones and numerous tribal and regional divides.

Thus, it is nonsensical to speak of backing "the Shi'ah" or "the Sunnis" in an Iraqi civil war, as those groups exist as meaningful "sides" only in the imagination of Westerners. The United States would first have to pick a faction within one of these communities and help it to slowly amass power by conquering or co-opting others before it represented a force large enough to be able to dominate Iraq. Given the historical difficulty in knowing a priori which groups will be able to generate the kind of military leadership that would enable them to succeed, this is an even more difficult proposition. Many nations have wasted huge sums of money trying to help one side in a civil war to dominate, only to find that the side that they picked simply did not have the wherewithal to prevail. Even Pakistan, a rare country that did eventually create a winner, first had to waste huge quantities of its scarce resources on a plethora of other Afghan militias before it hit upon the Taliban.

A second specific problem for the United States in trying to pick, or create, a winner in an Iraqi civil war is how, in practice, America would support them. Some Americans call for backing the Shi'ah on the grounds that they are the majority of Iraq's population. In reality, this would mean supporting a Shi'i faction in the hope that it could eventually unite the Shi'ah and then use their superior numbers (and resources, as most of Iraq's oil production lies in largely Shi'i territory) to secure the country. However, all of the Shi'i militias are strongly anti-American and/or closely tied to Iran, albeit more out of necessity than genuine feelings of amity. While some might be willing to sever those ties in favor of U.S. backing, most probably would not, and it is unclear how the United States would provide such backing. Specifically, none of Iraq's Sunni neighbors (Saudi Arabia, Kuwait, Jordan, and Turkey) would allow us to help a Shi'i militia gain control over Iraq. They were ambivalent at best about the Shi'ah dominating a democratic government; they would be apoplectic about letting a Shi'i militia win in a full-scale civil war. Indeed, their growing support for various Sunni militias is driven by their determination to *prevent* the Shi'i militias (and their Iranian backers) from dominating Iraq.

These Sunni neighboring states would be glad to help us support a Sunni Arab militia to gain control of the country, but there are at least two problems with this alternative. The Sunni Arab militias are closely aligned with al-Qaʿida in Mesopotamia and other *salafi jihadist* groups—the principal target of the U.S. war against terrorism, and leading foes of many of America's regional allies. Just as the United States would be foolish to expect Shi'i militias to cut their ties to Iran regardless of how much support America provided them, so too should the United States be skeptical that the Sunni Arab groups would evict the *salafi jihadists* even if the United States were supporting them. The Bosnian and Kosovar Muslims never evicted foreign fighters during the height of the struggle.

Moreover, the Sunni Arabs represent no more than about 18–20 percent of Iraq's population—a very narrow slice of the Iraqi demographic pie upon which to base a stable government. A Sunni Arab group would doubtless have to slaughter far more people to establish its hold on power than would a Shi'i group and, because of the Sunni Arabs' minority status, would have to rule with more of an iron fist than a Shi'i group. The brutality of Saddam's Sunni Arab–led dictatorship was partly driven by the difficulty of dominating Iraq from such a small power base.

The Kurds have greater cohesiveness than either the Sunni or Shi'i Arabs, but they are an even worse side to back in an Iraqi civil war. None of Iraq's neighbors would be willing to facilitate an American effort to enable the Kurds to conquer the rest of Iraq, so the problem of finding a conduit to provide this kind of aid is even harder. The Kurds also, for the most part, do not want to rule over the rest of Iraq—they want to secede. Nor would Iraq's Arab population willingly accept Kurdish domination, and the Kurds too represent only about 20 percent of the population.

Finally, attempting to back a winner in an Iraqi civil war would not avoid the problems of spillover, but would doubtless exacerbate them. Whichever group the United States chooses to support would have to slaughter large numbers of people to prevail and establish control over Iraq. In other words, they would have to fight out the civil war to a conclusion. Even if that conclusion came several years sooner than it otherwise might if the United States did not try to engineer a victory for one group or another, it would still mean several years of terrible bloodshed. That bloodshed would produce refugees and would radicalize neighboring populations. Whichever group the United States supported would likely find itself in alliance with some terrorists—foreign *jihadists* for Sunni groups, Hizballah for Shi'i groups, and the PKK for Kurdish groups. In return for the assistance of those terrorists in fighting against their internal foes, they would give their terrorist allies considerable assistance and freedom to conduct attacks abroad, just as the Taliban did for al-Qa'ida. It would similarly drive the other groups (those the United States was not backing) to more closely align with sympathetic terrorist groups of their own. Far from discouraging foreign intervention in an Iraqi civil war, the United States would be ensuring it, because whichever faction the United States backed, that group's external enemies would increase support to their proxies inside Iraq to neutralize U.S. support. Indeed, to further obviate U.S. backing, they might possibly provoke their proxies to support attacks against the United States or its interests, just as the Syrians and Iranians eventually moved to mount attacks against the United States because we backed their adversaries in Lebanon.

Avoid Active Support for Partition . . . For Now

In the end, after years of bloodshed and ethnic cleansing, a massive civil war in Iraq may eventually create conditions for a stable partition. However, a major U.S. effort to implement secession or partition today would probably trigger the massacres and ethnic cleansing that the United States seeks to avert. There are a number of well-intentioned plans according to which the United States would seek to partition Iraq—some under the aegis of a weak federal government, others without it.[66] While they may reflect the eventual outcome of an all-out civil war, that does not mean that the United States should purposely advocate such an approach, or even that it is inevitable if full-scale civil war erupts.

The basic problem with pursuing any version of partition in Iraq as a means of heading off or mitigating all-out civil war is that it is probably impossible to do so without either causing the all-out civil war it seeks to avoid in the first place—or deploying the hundreds of thousands of American and other developed country troops that should have been deployed as of 2003 for reconstruction to succeed. Other than the Kurds, few Iraqis want their country divided, nor do they want to leave their homes. While many are doing so out of necessity, and some are even doing it pre-emptively, this is not diminishing the impetus to civil war.[67] In fact, it is mostly doing the opposite. A great many of those who are fleeing their homes are not peacefully resettling in a more ethnically homogeneous region, but are joining vicious sectarian militias like Jaysh al-Mahdi in the hope of regaining their homes or at least extracting revenge on whoever drove them out.

Nor are Iraq's leaders particularly interested in partition, which is true for both the militia leaders and Iraq's current government. The Kurdish leaders want eventual independence but, as noted above, recognize that partition now would likely spark a civil war that would be disastrous for them and their people. Hakim, the political leader of SCIRI, has pushed for the nine predominantly Shi'i provinces of southeastern Iraq to form an autonomous bloc like that of the Kurds, but he is, in effect, alone among the Shi'i powerbrokers in favoring this solution, and other powerful groups, like the Sadr movement, Fadhila, and Da'wa (The Call, Iraq's oldest Islamist party), all oppose it. Moreover, many militia leaders, particularly the Sadrists, have made clear that they intend to fight for all of the land they believe is "theirs," which seems to include considerable land that the Sunnis consider "theirs."

Nor is it clear that a move to partition would result in the neat division of Iraq into three smaller states, as many of its advocates seem to assume. Even if the United States assumed that the main Kurdish parties, the Kurdistan Democratic Party (KDP) and the Patriotic Union of Kurdistan (PUK), were able to continue to put aside their long-standing feuds and jointly administer Kurdistan (which seems likely, although hardly guaranteed), there is absolutely no reason to believe that the same would hold for the rest of the country. As noted above, the Sunni and Shi'i Arabs are badly fragmented among dozens of different militias of widely varying sizes, but none of them large enough to quickly or easily unite their faction. Thus, far more likely than creating a new Sunni state and a new Shi'i state, Mesopotamian Iraq would splinter into chaotic warfare and warlordism. Eventually, larger concentrations would emerge as effective leaders found ways to assemble ever greater resources through conquest, coercion, and diplomacy. However, that might not transpire for many years, and the final regions that emerge might not look anything like the demographic divisions that proponents of partition suggest. Moreover, during this long period of fighting and conquest, the region would suffer from all of the effects of spillover.

Thus, the problem is not merely the large number of heavily mixed Iraqi population centers, but the animosity that ethnic cleansing inevitably creates. Put otherwise, merely eliminating the mixed-population cities would not eliminate the emotions driving the bloodshed and so would likely not eliminate the bloodshed either, although it might reduce the scale.

Of course, with enough military power it might be possible to draw ethnic and sectarian lines throughout Iraq, force the Iraqis to relocate to their respective zones, and then police those lines to prevent militias and terrorists from crossing over to exact revenge. Setting aside the problems with determining where mixed Sunni-Shi'i families—let alone individuals of mixed ancestry—would go, doing so would likely require roughly the same 450,000 troops as would preventing or ending the civil war, as the Bosnia example demonstrates. Moreover, the situation will be worse because the Iraqis will see the United States as imposing a highly unpopular partition on them. In Bosnia, in contrast, U.S. troops deployed to enforce an agreement that the key players had already accepted. If the United States attempted to impose partition after a long, bloody civil war, many Iraqis might be so desirous of simply stopping the fight that they would accept partition, just as the Bosnians did. However, to try to impose it beforehand might be the one good way to unite Iraqis (temporarily), by giving them a common enemy in the United States.

In short, plans to partition Iraq in one form or another as a way of heading off or ending a civil war make little sense because they are unlikely to do so absent a massive U.S. military commitment to Iraq. Lesser commitments of force are likely to create the worst of all possible worlds: failing to end the bloodshed and refocusing Iraqi anger at the United States because America will be imposing upon them a "solution" that very few of them accept, and are unlikely to do so until well into the horrendous suffering of an all-out civil war.

Finally, the United States needs to keep in mind that any American actions in Iraq depend on the support of its neighbors. It is not just that the United States requires basing and logistical support from Turkey, Kuwait, Jordan, and even Saudi Arabia, but that any plan the United States tries to implement can be undermined by the active opposition of Iraq's neighbors. None of

Iraq's neighbors support partition in any form. In late October 2006, the Saudi Ambassador to the United States, Prince Turki al-Faysal, announced, "Since America came into Iraq uninvited, it should not leave Iraq uninvited," and he argued that partitioning Iraq would result in "ethnic cleansing on a massive scale."[68] Only a few days later, the Turkish Foreign Minister declared "There are those who think that dividing Iraq might be better, that this chaos might end. This is what we say: Don't even think of such an alternative because that would lead Iraq toward new chaos."[69]

There is one potential exception to this rule, although it may be a modest one. Michael O'Hanlon, our Brookings colleague, has proposed that the United States back a policy of voluntary ethnic relocation, which would involve the U.S. and Iraqi governments providing economic incentives and physical protection for Iraqi families to leave mixed population areas and move to more homogeneous neighborhoods.[70] Even if it does not preclude an all-out civil war, voluntary relocation could still prove helpful in dampening the ferocity of a civil war in Iraq. Indeed, some Iraqis are already pre-emptively fleeing homes they consider unsafe, even going so far as to swap houses with members of other ethnic groups—Sunnis are "swapping" their homes in mostly Shi'i areas for those of Shi'iah in mostly Sunni areas. The numbers are small, but they do suggest that there is some room for this notion to have an impact.

Of course, this idea is far from perfect: most Iraqis seem unlikely to accept such offers until it is too late and they are driven from their homes by violence; thus, the program might actually become a form of refugee resettlement rather than voluntary relocation. In addition, like all partition plans, it has little to offer the many Iraqis of mixed ancestry or members of mixed families, and many more Iraqis will likely remain vengeful even if they relocate "voluntarily." The ranks of the worst militias and insurgent groups are being swollen by Iraqis fleeing their homes—voluntarily, pre-emptively, or at the end of the barrel of a gun.[71] Indeed, at present, one of the greatest impediments to this idea is the fact that Sadrists run the Iraqi Housing Ministry and they are using that power to ensure that any Iraqis who relocate as a result of the violence know that they were assisted by Jaysh al-Mahdi, not by the Iraqi government. Thus, many of those families involved in the voluntary house "swaps" are coming under the sway of some of the worst elements in Iraqi society.[72]

For these reasons, it seems unlikely that voluntary ethnic relocation will solve the problems that are pushing Iraq toward civil war. However, it might save lives—perhaps thousands or tens of thousands—and might help quicken the pace of ethnic separation while also lowering the body count. That is a positive good, in and of itself, and even if it does not solve Iraq's problems, it still makes it worthy of American support.

The time of partition may come, however, and the U.S. position with regard to Iraq's unity should not be dogmatic. The arguments about partition above represent a mixture of concerns in that it might escalate the violence and drag in Iraq's neighbors. However, in the long run much will depend on the strength and cohesion of the various parties involved. Should a Bosnia-like situation occur where the Kurds, Shi'ah, and Sunnis become unified communities (probably through a long process of killing, conquest, and alliance-forging) and increasingly tired of continued bloodshed, then partition might become more feasible—though the problem of external meddling would have to be carefully managed. Even outside powers may in the end see stable rump states as preferable to continued fighting for control over Iraq as a whole. Just as partition in the end proved necessary in the Balkans, so too it may be necessary in Iraq. Strife in Iraq may create de facto communal enclaves and has already led to massive population movements. At some point, after enough killing, it may be more feasible to try to enforce these de facto boundaries than to put the pieces of Iraq back together again.

Don't Dump the Problem on the United Nations

The United Nations can play a valuable role in helping legitimate international action in Iraq and providing technical expertise in certain humanitarian areas. When possible, the United States should try to gain UN support and assistance with regard to humanitarian aid and military action. However, the United Nations should not be expected to provide security, and it suffers from numerous bureaucratic limitations.

Most important of all, the United Nations has no independent capacity for military action. So-called UN forces are in reality the forces of its members, and the world's major military powers have already shown their unwillingness to increase their military presence in Iraq. Thus, expecting the United Nations to police refugee camps, dissuade foreign intervention, or otherwise handle difficult security tasks requires that major outside military actors, particularly the United States, be part of this effort. History is replete with feeble UN deployments. The United States or other outside powers decided that the international community should show the flag but were unwilling to pay the price of intervention, with failure or even disaster the result. Without the United States or its NATO allies, UN missions typically suffer because the troops provided by other nations rarely have the requisite skills. Moreover, because the United Nations is an organization intended to promote peace, not wage war in any manner, UN military missions (as opposed to those controlled by member states but UN authorized) are often politically constrained by limited goals and rules of engagement designed to maximize UN force protection, not help the force fight local combatants. For many years, Lebanon has hosted a UN force that has played little role in stopping the civil war (though several of its members have been kidnapped and killed).

Even when a UN-authorized force contains major American or other high-quality forces, the UN's very presence can create liabilities as well as benefits and has limits. In Somalia, the UN force had different levels of skill and equipment, making it difficult to coordinate military actions. Even worse, some members of the UN force sympathized with Aideed (or were less willing to engage in military action against him), making the overall effort dangerously incoherent.

UN administrative capacity is also limited. Although the WFP and UNHCR have many highly skilled professionals, these institutions as a whole move slowly in times of crisis. They often take months to fully establish themselves— months in which tens of thousands of refugees or others may die.

Because of these limitations, Americans should not expect the United Nations to pick up the reins and run refugee camps or otherwise manage critical tasks in the region. The United Nations can certainly provide some benefit—lending much-needed legitimacy to American efforts to deal with spillover and providing large numbers of personnel with critical skills to aid refugees—but the United Nations is not the answer to all our problems. Even if Washington believes that it is beneficial to have the United Nations nominally in charge of such operations, American personnel will have to play key leadership roles to compensate for UN shortcomings. The United

States should not assume, or even pretend to assume, that the world will clean up the mess the United States has made in Iraq.

PULL BACK FROM IRAQI POPULATION CENTERS

All-out civil war in Iraq will be horrific. Hundreds of thousands or even millions will die. Many more will be maimed and driven from their homes. It will probably make the current levels of violence appear tame by comparison. A great many people, including many Americans, will be anguished to see it unfold before their eyes every day through the lenses of the international media. It will be hardest on Americans because our country will ultimately be responsible for bringing civil war to Iraq.

Because of our moral responsibility, many will want the United States to do something to try to quell the violence in Iraq even after it has descended into an all-out civil war. Tragically, the history of such civil wars indicates that this would be a mistake. Painful examples are the various United Nations forays into Bosnia in the 1990s. In April 1993, the UN Security Council passed UN Security Council Resolution 819 which designated six Bosnian towns (Srebrenica, Sarajevo, Tuzla, Bihac, Zepa, and Gorazde) as "Safe Areas." The rationale was entirely humanitarian: to create protected havens where Bosnian civilians could flee and be protected from the slaughter and ethnic cleansing. The outcome was a disaster, with two of the safe areas falling to the Serbs, and thousands of Bosnians being killed or raped while the international community sat on its hands. The second United Nations Protection Force mission (UNPROFOR II), created to defend the safe havens, found itself caught in the crossfire, with inadequate troops, and without the requisite political authority to defend the "Safe Areas." In the end, the inability of these safe havens to serve their intended function, and the concern that more would fall, were major elements of NATO's reluctant decision to intervene.

The deployment of Western troops to Lebanon in 1982 was a similarly misguided effort. The U.S., French, Italian, and British forces deployed were too small to actually secure Beirut, let alone Lebanon, and so they simply became targets in the civil war, not peacekeepers. In both Lebanon and Bosnia, the small size of these forces (as well as pre-existing political hostility to them) made it impossible to quell all of the violence, forcing the peacekeepers to focus on only the worst culprits—which was seen as taking sides in the civil war, and which merely made them the enemy of the other warring parties. The result was loss of life for the peacekeepers without any real protection for the civilians.

While safe havens may prove to be an important element of a new American policy to deal with an all-out Iraqi civil war (see below), the United States should not assume that they can be created in the middle of the country, in the midst of the combat, to protect Iraqi population centers. As the tragic experience of Bosnia demonstrates, Iraqi cities would require huge numbers of troops to keep them safe—indeed, this was the principle behind the Baghdad Security Plan that kicked off in the summer of 2006 and was designed to secure the capital as the first step toward a gradual strategy of securing the country and enabling reconstruction. The Baghdad Security Plan failed because Washington refused to provide adequate numbers of American and properly trained Iraqi troops (as well as the political and economic support to lock in the security gains) to secure the capital.

Violence in Iraq's population centers cannot be controlled on the cheap. There is no force level that the United States can maintain in Iraq that is less than the numbers needed to give reconstruction a chance of success but large enough to prevent massacres in Iraq's cities: the same numbers are needed for both missions. Thus, if Americans are willing to commit the resources to actually securing Iraqi population centers and provide the people there with the political and economic institutions they need to survive, then reconstruction can succeed and the United States should be concentrating on that, not on how to deal with all-out civil war. But if the United States is not willing to provide such resources and so is faced with full-scale civil war in Iraq, it would be foolish to try to maintain or re-introduce lesser numbers of troops in the misguided belief that they might dampen the numbers of civilians killed.

Indeed, this gets back to the overarching problem of all-out civil war in Iraq: that the massive resources that would be needed to bring it to an end are effectively the same as those that would be needed for reconstruction to succeed now, thereby avoiding civil war in the first place. Since the United States does not appear willing to commit such resources now to avoid that descent into full-scale civil war, there is no particular reason to believe that Americans will be ready to commit those resources in the near future to end such a civil war, and therefore no reason to believe that the United States can meaningfully diminish the violence that will engulf Iraq's population centers if, or when, all-out civil war erupts.

Consequently, when the United States decides that reconstruction has failed and that all-out civil war in Iraq is upon us, the only rational course of action, awful and hateful though it will be, is to abandon Iraq's population centers and refocus American efforts from preventing civil war to containing it.

PROVIDE SUPPORT TO IRAQ'S NEIGHBORS

Radicalization of neighboring populations is frequently the most dangerous form of spillover, but it is also the most ineffable, making it very difficult to address. Yet there are historical cases where radicalization did not occur.

Where such radicalization did not occur despite the high probability of such a development, it seems to have been the product of socioeconomic prosperity and considerable government capacity and control among the communities likely to be affected. The Druze of Lebanon were major players in the Lebanese civil war and fought titanic battles against the Israeli-backed Maronites. Israel also has a significant Druze population that could easily have become enraged against Jerusalem as a result, but did not. The principal reason, along with widespread Shin Bet (then the General Security Service, Israel's domestic intelligence agency) monitoring, appears to be that Israeli Druze were relatively content with their lot politically, economically, and socially within Israeli society and either chose not to jeopardize it by opposing the government's policies or were less able to empathize with the Lebanese Druze because they did not feel the same degree of anger and desperation with their own situation. Similarly, there were large numbers of Romanians, Hungarians, and Bulgarians in the former Yugoslavia, and all three of these countries were affected economically and politically by the various civil wars there. However, none intervened in the fighting, largely because their socioeconomic situations were improving considerably as a result of aid and assistance from the European Union, coupled with the prospect of eventual EU membership.

This experience suggests that the more prosperous Iraq's neighbors are (and possibly the more that their populations are happy with their own political and social status), the less likely that their governments will feel the pressures of radicalization. For the United States, this would argue for providing assistance to Iraq's neighbors to reduce the likelihood that their own deprivation will create sympathy for, or incite emulation of, the actions of their ethnic and religious brothers and sisters in Iraq. The more content the people of neighboring states, the less likely they will be to want to get involved in someone else's civil war. Aid also provides some leverage with the government in question, making it more likely to hesitate before going against U.S. wishes. Generous aid packages can be explicitly provided with the proviso that they will be stopped (and sanctions possibly applied instead) if the recipient country intervenes in the Iraqi conflict.

Such aid could make a considerable difference to Bahrain, Jordan, and Turkey. Although it is often lumped in with the other Arab Persian Gulf states, Bahrain's standard of living cannot compare to Saudi Arabia, Kuwait, or the UAE because its hydrocarbon production is far smaller. While it does receive considerable subsidies from its fellow Gulf Cooperation Council (GCC) members, Bahrain is their poor relation. As noted above, Bahrain is already feeling the heat from Iraq through the radicalization of its majority Shi'i population, and it is particularly vulnerable to anti-Americanism because it has been a reliable U.S. ally and hosts the headquarters of the U.S. Fifth Fleet. Economic assistance to Bahrain could help dampen internal problems derived from, or exacerbated by, an all-out Iraqi civil war. Jordan is a small, poor country overburdened by its long-standing Palestinian refugee population. Absorbing hundreds of thousands of Iraqi refugees in addition might be the straw that will break the back of the Hashemite monarchy. Turkey is far better off than Jordan, but it too could benefit from U.S. economic assistance. What's more, Turkey's stronger economic position is, arguably, offset by the likelihood that its efforts to join the European Union will not bear fruit any time soon. This will likely be a source of great anger and frustration for many Turks, and generous American aid could help prevent those emotions from being further inflamed by spillover from Iraq. In addition, aid for these countries sends an important political message that the United States recognizes they are suffering from the war and seeks to help them. Thus, much of the foreign aid currently provided to Iraq itself may need to be redirected to its neighbors in the event of a full-scale civil war.

Of course, it is hard to imagine the U.S. Congress voting economic aid to Saudi Arabia and Kuwait. Nevertheless, there are steps that both states can take that would likely diminish the threat from radicalization, and the United States should encourage them—and find ways to help them—do so. Despite their wealth, neither of these societies is idyllic. Many Saudis and a lesser number of Kuwaitis feel frustrated because they are unable to get jobs and enjoy the privileged positions in society to which they believe that they are entitled. This is particularly true for the Shi'ah in both countries, who tend to be discriminated against in a variety of subtle ways. While this is not the place for a lengthy discussion of the ills of Saudi Arabian and Kuwaiti society, it is worth noting that some leaders of both countries recognize the need for wide-ranging economic, political, educational, legal, and social change. Unfortunately, conservatives in both countries are resisting the calls for reform and the high price of oil has allowed them to argue that such reforms are no longer necessary. This is terribly short-sighted because high oil prices will not solve their structural problems and because spillover from an all-out Iraqi civil war could be equally devastating.

In the wake of the disastrous results of "illiberal democracy"[73] in Iraq, Lebanon, and the Palestinian territories, it is important to acknowledge that political, economic, and social reform in the Arab world is not without its problems. Reforms do create instability by themselves. This is one important reason, albeit not the only one, that Arab autocrats have shied away from them. Nevertheless, not reforming is equally dangerous and, in the context of an Iraqi civil war, the potential perils of both acting and not acting will rise. All of the Muslim states of the Middle East are fragile, and spillover from Iraq could stress them beyond their breaking point. But reform poses a similar risk, at least in the short term. The reason to pursue reform, nonetheless, is that it holds out the promise of strengthening these states over the mid- to longer term to the point where they can withstand the effects of spillover—not to mention providing a better life for their citizens and greater peace and stability throughout the region. Thus, the United States must encourage such reform despite the potential for it to cause instability itself, and so must help the states of the region to enact reforms in such ways that they minimize the likelihood of causing instability. That means a gradual process, helped by considerable Western aid in all its forms, and one that seeks to foster progressive change from within the societies themselves by helping indigenous reformers, rather than imposing Western solutions from the outside.

Consequently, the United States should continue to press both Saudi Arabia and Kuwait to continue their reform programs as these create the best circumstances in which popular radicalization can be dampened. Unfortunately, in the midst of an all-out civil war in Iraq such U.S. encouragement will become even more difficult. In addition to the fear that such reforms will cause instability, many throughout the region associate these kinds of progressive reforms with Western policy and culture. The utter failure of the United States in Iraq (which the descent into all-out civil war would represent) will make it even more difficult for the Saudi Arabian and Kuwaiti governments (or other Arabs governments, for that matter) to continue to advocate Western-sounding reforms, no matter how beneficial they might be.

For that reason, the most that the United States might be able to do could be a combination of quiet encouragement, minimizing U.S. demands on Kuwait and Saudi Arabia, and taking other actions that would make pursuing meaningful reform more palatable. U.S. diplomats should continue to stress the importance of these reforms for Saudi Arabian and Kuwaiti long-term stability, especially in the face of new challenges from Iraq. The United States should try to limit its demands on Saudi Arabia and Kuwait so that these governments do not feel the need to decelerate reform programs to save domestic political capital for other American initiatives that they may have to deliver on. A perfect example is major American military equipment sales to Saudi Arabia, which the country generally does not need and sometimes does not request. That may be bad for U.S. business, but it will be much better for U.S. interests if the Saudi Arabian government does not need to explain major equipment purchases to an unhappy populace at such a delicate time. Finally, the United States should consider other feasible measures that will create political "space" for Saudi Arabia and Kuwait to pursue domestic reform by ameliorating other sources of instability and animosity. The most useful such initiative would be for the United States to make a major good-faith effort to revive an Israeli-Palestinian peace process (if not a broader Arab-Israeli peace process, discussed below). This is an issue of major concern to Arabs across the region, and their governments have repeatedly told us that their ability to pursue what are seen as "Western" reforms would be greatly enhanced by real movement on the Israeli-Palestinian issue. As Americans have learned from hard experience, the absence of such a process over the past six years has helped undermine the stability of the Middle East, so there are other reasons to embrace this cause. However, the United States should also make such a push because it would make it easier for the Arab states to pursue the kinds of reforms that would make the radicalization of their populations from a full-scale civil war in Iraq less likely.

Most of the economic aid helps at the national government level, demonstrating U.S. support for its allies and enabling leaders to shore up their power in the face of the possibility of increased popular frustration. But it is also necessary to help governments build regime capacity, a key determinant of the likelihood of overall rebellion.[74]

Capacity has many forms and, unfortunately, the United States usually focuses on military capacity, in part because it has many programs in this area. However, for internal rebellion, police and intelligence forces are usually more important than military ones, particularly in the early stages before a revolt becomes widespread. The United States should try to augment allied security services and administrative capacity through training programs and technical aid. In addition, Western technical expertise can assist the bloated and inefficient bureaucracies of the Middle East to better deliver services to their people.

Bolster Regional Stability

An all-out civil war in Iraq will increase instability throughout the region, possibly to disastrous levels, as a result of spillover. Consequently, it will be of considerable importance that the United States do whatever it can to remove other sources of instability in the region and otherwise increase its stability. Unfortunately, at this point there are a number of other problems that are adding to the general instability of the region. Two that loom large include the ongoing deadlock in Lebanon and the worsening state of Israeli-Palestinian affairs.

A full program to bring peace to Israel and its Arab neighbors or to resolve the Lebanese confrontation is beyond the scope of this paper. Moreover, either or both may be impossible to achieve for many years, and even if they could be solved, by themselves, their solution would not eliminate the problems of spillover from an Iraqi civil war. However, they are not irrelevant either. Their own problems will magnify the shockwaves coming from

Iraq, and therefore the threat of spillover from an Iraqi civil war ought to add a strategic imperative to the diplomatic and humanitarian considerations pushing the United States to make a greater effort to stabilize Lebanon and revitalize a Middle East peace process.

Especially on this latter point, it is important to recognize that the absence of a peace process between Israelis and Palestinians bolsters radical forces in the region and hurts the credibility of U.S. allies. Popular sentiment in the Arab world is rabidly anti-American, in part because of the violent limbo in which many Palestinians remain caught. Many moderate voices who might otherwise be pro-American feel that their opinions on Iraq or other issues are discredited because their opponents can paint them as U.S. stooges, and thus opponents of the Palestinians.[75] Throughout the 1990s, the appearance of a vital peace process made it easier for the United States to deal with any number of ultimately unrelated problems in the Middle East, and a revival of that process would likely do so again, particularly with regard to coordinating regional efforts to contain spillover from civil war in Iraq.

Of course, while it would be highly beneficial for the United States to make a determined effort to restart peace negotiations between Israel and the Palestinians because it would aid American efforts to contain the spillover from an all-out Iraqi civil war, it would be a mistake for Washington to pressure either side to accept aspects of a peace agreement they do not like. Not only will this alienate the participants, but it is unlikely to produce a lasting peace. The United States must help its Israeli ally so that Jerusalem will be willing to take risks for peace, and must help empower a new, moderate leadership among Palestinians able and willing to make peace.

Similarly, the United States must make a more determined effort to build a capable Lebanese government able to provide its citizens with the security and basic services they often lack—and which, among the Shi'ah, has driven so many into the arms of Hizballah. Although Washington must also hold firm to its determination to see Hizballah disarmed, it should not hold the provision of aid to the Lebanese government and people hostage to this requirement. Doing so simply bolsters Hizballah's position both rhetorically and materially. Washington has made a number of good pledges since the Israeli-Hizballah fighting of the summer of 2006; now it needs to live up to both their letter and their spirit.

Moreover, Americans should recognize that a peace process and greater involvement in rebuilding Lebanon's state and society are not panaceas but do help improve the U.S. image among many Arabs. More important, they will allow more moderate voices to move closer to Washington without being discredited. This will be vital as many of the recommendations in this paper call for close, open, and continual cooperation with Iraq's Arab neighbors.

DISSUADE FOREIGN INTERVENTION

The United States, hopefully along with its EU and Asian allies, will have to make a major effort to convince Iraq's neighbors not to intervene in an Iraqi civil war. Given the extent of their involvement already, this will be difficult to do. Only a combination of large positive incentives and equally large negative ones will have any chance of succeeding. The positives should consist of the economic aid described above, as well as specific benefits tailored to the needs of the individual countries. For Jordan and Saudi Arabia, it might be an effort to reinvigorate Israeli-Palestinian peace negotiations, thereby addressing one of their major concerns. For Turkey, it might be pushing harder for acceptance into the European Union. For Syria and Iran, it might be an easier road to rehabilitation and acceptance back into the international community. Economic assistance will likely be important to some of these countries, but the United States should not assume that it will be sufficient for any of them.

In addition, Washington and its allies are going to have to level some very serious threats at Iraq's neighbors to try to keep them from intervening too brazenly. Multilateral sanctions packages could be imposed on any state that openly intervenes. At the very least, there should be a general embargo on the purchase of any Iraqi oil sold by any country or organization other than the Iraqi government or a publicly licensed unofficial entity. This would be hard to enforce because of the ease with which Iraq's oil-rich neighbors could play shell games with oil stolen from Iraq if they chose to do so. However, it might help remove some of the incentive to seize Iraq's oil fields.

In addition, specific disincentives will have to be crafted to affect the thinking of specific states. Jordan could be threatened with the loss of all Western economic assistance, and Turkey with support for its EU membership bid. Saudi Arabia and Kuwait would be extremely difficult for the

United States to coerce, and the best Washington might do is to merely try to convince them that it would be counterproductive and unnecessary for them to intervene—unnecessary because the United States and its allies will make a major exertion to keep Iran from intervening, which will be one of Riyadh's greatest worries.

LAY DOWN "RED LINES" TO IRAN

Preventing Iran from intervening, especially given how much it has already intruded into Iraqi affairs, will be the biggest headache of all. Given Iran's immense interests in Iraq, some level of intervention is inevitable. For Tehran (and probably also for Damascus), the United States and its allies will likely have to lay down "red lines" regarding what is absolutely impermissible. This should include sending uniformed military units into Iraq, laying claim to Iraqi territory, or inciting Iraqi groups to secede.

The United States and its allies will have to lay out what they will do in the event that Iran crosses any of these "red lines." Economic sanctions would be one possible reaction, but they are likely to be effective only if the United States has full EU cooperation and the participation of Russia, China, and India (if only because the United States has basically exhausted the list of possible sanctions it could impose on Iran). Alone, the United States could employ punitive military operations, either to make Iran pay an unacceptable price for one-time infractions (and so try to deter Iran from additional breaches) or to convince Iran to halt an ongoing violation of one or more "red lines." Certainly the United States has the military power to inflict tremendous damage on Iran; however, the Iranians probably would keep their intervention covert to avoid providing Washington with a clear provocation. In addition, all of this would be taking place in the context of either a resolution of, or ongoing crisis over, Iran's nuclear program, either of which could add enormous complications to U.S. willingness to use force against Iran to deter, or punish, it for intervening in Iraq.

ESTABLISH A CONTACT GROUP

It is long overdue for the United States to convene a formal, standing group consisting of Iraq's neighbors (possibly to include other great powers, like the five permanent members of the UN Security Council) to consult and act collectively to help stabilize (and increasingly) manage spillover from Iraq. It is something that the United States should have put forward even before the invasion of Iraq. It is something that could have helped the process of reconstruction, and at some future point, it could be critical to mitigating the impact of spillover from an all-out Iraqi civil war.

Civil wars tend to breed suspicion among neighboring countries. Invariably, countries believe that others are providing covert assistance to one group or another in the civil war, and they fear that the other countries are somehow gaining an advantage over them. Those fears will be greatly multiplied in the case of Iraq because of the importance of its oil wealth, geographic position, water and farmland, and religious shrines. All of its neighbors may covet parts of Iraq and, at the very least, will be determined to prevent other countries from acquiring them. This frequently leads to mistrust, misperception, and exaggeration of other states' allegedly bad behavior. Indeed, this is already going on in Iraq: while there is no question that Iran is backing many, perhaps even all, of the Shi'i militias, the Kurds and the Sunni states neighboring Iraq seem to believe that the Iranians are *controlling* all of these groups. Thus, the first role of a Contact Group for Iraq would be to provide a forum where the neighbors could air their concerns, address each other's fears, and discuss mutual problems. This alone might go some way to allaying suspicions about the activities of others, and so prevent the kinds of interventions that would add fuel to the fire of an Iraqi civil war.

It will be particularly important to invite Iran and Syria to participate. Iran is the only country in the region that holds genuine influence with Iraq's various Shi'i factions, while Syria has provided important support to Sunni Arab insurgents in al-Anbar province. In many cases, it may prove impossible to convince some of Iraq's neighbors to take painful steps to deal with the problems of spillover if other neighbors refuse to do so. Thus, the kind of collective action by Iraq's neighbors ultimately envisioned as the goal of the Contact Group requires that these two key actors participate if there is to be any hope of reaching consensus on necessary actions.

In addition, some problems like terrorism, refugees, and secessionist movements will benefit from being addressed multilaterally. The best way to get each of Iraq's neighbors not to support "friendly" terrorists is to have all of them relinquish assistance to their terrorist proxies. Put otherwise, the mutual trade-offs will be that they all agree that Iran won't support Hizbal-lah in Iraq, that the Sunni Arab states will agree not to support Sunni terrorists in Iraq, and that the Kurds will agree not to support the PKK. As hard as this may be, it is impossible to imagine them refraining from sup-porting their own terrorists any other way. Likewise, if all present agree not to recognize or assist secessionist movements until all are ready to do so, it will likely dampen the ardor of groups considering secession.

If, at some point, the United States (or the United Nations, or another actor) believes that it is necessary to end the civil war, a Contact Group would likely prove invaluable, just as it did in the former Yugoslavia in bring-ing both the Bosnia and Kosovo wars to a close. The Contact Group for Iraq would provide a standing mechanism by which assistance from Iraq's neigh-bors could be coordinated to try to end the fighting. Finally, the Contact Group's existence would be a diplomatic and public opinion boon for the United States, as it would allay suspicions of U.S. intentions that were height-ened by U.S. unilateralism in Iraq.

PREPARE FOR OIL SUPPLY DISRUPTIONS

One of the principal reasons that an all-out civil war in Iraq could be disas-trous to the United States, unlike other failed interventions and civil wars, is because of its potential impact on global oil markets. At its worst, an Iraqi civil war could cause civil wars in neighboring states or escalate to a regional war—which could result in large-scale disruptions of Persian Gulf oil pro-duction. During the Iran-Iraq War, both sides attacked each other's oil production and export capacities, while during the 1979 Iranian Revolution that country's oil production dropped from over 6 million b/d, to just over 1 million b/d. Thus, regional war or civil war spreading to neighboring states could have severe consequences for Persian Gulf oil exports.

Even if spillover from an Iraqi civil war does not reach such levels, lesser problems, such as terrorist attacks on oil infrastructure of the kind con-ducted daily in Iraq (or the 2006 attack on the Abqaiq facility in Saudi Arabia), could still cause oil price volatility with repercussions for the global economy. The economic impact of such attacks could be considerable. A fur-ther reduction in Iraqi oil production might put upward pressure on world oil prices. Of far greater concern, however, is the risk of attacks on Saudi Arabian production and transit facilities. Disruptions in Saudi Arabian supply would very likely send prices soaring. Even the greater risk of attacks would lead to an instability premium being built into oil prices.

In its own planning exercises and as part of its global efforts, the United States should be prepared for potential supply disruptions. Washington should consider building up the Strategic Petroleum Reserve to reduce the impact of price spikes. Washington should also encourage the International Energy Agency to develop contingency plans so that leading oil-consuming countries can better manage the risk of disruptions. Together, such efforts might even reduce incentives to attack oil production and transit facilities, though these facilities will still be a priority target.

Manage the Kurds

Because of the ease with which secessionism can spread, and the number of groups in the Persian Gulf that could easily fall prey to such thinking, it will probably be necessary for the United States to persuade the Iraqi Kurds not to declare their independence anytime soon. Iraq's Kurds (and all of the Kurds of the region) deserve independence, but this should come only as part of a legal process under conditions of peace and stability. In the run-up to, or in the midst of, a massive civil war, it could create destabilizing problems well beyond Kurdistan.

To some extent, Kurdistan must nevertheless be managed as if it were independent—as if it were one of Iraq's neighbors. Since the *peshmerga* are fully capable of keeping the chaos from a civil war in the rest of Iraq out of their territory, Iraqi Kurdistan is likely to look and feel like a different country. The Kurds are likely to share the same problems as Iraq's neighbors in terms of refugees flowing their way, terrorist groups striking out against them (and using their territory to conduct strikes), and the radicalization of their population. In particular, hundreds of thousands of Iraqi Kurds live in Baghdad, Mosul, and other cities beyond the borders of Iraqi Kurdistan proper. Many of these people may flee to Kurdistan, while many Kurds will demand that the PUK and KDP mount military operations into the rest of Iraq to try to protect Kurdish civilians or punish the Arab attackers.

Consequently, the United States will have to help the Kurds deal with their own problems of spillover from the civil war in the rest of Iraq and convince the Kurds not to "intervene" in it. That will mean helping them deal with their refugee problems, providing them with considerable economic assistance to minimize the radicalization of their own population, and likely providing them with security guarantees—or, better still, U.S. military forces—to deter either Iran or Turkey from attacking them. Indeed, one U.S. "red line" for Iran ought to be no attacks, covert or overt, on the Kurds.

The price for this assistance must be that the Kurds agree to forswear declaring independence in the near term and to take actions like policing their own borders to minimize other spillover problems. In particular, the United States should press the Iraqi Kurds to cooperate with Turkey to stop the PKK from using Iraqi Kurdistan as a rear base for its operations.

Thus far, Kurdish politicians have often behaved with remarkable forbearance and perspicacity regarding both Iraq's future and their role in it. They understand how difficult it will be for them to secede while Iraq is in a state of upheaval, but there is a powerful popular desire for independence now. If the rest of the country falls into true chaos, it may be difficult for even the most statesman-like of Kurdish leaders to resist demands for independence. Moreover, there are large numbers of Kurds living in the mixed-population areas of Baghdad and central Iraq who will be threatened by civil war, while many Kurds harbor irredentist designs on Kirkuk and a number of other towns. These forces too will push them to intervene. Thus, the United States has to stop being so churlish with its support for the Kurds; the only way to keep them in Iraq, at least temporarily and technically, will be to ensure their security and prosperity.

STRIKE AT TERRORIST FACILITIES

Should Iraq fall into an all-out civil war, Washington will have to recognize that terrorists will continue to find a home in Iraq and will use it as a base to conduct attacks abroad. All of the different militias are likely to engage in terrorist attacks of one kind or another, and will just as likely try to ally with transnational terrorist groups to enlist their support. And the more that the United States recedes from an Iraqi civil war, the fewer the disincentives for them to do so.

Nevertheless, the United States should continue to try to limit the ability of terrorists to use Iraq as a haven for attacks outside the country. The best way to do that will be to retain assets (air power, Special Operations Forces, and a major intelligence and reconnaissance effort) in the vicinity to identify and strike major terrorist facilities like training camps, bomb factories, and arms caches before they can pose a danger to other countries. Thus, the United States would continue to make intelligence collection in Iraq a high priority, and whenever such a facility was identified, Shi'i or Sunni, U.S. forces would move in quickly to destroy it. When possible, the United States would work with various factions in Iraq that share our goals regarding the local terrorist presence.

This requirement is difficult, however, as it does not remove the U.S. military presence from the region. If such strike forces were based in Iraq's neighbors, they would upset the local population and likely face limits on their ability to operate in Iraq by the host governments. This was exactly the set of problems the United States encountered during the 1990s, and which led Washington to eliminate many of its military facilities in the region after the invasion of Iraq.

On the other hand, maintaining American troops in Iraq, even at reduced levels, will have negative repercussions on the terrorism threat as well. It will allow the *salafi jihadists* to continue to use the U.S. presence in Iraq as a recruiting tool, although the diminished U.S. military footprint will make this slightly harder. It will also mean that American troops will continue to be targets of terrorist attacks, although redeploying them from Iraq's urban areas to the periphery would diminish the threat from current levels.

Finally, the United States will have to recognize the military limits of what can be accomplished. Terrorism in Iraq has flourished despite the presence of 140,000 U.S. troops: it is absurd to expect that fewer troops could accomplish more. The hope is to reduce the frequency of attacks and the scale of the training and other activities, but our expectations must by necessity be modest.

Consider Establishing Safe Havens or "Catch Basins" along Iraq's Borders

A priority for the United States would be to prevent the flow of dangerous people across Iraq's borders in either direction—refugees, militias, foreign invaders, and terrorists. This will be among the hardest tasks for the United

States: we present it below and highlight its difficulties as well as its advantages. A half-hearted effort on this front that ignores the potential problems may be the worst outcome of all.

One option might be to create a system of buffer zones with accompanying refugee collection points inside Iraq manned by U.S. and other Coalition personnel. The refugee collection points would be located on major roads preferably near airstrips along Iraq's borders—thus, they would be located on the principal routes that refugees would take to flee the country—and would be designed with a good logistical infrastructure to support facilities to house, feed, and otherwise care for tens or even hundreds of thousands of refugees. At these refugee collection points, the United States and its allies would stockpile massive quantities of food, medicine, and other supplies, and would build tent cities or other temporary housing. Iraqi refugees would be gathered at these points, and held and cared for. The Coalition (principally the United States) would also provide military forces both to defend the refugee camps against attack and to thoroughly pacify them (by disarming those entering the camps and then policing the camps afterwards). As the United States learned in the Balkans, and the world learned in Congo, disarming refugees and pacifying refugee camps are very onerous tasks, but failure to do so can lead the camps to become militia bases, and their attacks will worsen the conflict and then invite retaliation against the camps.

Another key mission of Coalition military forces could be to patrol large swathes of Iraqi territory along Iraq's borders beyond the refugee collection facilities themselves. One purpose of these patrols would be to prevent both refugees and armed groups from skirting the refugee collection points and stealing across the border into a neighboring country. However, a second but equally important goal of these buffer zones would be to prevent military forces (and ideally, intelligence agents and their logistical support) of the neighboring countries from moving into Iraq. Historically, even our closest allies have shied away from an open confrontation with American military forces when they were manning such buffers. Indeed, on a few occasions in Lebanon, U.S. Marines forced Israeli units to halt combat operations by simply interposing themselves between the Israeli forces and their intended target. In Iraq, powerful U.S. forces defending these buffer zones would likely deter any of Iraq's neighbors from directly moving through their areas of operation into Iraq proper.

These buffer zones and their refugee collection points would thus serve as "catch basins" for Iraqis fleeing the fighting, providing them with a secure place to stay within Iraq's borders and thus preventing them from burdening or destabilizing neighboring countries. At the same time, they would also serve as buffers between the fighting in Iraq and its neighbors by preventing some forms of spillover from Iraq into their states, and by preventing them from intervening overtly in Iraq (and hindering their ability to do so covertly). Of course, because they are designed to address the problem of spillover, catch basins cannot be used to quell the violence that would consume much of central Iraq.

It would be important to have these catch basins on the periphery but inside Iraqi territory to ensure coalition freedom of action, hinder the terrorists and militias from crossing into neighboring states, and reduce the legal burdens that those fleeing the violence would acquire if they crossed an international border. Moreover, the United States would not want the refugee camps to be on the territory of Iraq's neighbors, because this would allow them to arm and manipulate the refugees and would not allow the catch basins to serve as a barrier should they decide to intervene directly in the conflict with their own forces. American forces operating on the soil of another country would have considerably more difficulty preventing the forces of that country from intervening in Iraq than if the American units remained on Iraqi soil.

Overall, a force of roughly 50,000–70,000 Coalition troops in country with another 20,000–30,000 providing logistical support from elsewhere in the region would probably be necessary to support the "catch basin" concept. Most of the catch basins themselves would be manned by military forces of roughly Brigade Combat Team (BCT)/Marine Regimental Combat Team (RCT)/or Armored Cavalry Regiment (ACR) size, coupled with large numbers of civilian personnel—ideally from international NGOs as well as the Coalition. In addition, as much as a full division might be needed in southern Iraq near Safwan and az-Zubayr. This region would be closest to Iraq's populated areas, and would be a logical destination for refugees fleeing some of Iraq's largest cities—like Basra, an-Nasiriyah, as-Samawah, and ad-Diwaniyah. In addition, Iraq's massive Rumaylah oilfield lies in this area and the Coalition might want to defend it either to prevent its destruction or capture, or conceivably to pump oil from the field. The greater complexity of the challenges in this area, coupled with the potential for greater numbers of refugees, would call for a larger commitment of forces.

In addition to this full division deployed in the south of Iraq and four to seven BCT/RCT/ACR-sized catch basins along the Saudi Arabian, Jordanian, and Syrian borders, the United States would have to decide whether to establish similar zones along the Kurdish borders with the rest of Iraq. As noted above, a key element of keeping the Kurds from seceding, and from intervening in central Iraq proper, will be helping them to deal with the problems of spillover. The Kurds will also have refugee and terrorism problems. They too will be tempted to mount military operations into the rest of Iraq on behalf of the many Kurds living outside Kurdistan. And they too will face the threat of attack from the Turks, Iranians, and Syrians. Establishing three to five additional catch basins along the inside of the borders of Iraqi Kurdistan would help solve all of those problems, but at the cost of committing the United States to the security of Kurdistan.

Although the United States has never attempted precisely this type of operation before, there are some historical analogies. In northern Iraq in 1991, the United States launched Operation Provide Comfort, which was a massive effort to care for and protect Iraqi refugees (overwhelmingly Kurds) fleeing Saddam's Republican Guards after the Gulf War and the subsequent Shi'i and Kurdish revolts. Although Operation Provide Comfort did not disarm the Kurds, it established refugee camps in Iraqi territory (to prevent the Kurds from fleeing into Turkey and Iran), successfully saving over a million people and preventing the Iraqi Army from attacking them. Likewise, during the Yugoslav civil wars, NATO and the United Nations helped establish refugee camps in Albania and Macedonia to protect and provide for hundreds of thousands fleeing the fighting, especially from the Kosovo war. The "catch basin" approach would build on these and other examples, taking the overarching concept to the next level so that it is properly tailored to meet both the humanitarian needs of the refugees and the strategic imperative to diminish spillover.

However, the catch basin concept has significant drawbacks as well, and Americans should not fool themselves that it is a panacea for the problems of spillover or that it can be done at little cost. Even in the strategic realm, the idea has at least one big problem: Iran. Unlike Iraq's borders with Syria, Jordan, Kuwait, and Saudi Arabia, the Iranian border is simply too long and

Schematic of Catch Basin Concept

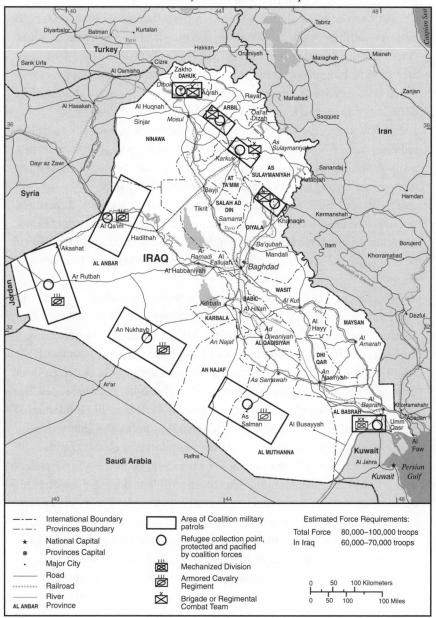

–·–·–	International Boundary	
–··–··–	Provinces Boundary	
★	National Capital	
◉	Provinces Capital	
•	Major City	
——	Road	
+++++++	Railroad	
——	River	
AL ANBAR	Province	

▭	Area of Coalition military patrols
◯	Refugee collection point, protected and pacified by coalition forces
⊞	Mechanized Division
⊠	Armored Cavalry Regiment
⊠	Brigade or Regimental Combat Team

Estimated Force Requirements:

Total Force 80,000–100,000 troops

In Iraq 60,000–70,000 troops

0   50   100 Kilometers

0   50   100   100 Miles

has too many crossing points for it to be policed effectively by smaller numbers of Coalition troops. Iran will never allow the United States the access across its territory, let alone logistical support, that would be necessary to make establishing catch basins along the Iraq-Iran border realistic. Thus, employing this scheme could have the effect of making it look like the United States was turning Iraq over to the Iranians; the catch basins could prove very effective at preventing intervention by any of Iraq's Sunni neighbors while doing nothing to stop Iranian intervention.

For this reason, the United States would have to be able to lay down clear red lines to Iran about non-intervention (at least overt) and then be in a position to enforce this assiduously. This might not be realistic given the many complicating factors in the U.S.-Iranian relationship.

The refugee safe haven concept also has significant logistical difficulties. It is intended to keep the refugee problems out of neighboring countries and major urban areas. However, this requires establishing camps in the deserts near Syria and Kuwait, a challenging (though not impossible) logistical effort.

If the strategic and logistical problems with the catch basin concept seem unpleasant but manageable, the political drawbacks may not be. The concept requires a willingness on the part of the American people to endure ongoing high costs in Iraq, albeit at reduced levels from the present and with the intent of diminishing the costs that the United States would pay if spillover from an Iraqi civil war were expected to destabilize other regional states. The concept also may face legal problems, as individuals have the fundamental right to leave their country to seek asylum, and any policy that interferes with this is open to legal challenge. Thus, American forces probably could do no more than encourage Iraqis fleeing the violence to go to the refugee collection points—and facilitate their transport—while making the facilities for housing and caring for refugees reasonably desirable. The United States would still have to deploy tens of thousands of troops to Iraq (albeit on its periphery), and provide supplies and otherwise help feed and care for hundreds of thousands of refugees. Because the United States would still occupy parts of Iraq, the catch basins might not help at all with the problem of terrorism. As with U.S. efforts to strike at terrorists, the U.S. presence would, to an extent, remain a recruiting poster for the *jihadist* movement. Finally, all of these costs would have to be endured for as long as the war rages or some other solution could be devised: refugees from the wars in Afghanistan lived away from their homes for over 20 years.

Finally, the policy might prove difficult to sustain for humanitarian reasons. The catch basin scheme would have to concede that the center of Iraq, where the vast majority of its population lives, would be a raging inferno of civil war, with innocent men, women, and children potentially dying by the thousands on a daily basis. It will be awful enough if the United States simply walks away from the nightmare it will have created, but it will be far harder to maintain tens of thousands of troops along Iraq's borders and have them do nothing to stop the fighting that may be taking place only a helicopter ride away. Any goodwill the United States would gain from taking care of the refugee problem could dissipate as many would hold Washington responsible for the problem's creation.

In October 2006 the Saban Center for Middle East Policy at Brookings ran a war game in which a group of former senior U.S. officials took on the roles of the National Security Council (NSC) and were faced with a series of challenges from an Iraq slipping into full-scale civil war (see "An Ugly Practice Run" on page 94). This mock NSC debated the options open to the United States and fairly quickly adopted a version of the catch basin concept, precisely because it offered the United States the chance to get out of the way of Iraq's civil war and hold down American casualties and other costs, while simultaneously mitigating the impact of spillover on Iraq's neighbors. However, after the game was over, several of the participants confided that even though the approach made such strategic sense, they felt it would be hard to sustain in reality because of the "optic" of having American troops sitting on their hands so close by when so many were dying. Of course, that is the terrible reality of civil war in Iraq; it will likely make us choose among options so awful that they could make the current debate seem easy and straightforward by comparison.

Take Decisive Steps Early and Be Wary of Half-Measures

In the cases of all-out civil wars, history demonstrates that incremental steps and half-measures frequently prove disastrous. The UN intervention in Bosnia had too few troops, an unclear mission, and lukewarm support from member states. The result was the disasters at Srebrenica and Gorazde. Indeed, between April 1992 and October 1993, the UN Security Council passed 47 resolutions related to the former Yugoslavia, none of which had any discernible impact on the fighting. In Lebanon, both the Israelis and the Syrians tried half-measures—arming proxies, mounting limited interventions, striking at selected targets—to no avail. U.S. and international attempts to bring order to Somalia with a small military force with a limited mission proved similarly disastrous. America's own determination to stabilize Iraq on the cheap has contributed to the disasters that have unfolded there since 2003.

A related aspect of this caveat is the need to deal with problems promptly when they arise, rather than letting them fester. One of the principal lessons of the Iraq Civil War simulation was the importance for the United States of dealing with Iran early on. As the civil war playing out in the simulation worsened, the U.S. side found its leverage diminishing and Iran's rising. This is likely to be the case in reality, and it argues for deciding early on whether the United States should take a confrontational or cooperative (even tacitly) approach toward Iran and then pursuing it aggressively.

An Uncertain End Game

Even if taken together, the recommendations outlined above are not a panacea. If Iraq descends into an all-out civil war, the United States will only have a choice between terrible options and worse ones. Those listed above could all help ameliorate the problems of spillover from a full-blown Iraqi civil war, but they are not guaranteed to solve the problems, and they will create other costs, risks, and complications of their own. Unfortunately, that is the nature of dealing with Iraq and civil war, and as bad as these choices may be, we believe that the opposite—simply walking away from Iraq in the hope that somehow spillover will not occur or will not have much of an impact—is even worse.

However, it is important to recognize that all of the measures proposed above are simply designed to contain a civil war in Iraq, not shut it down. There is no end game inherent in these options. Instead, the goal of the United States would have to be to contain the Iraqi civil war until one of two things became possible. The first is that the war would burn itself out, making possible a (modest) international effort to resolve it and set the country back on a path toward stability. Every civil war must end, but that can take decades. The alternative would be for the United States and its allies in the region to try to contain an Iraqi civil war long enough for the international community (including the U.S. government) to summon the will to intervene with the kind of force and resources that could actually shut it down. If the first option seems like a poor goal because it may take a very long time to occur (and all the while we will have to do many of the things listed above), the second seems even worse because it seems so unlikely that any country or combination of countries would contribute the 450,000 or so troops that probably would be needed.

This is one illustration of just how bad a situation we will have created for ourselves in Iraq if we allow that country to implode in all-out civil war: that the best courses of action we will have open to us will be to try to contain horrific violence there long enough for it to burn itself out, or for the United States and the rest of the world to summon the will to do what they have been unwilling to do from the very start.

How we got to this point in Iraq is an issue for historians (and perhaps voters in 2008); what matters now is how we move forward and prepare for the enormous risks an Iraqi civil war poses for this critical region. As we prepare, we must remember that Iraq's descent into the abyss does not relieve us of our political, military, and financial responsibilities: dealing with the problems of spillover is likely to be costly, painful, and bloody. But ignoring the risks could be even worse.

AN UGLY PRACTICE RUN

On October 4, 2006, the Saban Center for Middle East Policy conducted a one-day crisis simulation to test U.S. policy options under a scenario in which Iraq was sinking into an all-out civil war.[76] We gathered 11 former high-ranking U.S. government officials to play the parts of a mock Principals Committee (PC) of the NSC. The game consisted of three moves, each roughly six months apart in game terms. The group's members consisted of former officials in both Republican and Democratic administrations, who were instructed to think in non-partisan terms. Saban Center fellows were the game's Control.

SCENARIO AND COURSE OF THE SIMULATION

The scenario began with a series of events that led to the rapid dissolution of the Iraqi armed forces and a request by the U.S. commander of the Multi-National Force-Iraq for approximately 60,000 more U.S. troops to substitute for the evaporating Iraqi formations and to stabilize the situation. Although the Principals recognized the gravity of the situation, they were initially unable to agree on how to respond, with different members proposing radically different, but equally dramatic changes. The result, at least initially, was a decision to compromise with a tweaked "muddle-through" approach for the time being while they set in motion a formal policy review process to decide among the different alternatives.

This initial decision created additional problems on the ground, including a threat by the Kurds to declare independence, growing numbers of refugees coupled with the incipient problems in Saudi Arabia and Kuwait, greater internecine warfare both among and within Iraq's various ethnic and religious communities, growing Iranian involvement in southern Iraq, efforts by Iraq's Sunni Arab neighbors to try to match the Iranians by providing corresponding levels of support to Sunni insurgent/militia/terrorist groups, and a decision by the Iraqi prime minister to roll the dice on a national reconciliation conference—the failure of which was expected to bring down his government. These developments, and additional conversations that amounted to the resolution of the policy review process, resulted in the PC adopting a radically different course. The PC opted to simultaneously back the Iraqi prime minister's plan for a national reconciliation conference to the hilt, secure diplomatic support for it from all of Iraq's neighbors, which was to be followed by a major redeployment of Coalition military forces out of Iraq's population centers and to its periphery, along the lines of the catch basin approach outlined above.

The result of all this was that the regional conference failed—most of the neighbors were unwilling to make serious commitments, the Iranians opted not to attend, and the Iraqi participants could not come to any agreement on power-sharing or other measures. However, this then provided political cover for the redeployment, which initially went quite smoothly. Indeed, the catch basin scheme seemed to do well in preventing Kurdish secession; refugee problems; and foreign intervention from Saudi Arabia, Turkey, and Jordan. It also diminished U.S. casualties, although it did not eliminate them entirely. However, to test a few of the potential weak points of the catch basin scheme, Control decreed that the Iranians were deploying large numbers of Revolutionary Guards with their heavy weapons to Iraq in the guise of a new Shi'i militia called Iraqi Hizballah.

In the final move of the game, the catch basins were holding the line with the refugee problem and preventing foreign interference from the Sunni states, but Iraqi Hizballah (because of its massive Iranian backing) was making huge gains in the center of the country against both Sunni Arab groups and other Shi'i groups. This was making the Sunni regimes nearly apoplectic. The game ended with the PC deciding to make a direct demarche to Tehran to warn it to cease its aid. If, as the group expected, that failed, the United States would begin to help the Saudis, Kuwaitis, and Jordanians to arm the Sunni Arab militias (and any other Shi'i militias who would accept aid from the United States and to whom the United States could find ways to provide such aid) to help them defeat Iraqi Hizballah. In short, civil war in Iraq had become a very thinly veiled proxy war between the United States and Iran, with Iran having huge advantages in terms of the strength of the group it was supporting and the logistical ease of supplying it. The U.S.-Iranian confrontation dominated the final session, with other fallout from Iraq, including the collapse of the British government (by then led by Gordon Brown) and Sunni regime support for Sunni Arabs in Iraq linked to foreign *jihadists* falling by the wayside.

LESSONS FROM THE SIMULATION

Any conclusions from the game would have to be seen as highly context-dependent as the game was run only once and was designed to allow for multiple policy directions by the United States. For example, the game did not test what would happen if a massive terrorist attack was organized and planned from Iraq and resulted in significant U.S. casualties—an event that could fundamentally change U.S. perceptions of the stakes and priorities in Iraq. That said, the simulation did seem to demonstrate certain points.

PROS AND CONS OF THE CATCH BASINS

The redeployment of U.S. military assets along the lines of the catch basin approach appeared to perform reasonably (at least for the 12 months during which it was employed in the game) in handling those missions for which it was designed: preventing refugees from creating spillover problems, hindering the movement of terrorists and militias, and preventing overt intervention by most of Iraq's neighbors. All of these were very positive developments that should not be underestimated. However, the game also highlighted two of its most important potential drawbacks:

—The catch basin approach has little ability to prevent Iranian interference in Iraq, and by efficiently preventing the intervention of other states could cause these states to focus their anger on the United States. Preventing the intervention of most of Iraq's neighbors is an absolute positive—especially since history suggests such interventions tend to be harmful, potentially disastrously so, and greater Iranian intervention could prove extremely dangerous to Iran itself in the medium or long-term.

Whatever its actual long-term impact turns out to be, however, giving Iran a free hand in Iraq will certainly be perceived as being harmful to the interests of all the other neighbors, to Iraqis themselves, and to the United States. This demonstrated that employing the catch basin approach places a premium on finding other ways to limit Iranian involvement, either by threatening Iran (including the use of "red lines") or by persuading Iran (possibly by making concessions to them on other issues).

—The catch basin approach could face considerable political pressure both at home and abroad because of the humanitarian "optics." It did nothing to stem the flow of refugees from Iraq's population centers (and may indeed have led more to leave, as they could go to an area of relative safety). Under such a plan, 60,000 to 80,000 U.S. troops would remain on the periphery of a war zone, guarding large chunks of Iraq's borders as well as huge numbers of refugees. But that would not stop the carnage in Iraq's cities just hundreds (or even just tens) of kilometers away, and there would be no end in sight for either the war or their mission.

Dealing with Iran

In part because of the effectiveness of the catch basins in eliminating several other forms of spillover (at least for some time), the course of the game focused increasingly on U.S-Iranian competition. By the end, that was the only issue on the table, and it had become an extremely prickly one. This development suggested one specific lesson, and one general one, regarding U.S. policymaking as Iraq descends into all-out civil war.

The general lesson is that U.S. leverage with any of the parties involved in Iraq is likely to erode quickly as the slide toward civil war accelerates—which it historically almost always does. During the first move of the game, the United States had considerable leverage with Iran; by move three it had almost none and was reduced to either threatening to back the Sunni Arab insurgents or else trying to buy off Iran by agreeing to Iranian demands on other issues, most likely the Iranian nuclear program.

The specific lesson is that the outbreak of an all-out civil war in Iraq eliminates one of the most important mutual interests between Iran and the United States. It effectively makes Iran into the United States' unambiguous adversary. Concerns about Iraq no longer serve as a caution against U.S. military action against Iran, and U.S. regional allies' perceptions of a Sunni-Shi'i schism invariably seem to propel the United States into clear alignment with Saudi Arabia, Jordan, Kuwait, and Turkey (its more traditional allies) against Iran.

DITHERING AND HALF-STEPS ARE DISASTROUS

The lessons for U.S. policy toward Iran are more easily observed than practiced. In part because U.S. leverage from its presence in Iraq would diminish rapidly, the game emphasized the need for the United States to take decisive action when confronted with Iraq sliding into all-out civil war. The PC actually made decisions more adroitly and faster than many do in real-life (including the actual PCs in which many game participants had actually served), but it was still not fast enough to avoid squandering important relative advantages that the United States held early on.

Unfortunately, bureaucracies have great difficulty making dramatic changes rapidly. This is particularly so in the case of events like civil wars because the evidence is typically very ambiguous. The participants in our simulation knew generally where the game was headed, and thus had a clearer perception of the future, than the United States will have when Iraq descends into all-out civil war. Nevertheless, because of the importance of this point, it is still worth highlighting in the hope that it will be clearer when the moment comes and so will inject some greater urgency into U.S. decisionmaking at that point.

PART II
───────

CIVIL WAR
CASE STUDIES

4

AFGHANISTAN
AFTER THE SOVIET WITHDRAWAL

The civil war that consumed Afghanistan led to all of the types of spillover discussed in this book. Indeed, Afghanistan is one of the worst modern instances of a civil war, not only devastating a country, but also wreaking havoc upon its neighbors and other states. For U.S. purposes, perhaps the most important form of spillover was terrorism. Al-Qa'ida was born in Afghanistan, and the 9/11 attacks were orchestrated from this base. But terrorism cannot be separated from the other forms of spillover. The Taliban, an organization that emerged from Pakistani refugee camps and was nurtured by the Pakistani government, sheltered and aided Bin Laden. This support occurred in part because the years of conflict in Afghanistan had further radicalized Pakistani politics, fostering chaos and extremism there. Terrorism also led to foreign interventions—most notably the 2001 U.S. military campaign that toppled the Taliban.

OUTBREAK

The Soviet invasion of 1979 plunged Afghanistan into a bloody period of strife and resistance. For a decade, Afghan fighters, acting in the name of God, waged a deadly insurgency against

the foreign invaders. In a victory that surprised the world, the Soviets withdrew in defeat in 1989.[77]

The Soviet occupation had been a bitter one, but when Soviet troops
withdrew, the already unstable Afghanistan exploded into a full-scale war.
Much of the country, particularly outside the cities, was in the hands of one
of the many bands of Afghan resistance forces. These forces fought the Soviets stubbornly, but they also fought one another regularly.[78] Many of the
warlords who played a key role in resisting the Soviets (or fighting on their
behalf) became leading figures in the post-Soviet period. These included
Ahmed Shah Massoud, the Tajik warlord; Gulbuddin Hekmatyar, a Pashtun
Islamist with close ties to Pakistani intelligence; and General Abdul Rashid
Dostam, an Uzbek warlord who had once worked closely with the Soviets.

When the Soviets withdrew, the frictions and occasional skirmishes
among these various insurgent groups erupted into a massive civil war.
Moscow left behind a puppet regime, which barely last three years before it
was toppled by the same forces that had chased off the Soviet Army. At that
point, with no foreign foe to fight, the *mujahidin* fell upon one another,
ushering in a disastrous period of civil strife and warlordism. Different military commanders took control of a fragmented country, drawing primarily
on ethnic and tribal loyalists to ensure their rule. Afghanistan was split into
autonomous mini-states, and in several of these, particularly in the south
where Afghanistan's once-dominant Pashtun community lived, rival warlords battled for control. Pakistan, Iran, Saudi Arabia, Russia, and other
states poured weapons and money into the country to support their proxies. In a Hobbesian struggle, commanders fought one another constantly,
while the traditional leadership of Afghanistan—religious leaders, tribal
chiefs, and others—declined in importance.[79]

In social science terms, the post-Soviet civil war in Afghanistan was
overdetermined. The opposition to the Soviets was divided along ethnic,
tribal, ideological, and personal lines and was (barely) united only by its common hatred of the Soviet occupiers. The country was awash in weapons, and
the government had always been weak, even in times of peace. Geography
compounded this problem, with Afghanistan's mountainous terrain and poor
infrastructure giving guerrillas and local militias numerous advantages.

The war with the Soviets and the subsequent civil war shattered
Afghanistan and profoundly changed its politics. Over one million Afghans

died in the struggle, and as much as one-third of the population fled, with almost two million refugees settling in Iran and perhaps three million moving to Pakistan. For many years, there were more refugees from the Afghan struggle than from any other conflict in the world. Afghanistan's rudimentary infrastructure and weak political institutions quickly collapsed, leaving the country devastated. Afghans were always pious, but their traditional form of Islam was tolerant and allowed Hindu, Sikh, and Jewish communities to exist—a tolerance that ended in the 1990s as the war increased the country's zealotry. The war also shifted the communal balance of power, giving Tajiks, Uzbeks, the Shi'i Hazaras, and others their own weapons and power, ending the dominant position of Afghanistan's Pashtun. Tribalism and banditry increased, while the always-weak central government in Kabul became completely powerless.[80] Most of the violence remained ethnic, sectarian, and tribal in nature, although over time the Afghan civil war gave rise to an incredible series of alliances and betrayals.

The conflict also led to what Barnett Rubin calls the "microsegmentation" of Afghan society. Warlord factions were divided along both ethnic and regional lines. After the Soviet withdrawal, "Hekmatyar's conventional force, known as the Lashkar-i Isar (Army of Sacrifice), developed into the only *mujahidin* military force other than Massoud's Islamic Army (his *mujahidin*) that bypassed local and tribal (though not ethnic) segmentation."[81] On the one hand, there obviously was an ethnic and regional dynamic to the fighting. But on the other hand, understanding this dynamic is complicated by the fact that a number of the guerrilla groups (for example, Dostam's militia) switched sides during the fighting and were at one time or another aligned with Pashtuns, Uzbeks, and Tajiks.

Compounding this problem further, Afghanistan's neighbors meddled constantly in the fighting. Pakistan supported a bewildering array of groups. The one thing they all (mostly) seemed to have in common was that they were generally Pashtun groups with extreme Islamist tendencies. But even this was not fully consistent as Islamabad did modulate its support and even worked with a number of rival groups too. Iran worked primarily with Shi'i Hazara groups, trying to unify them and make them stronger. Russia and Uzbekistan also worked with various groups to protect their interests, although over time they increasingly settled on Dostam's forces and Ahmed Shah Massoud's Northern Alliance.

This period also saw an endless procession of negotiations, ceasefires, and alliances as groups jockeyed for tactical advantage. In March 1993, for example, several *mujahidin* parties signed the "Islamabad Accord," a Pakistani-imposed ceasefire. According to one observer, "The Islamabad agreement can be seen as an attempt by Pakistan to prevent ethnic discord in Afghanistan from spilling over into its own frontier regions where the Pashtuns form a large part of the population."[82] But all these accords failed, as both the Afghan warlords and neighboring states saw them only as a way to gain breathing space to better arm and prepare for the next round of fighting.

The Taliban Emerges

The Taliban was born among the Afghan refugee population of Pakistan. The Jamiat-e Ulema Islam (Assembly of the Clergy), which had close links to the government of Benazir Bhutto which took power in Pakistan in 1993, ran hundreds of religious schools in Pashtun areas in Pakistan. The Taliban emerged as a student movement from these schools. These students represented the new generation of Afghans rather than the leaders who had emerged as the established resistance to the Soviet Union. The schools, and later the Taliban, emphasized an extreme version of Islam along with elements of *pashtunwali,* the ancient tribal credo of Pashtun tribes that glorifies hospitality as a key component of honor.[83]

Led by Mullah Muhammad Omar, the Taliban began as a small group of fighters who achieved a reputation for decency by supposedly hanging from a tank barrel a local commander whose forces had abducted and raped two teenage girls, a move that led to appeals for help from neighboring communities afflicted by former *mujahidin* turned bandits.[84] After a brief period of inactivity, the Taliban began to act as guards for local merchants, particularly those trading in Pakistan. It then moved to Qandahar and quickly captured the rest of the city.[85] Qandahar was Afghanistan's second largest city and the heart of the Pashtun area. By establishing control over Qandahar, the Taliban had emerged as the champion of the Pashtun community.

The movement had a reputation both for its faith and for its honesty, the latter being a particularly rare quality among political and military leaders in Afghanistan in the 1990s. Moreover, the Taliban imposed order and disarmed warlords wherever they went, a welcome relief from the years of strife under the Soviets and then the rampaging warlords.[86] The Taliban also had a financial advantage, gaining money from Saudi Arabia, from donors linked to Bin Laden and his network, and from its collusion with smugglers—who appreciated the Taliban's efforts to end banditry, which helped facilitate organized smuggling in the south. Finally, the movement could draw on Pakistan's substantial military assistance. This reputation and these resources, combined with its solid support in Pashtun areas, appealed to many Afghans battered by two decades of war.[87] As Ahmed Rashid has noted, Afghans accepted the Taliban with "a mixture of fear, acceptance, total exhaustion, and devastation."[88]

The Taliban quickly spread across Afghanistan, particularly in the south, where many of the 40 percent of Afghanistan's population who are Pashtuns live. The movement drew on its already strong ties to Pakistan, gaining money, weapons, and at times direct military aid. The Taliban bribed many local commanders to gain their support, while others bowed to its large forces and growing popularity. The movement's lightning successes transformed it from a band of 30 men in the spring of 1994 to an army of 25,000 a year later.[89] The Taliban army numbers subsequently hovered between 25,000 and 30,000 men, roughly one-third of whom were students from Pakistani religious seminars.[90]

The Taliban found resistance far stiffer when it pushed on beyond Afghanistan's Pashtun-dominated areas. Tajiks, Uzbeks, and other Afghan minority communities feared that the Taliban represented a virulent form of Pashtun nationalism and Sunni fundamentalism, despite its protestations to speak for all Muslims. When the Taliban conquered these non-Pashtun areas, it often ruled as an occupier, not as a liberator. It also distrusted the more sophisticated citizens of Kabul and ran the country from Qandahar. Most ominously, the movement saw the Shi'ah, 15 percent of Afghanistan's Muslims, as heretics. At times, Taliban fighters massacred them by the thousands.[91] Even in areas where their supporters lived, the Taliban ruled brutally, imposing a harsh form of Islamic law, denying women the most basic rights, and engaging in numerous human rights abuses. Afghanistan's infant mortality rate remained high, while its life expectancy was short.[92]

The Taliban were highly ideological, even before they came into contact with Bin Laden. Their leader, Mullah Omar, appeared to genuinely believe that Afghanistan's foreign and domestic policies should follow his interpretation of Islam, not *realpolitik* or domestic politics. Thus, he refused to conciliate his enemies at home and did not hesitate to anger foreign governments. Mullah Omar declared that the Taliban seeks "to establish the laws of God on Earth and prepared to sacrifice everything in pursuit of that goal." As Olivier Roy noted in 1997, "Of course, the problem with the Taliban is that they mean what they say."[93]

The movement appeared to grow more extreme as it consolidated power. For instance, the Taliban were not initially hostile to the United States. Writing in 1998 (and drawing on evidence collected before that), Peter Marsden observed that the Taliban sought "purification of Afghanistan alone" and did not want to export their system.[94] Visitors to Qandahar in the mid-1990s noted that people were not required to pray and that some women did not wear burqas—a tolerance that eroded as the decade wore on.[95]

In parallel with their growing intolerance, the Taliban's cooperation with, and reliance on, Arab and other foreign fighters linked to al-Qaʻida grew. Before the capture of Kabul in September 1996, the Taliban had few contacts with "Arab Afghans." After Bin Laden relocated to Afghanistan from Sudan in May or June 1996, however, his group and the Taliban began to cooperate with increasing frequency. The Taliban also opened Afghanistan's doors to hosts of militants, not just those who were part of al-Qaʻida.[96] Among the many groups hosted by the Taliban were fighters from the Islamic Movement of Uzbekistan, Pakistanis mounting operations into Kashmir, radical Sunni Pakistanis bent on killing Pakistani Shi'ah, Chechen fighters battling Russia, and Sunni Muslims opposed to Iran's Shi'i government. These groups continued fighting their wars from bases in Afghanistan. At the time, the Taliban "played host" to many of the extremist Islamic groups in the Muslim world.

The Taliban steadily conquered much of Afghanistan. One by one, non-Pashtun areas fell to the Taliban. By September 11, 2001, the movement controlled approximately 90 percent of the country and appeared poised to unify Afghanistan under their dominance.

The Taliban's fall from power came suddenly. The terrorist attacks of 9/11 were quickly tied to al-Qaʻida, and the United States moved almost immediately to destroy the regime. The United States began a military campaign that relied on precision bombing combined with the use of Special Operations Forces and the anti-Taliban National Islamic United Front for the Salvation of Afghanistan (aka the Northern Alliance). The bombing commenced on October 7, 2001, and by November 9, 2001, the northern city of Mazar-e Sharif had fallen to the Northern Alliance. Four days later, Kabul fell, and on December 6, 2001, the Taliban lost their stronghold, Qandahar.[97]

SPILLOVER

The Afghan civil war had numerous spillover effects.

Terrorism

The Afghan *jihad* was responsible for the birth not only of the Taliban, but also of al-Qa'ida. After the Soviet invasion of Afghanistan in 1979, Muslim volunteers, particularly from the Arab world and Pakistan, flocked to join the Afghan resistance. Tens of thousands of foreign Muslims participated, and the experience forged deep bonds among them.

Although the contribution these volunteers made to the defeat of the Soviet Union was negligible, their participation had a lasting effect on the Muslim world's consciousness. A small band of dedicated fighters, acting in the name of God, had defeated a seemingly invincible superpower. These *jihadists* were hailed around the Muslim world, emerging as popular heroes and publicly lauded by governments that in private would have rejoiced in their deaths.

Al-Qa'ida sprang up in Afghanistan around 1988. Founded by the Palestinian religious leader Abdullah Azzam in cooperation with Usama Bin Laden, it sought to unify the many Muslim fighters who had come to Afghanistan. The movement drew on the Maktab al-Khidmat (Bureau of Services), which operated a recruiting and logistics network for *jihadists* fighting the Soviet Union in Afghanistan. One of al-Qa'ida's own internal histories noted that it initially sought to keep "alive the Jihadist spirit among Muslims in general, and Arabs in particular, by opening bases for their Jihad along with maintaining contact lines with them" after the Afghan struggle against the Soviets ended.[98] It initially sought to raise money, facilitate travel for *jihad*, provide training, and offer logistics.

When Bin Laden took over the movement after Azzam was murdered in 1989, however, his aims were broader. The movement took on an operational role as well as backing associated causes. Bin Laden sought to bring *jihad* to other parts of the Muslim world he saw as oppressed and to overthrow corrupt Muslim regimes. One of its most unusual goals, however, was to strike at the United States, which Bin Laden blamed for stationing troops on the holy soil of the Arabian peninsula, for backing Israel, for starving the people of Iraq through sanctions, and for a host of other grievances linked to the perceived denigration of the Muslim world.[99]

Al-Qaʻida was small initially, but it gradually grew in Afghanistan until 1992, and then in Sudan, where it was based from 1992 to 1996. During this time, al-Qaʻida forged ties to a host of like-minded (and initially not so like-minded) Sunni insurgent and terrorist groups. It sought to support their efforts against various regimes in the Muslim world and spread a call for anti-American *jihad,* as well as to conduct its own operations.

Bin Laden relocated to Afghanistan in May or June of 1996, bringing with him the leadership core of al-Qaʻida. It already had training camps in Afghanistan, from where it supported the insurgencies in Chechnya, Kashmir, and Tajikistan. The Afghan *jihad* was a cause célèbre in the Muslim world during the 1980s, bringing together Muslims from around the world. Moreover, Bin Laden and other al-Qaʻida members appeared to have a genuine admiration for the Taliban's efforts to bring the rule of Islamic law to Afghanistan and for Mullah Omar himself. After several years, Bin Laden may have even sworn loyalty to Mullah Omar.[100]

Bin Laden initially located himself in Jalalabad, which was not under the Taliban's control—a sign, perhaps, that he and the Taliban initially were not close. The Taliban initially welcomed Bin Laden, despite his links to terrorism. Bin Laden was widely admired for his participation in the anti-Soviet struggle during the 1980s. Moreover, the Taliban saw his support for various *jihads* as laudable. In addition, Bin Laden brought considerable financial resources with him. A senior al-Qaʻida leader informed other *jihadists* that the Taliban was exceptionally welcoming of Arabs who had fought the Russians in Afghanistan.[101]

The Taliban willingly provided a haven to al-Qaʻida, and together the two hosted a wide variety of groups as well as built up al-Qaʻida's international networks. The Taliban appear to have imposed few if any restrictions on al-Qaʻida, a freedom rare in the annals of state-terrorist group relations. Al-Qaʻida fighters could enter or exit Afghanistan without visas and travel freely within the country's borders.[102] From its base in Afghanistan, al-Qaʻida was exceptionally active. It planned operations, trained operatives for its own organization and others, seeded new insurgencies and terrorist groups throughout the world, propagated its *jihadist* ideology, and otherwise pursued its ambitious agenda.

Some of its actions included:

—Conducting a series of lethal and highly skilled terrorist attacks, including (but by no means limited to) the August 7, 1998, bombings of U.S. embassies in Kenya and Tanzania, killing over 224 (among them 12 Americans) and wounding over 5,000, many of whom were permanently blinded; the October 12, 2000, attack on the *USS Cole* that killed 17 U.S. Navy sailors; and overseeing the September 11, 2001, attacks that killed almost 3,000 people.

—Training Arabs, Uzbeks, Chechens, and other Muslims to fight in the Caucasus and Central Asia. This included guerrilla and terrorist training for groups fighting in Chechnya and Uzbekistan, which have waged a long-running insurgency and conducted numerous terrorist attacks.

—Backing Kashmiri and other radicals fighting against India. These groups have conducted a long-running insurgency in Kashmir and also made numerous attacks on civilian targets in India itself.

—Sponsoring a host of small terrorist groups throughout the Arab and Muslim world, such as the Islamic Aden-Abyan Army in Yemen, Ansar al-Islam in Iraq, and Asbat al-Ansar in Lebanon.

—Supporting Islamist insurgencies in Southeast Asia, including the Abu Sayyaf Group in the Philippines and the Jamaat Islamiyya in Indonesia.

—Developing a global network of radicals that is active in dozens of countries in Africa, Asia, and Europe as well as the Middle East.[103]

As the above list suggests, from his Afghan safe haven, Bin Laden trained a small army to wage insurgencies around the world. Al-Qa'ida had dozens of training camps in Afghanistan. U.S. officials believe that 10,000–20,000 foreign volunteers trained in Afghanistan after Bin Laden relocated there in 1996.[104]

Much of the training consisted of teaching guerrilla tactics in preparation for helping the Taliban defeat the Northern Alliance. Al-Qa'ida veterans gave classes on small unit tactics, the use of plastic explosives such as C-3 and C-4, the calculation of artillery fire ranges, first aid, the mining of roads, and other necessities for guerrilla war. Al-Qa'ida also amassed knowledge on a range of topics useful to *jihadists* such as small unit tactics, explosives, and the manufacture of chemical and biological weapons, in part by acquiring and translating U.S. military training manuals. By 2001, the training was very sophisticated: Pakistani groups, for example, would learn how to use M-16s, because these are used in Kashmir, while other groups would learn on AK-47s, which are more common elsewhere.[105]

Al-Qa'ida members in Afghanistan pursued chemical and biological weapons, though the effort appears to have made little overall progress. Al Qa'ida leaders had a start-up program and were corresponding with scientists in Egypt and elsewhere. In Afghanistan, al-Qa'ida members, at times working in conjunction with Pakistani scientists, plotted how to acquire, weaponize, and use anthrax, cyanide, and other chemical and biological agents. Disturbingly, al-Qa'ida's number two figure, Ayman Zawahiri, lamented that the organization became aware of the lethal power of these weapons only after Americans repeatedly noted that they could be easily produced.[106]

The sanctuary also was a place for a much smaller group of select recruits to learn specialized skills that would make them more formidable terrorists as well as guerrilla fighters. An FBI official estimates that "hundreds" of terrorists were trained, as opposed to "thousands" of guerrillas.[107] Small groups of fighters trained in Afghanistan were selected to learn how to observe foreign embassies, assassinate guarded officials, recruit agents, make explosives, and other tricks of the terrorist trade.[108] Some camps taught bomb-making, surveillance, and sabotage.[109] These camps churned out skilled terrorists in large numbers, and they conducted operations around the world. As Michael Sheehan, the State Department's former coordinator for counterterrorism, noted, "Afghanistan was the swamp these mosquitoes kept coming out of."[110]

From Afghanistan, al-Qa'ida began to realize one of its chief objectives: knitting together different Islamist militant groups and focusing them on the United States and other Western powers. Although *jihadists* had trained in Afghanistan long before Bin Laden relocated there, none of the training focused on the United States until Bin Laden's arrival.[111] Much of the training al-Qa'ida provided consisted of videos, pamphlets, and talks intended to inspire and indoctrinate new recruits with the same worldview, not just to give them a better skill set. The instruction emphasized the supposedly illegitimate nature of many Arab regimes and the claimed evil of Israel and the United States. The Afghan sanctuary also gave activists a location to forge new ties, increasing the importance of the indoctrination effort. Recruits from over 20 countries came to Afghanistan in the 1990s. Al-Qaʿida helped activists network within their countries and more globally.[112]

Afghanistan also served as a logistics center for planning various operations. Two of the most significant al-Qaʿida attacks before 9/11—the August 7, 1998, strikes on U.S. embassies in Kenya and Tanzania, and the October 12, 2000, attack on the *USS Cole* were planned and coordinated by operatives from Afghanistan, many of whom returned there after the attack. Al-Qaʿida members also were given Afghan passports.[113]

Over time, the Taliban also came to share al-Qaʿida's enthusiasm for exporting *jihad.* The Taliban renamed the country "The Islamic Emirate of Afghanistan." In addition to al-Qaʿida, the Taliban also hosted a range of Islamist insurgent groups active against neighboring countries. By September 2001, the Taliban were supporting revolutionary groups fighting the neighboring governments of Iran, Uzbekistan, China, and Tajikistan, as well as al-Qaʿida and its affiliates.

Thus, by September 2001, a common ideology bonded al-Qaʿida and the Taliban. The Taliban, like al-Qaʿida, rejected any accommodation with Muslim moderates, let alone the infidel West.[114] As Julie Sirrs argued before the overthrow of the Taliban, "the Taliban are sheltering Bin Laden first and foremost because of a shared worldview."[115]

By 9/11, the two movements and their leaders had become exceptionally close. The distant admiration of 1996, and the reported tension of early 1998, were long gone. In its place was a tight alliance between al-Qaʿida and the Taliban, bound by a shared ideology and mutual respect. The Taliban would go to any length for al-Qaʿida. Mullah Omar declared to Western reporters in 2001, "Half my country was destroyed by 23 years of war. If the remaining half of Afghanistan is destroyed in trying to save Bin Laden, I am ready."[116]

The mixing of the Taliban and al-Qaʿida also suggests a particularly important but unusual form of spillover: cross-fertilization. Over time, al-Qaʿida ideas transformed the Taliban from a group that had at most a limited anti-U.S. agenda to one that was at the forefront of the anti-U.S. struggle. In addition, the Taliban embraced an array of groups and policies that went beyond its origins in the Afghan refugee camps.

Radicalization of Populations

The Afghan civil war radicalized parts of Central Asia, Iran, and in particular Pakistan.

PAKISTAN. The strife in Afghanistan and the Taliban's activities weakened the Pakistani state, contributing to economic problems and social unrest. Chaos in Afghanistan and the flood of refugees to Pakistan led to an epidemic of smuggling and narcotics trafficking, weakening the already decaying Pakistani state. Pakistan also lost revenue from tolls and tariffs, as smuggling from Afghanistan replaced legitimate commerce.

The Taliban encouraged both Pashtun nationalism and Islamic extremism in Pakistan itself, further fraying an already weak social fabric. In 1998, the Taliban provided sanctuary for the Sipah-e-Sahaba ("Corps of the Prophet's Companions") Pakistan, a murderous anti-Shi'i group that had split from the Jamiat-e Ulema Islam and was hounded from Pakistan after it killed hundreds of Shi'ah there. Thousands of Sipah-e-Sahaba members joined the Taliban's ranks.[117] Because the Taliban's activities risked radicalizing its patron, some commentators began to talk of the "Talibanization" of Pakistan.[118]

IRAN. Although Iran did not suffer the same level of radicalization as did Pakistan, the situation in Afghanistan did raise serious problems for Iran. In particular, the Taliban's brutal treatment of the Shi'i Hazara minority and Sunni chauvinism almost led Iran to invade the country in 1998. As the Taliban defeated the Shi'ah in the civil war, they regularly massacred them and, in the process, killed and captured several Iranian diplomats. Iranians were outraged and massed troops on the Afghan border, though they did not invade in force, as discussed below under "foreign interventions."

CENTRAL ASIA. The chaos in Afghanistan also proved a major problem for Central Asia. Most important, Islamists took shelter in Afghanistan and used it as a base in the civil war in Tajikistan. Several terrorist groups took shelter in Afghanistan and from there planned attacks against Central Asian states, particularly Uzbekistan. Dostam, on behalf of Russia and Uzbekistan, in the spring of 1994 tried to influence the conflict next door in Tajikistan by using his militia to pressure the Tajik government into making sacrifices at the peace negotiations in Moscow.[119] Fighters with the anti-government Islamic resistance in Tajikistan also made a base in Afghanistan, as did fighters opposing the government of Uzbekistan. Ahmed Rashid has argued that the crisis in Afghanistan was "the single most important external factor in the growing instability in Central Asia" in the 1990s.[120]

ARAB STATES. A generation of *mujahidin* trained and fought in Afghanistan and later returned to their home countries to undertake *jihad*, but estimates vary as to the numbers involved. In this respect, during the 1990s Afghanistan evolved from a regional problem to a global one.

Spillover also took on a psychological form. In Muslim countries around the world, Afghan Arabs returned and were convinced that their defeat of the Soviets was God's will. In turn, they advocated violent resistance along Afghan lines to various local regimes, energizing opposition and making it far more violent. The impact was particularly profound in Central Asia, with groups in Uzbekistan and Tajikistan seeing Afghanistan as a model for their own struggles.

Refugees

As part of the largest exodus in the world since 1945, Afghan refugees fled to Peshawar and Quetta in Pakistan and to Mashhad and Tehran in Iran.[121] Olivier Roy has argued that the flood took on an ethnic dimension, with Pashtuns accounting for a larger proportion of refugees.[122] According to Barnett Rubin, the total number of refugees during the Afghan-Soviet war was between five and six million—more than a third of Afghanistan's population at the time.[123] Roughly half, some three million refugees, sought haven in Pakistan.[124] While Afghanistan was consumed by civil war, these refugees did not return.

Foreign Interventions

Iran, Russia, and particularly Pakistan were all active in backing various warlords in the early 1990s, as all sought to influence the country and to counter their rivals' influence. All were frustrated by the proxies' unwillingness to heed their wishes.

Not surprisingly given its support for so many terrorist and insurgent groups, the Taliban came to have many enemies. The fractious warlords of Afghanistan coalesced into the Northern Alliance. The alliance at times drew backing from Iran, India, Russia, Uzbekistan, the Kyrgyz Republic, Turkey, Kazakhstan, and Tajikistan, all of which opposed the Taliban's efforts to back radicals in their own countries, sought to support their favored communal groups against the Pashtun-dominated Taliban, and counter what they saw as undue Pakistani influence in Afghanistan.[125] Over time, this created a vicious circle: regimes backed opponents of the Taliban because the Taliban had backed radicals in their countries; in turn, the Taliban increased its support for radicals.

In this way, by the late 1990s, civil war in Afghanistan had become a regional war by proxy, stemming from one central problem: all of Afghanistan's neighbors believed their security interests were directly threatened by the Afghan civil war. According to Paula Newberg, Pakistan at the time saw Afghanistan as "an element of its India policy" and sought to protect its western border.[126] Moreover, the Central Asian republics felt threatened by the potential spread of anti-regime Islamic elements. Tajikistan and Uzbekistan in particular perceived a direct security threat, with opposition members from both countries basing themselves in Afghanistan. For Tajikistan, the presence of Tajik anti-regime militants so close to its borders prolonged the civil war and hampered efforts to put the peace agreement into effect.[127]

In addition to frequent clashes along the Tajik-Afghan border, there were a number of high-profile skirmishes with the Iranians in October 1998. After capturing Mazar-e Sharif on August 8, 1998, Taliban fighters killed eight Iranian diplomats and an Iranian journalist stationed there. In early October 1998, Tehran moved more than 200,000 troops to its Afghan border and began large-scale military exercises. The Taliban responded by moving 20,000 troops into the area. According to the Iranians, their military clashed with Taliban forces along the Afghan border on October 8, 1998, "completely destroy[ing]" three Taliban border posts around 110 miles away from the major Iranian city of Mashad.[128]

Pakistan was by far the most active outside player in Afghanistan. Pakistan had an ancient history of meddling in Afghanistan's politics. Pakistan had long, if bizarrely, seen Afghanistan as a "strategic reserve" should its troops need to redeploy in the event of an Indo-Pakistani conventional conflict (Pakistani forces would presumably regroup in Afghanistan if pushed back by Indian forces). In addition, Pakistan worried that Afghanistan's Pashtuns would revive irredentist claims to Pashtun areas on the Pakistani side of the border. As religion came to play more of a role in Pakistan, domestic groups (and politicians who courted them) sought to enhance the power of groups with similar sympathies in Afghanistan. But of greatest importance, Pakistan saw Afghanistan as its backyard and believed it was the rightful hegemon there. Pakistan typically worked with multiple groups and tried to keep any from being too strong. However, in 1994 it began to work with the Taliban and over time backed it to the exclusion of its rivals.

Indeed, the story of the Taliban's rise cannot be told without recognizing the central role played by its foreign patron, Pakistan. After the withdrawal of the Soviets in 1989, Pakistan backed various *mujahidin* leaders, such as Hekmatyar, with whom it had worked during the anti-Soviet struggle. By 1994, Islamabad's proxies had shown themselves to be dismal failures: brutal, riven by infighting, and—most important, from Pakistan's perspective—incompetent. Moreover, Pakistani Prime Minister Benazir Bhutto, who took power in 1993, correctly saw several of Pakistan's then proxies as tied to political movements and bureaucratic elements in Pakistan that opposed her rule.[129] She favored the Taliban, in part, to aid her own domestic political maneuvering.

The extent of Pakistan's role in the Taliban's creation and initial successes remains unclear, but as the movement gained strength it increasingly became Islamabad's favored proxy. Pakistan's military and intelligence service provided arms, ammunition, supplies for combat, financial aid, and training. Pakistan also helped recruit fighters for the Taliban, often working with domestic religious associations. The Pakistani government at times even tried to represent the Taliban's interests overseas.[130]

The extent of Pakistani support was considerable. Pakistani military advisers trained the Taliban, boosting its tactical and logistical capabilities to be able to prosecute a massive war effort. In 1997, the year after the Taliban captured Kabul, Pakistan gave the movement $30 million in aid, including weapons, food, fuel, and other necessities. Pakistan provided $10 million to the Taliban to pay the salaries of government officials. Pakistani soldiers at times may have fought alongside the Taliban, aiding it in key battles.[131] Pakistani diplomats defended the Taliban at the United Nations and other international fora, and fought against sanctions and other forms of punishment.[132]

Support for the Taliban went far beyond official government circles and included major political parties, religious networks, and many ordinary Pakistanis. When the Taliban first emerged, hundreds of Pakistani volunteers joined the Afghan refugee fighters who made up much of the Taliban's fighting force—Larry Goodson estimates that Pakistanis comprised one-quarter of the Taliban's forces, and several other estimates are even higher.[133] Pakistani political parties and religious movements outside the government also aided the Taliban. The Jamiat-e Ulema Islam, of course, established the religious schools that gave birth to and nurtured the Taliban and shaped its ideology. Parties like the Jamiat-e Ulema Islam did not distinguish between Kashmir, Pakistan, and Afghanistan when pursuing their ambitions.

Over time, these parties and privately run schools provided much of the manpower for the Taliban. One Taliban official noted that the "*madrasa* network"—the network of religious seminaries—in Pakistani areas near the border sent "thousands" of recruits to join the Taliban. At decisive points, such as the July 1999 offensive in northern Afghanistan, up to 8,000 Pakistani volunteers participated.[134]

As the Taliban swept through Afghanistan, the movement gained the support of much of Pakistan's political establishment. Even though Pakistan's political groups fought bitterly against one another—and the military, the true power, distrusted politicians of all stripes—they all supported the Taliban when they were in power. For Islamabad, the Taliban represented a force that could unify Afghanistan while keeping it close to Pakistan. Moreover, the Pashtun-dominated movement sat well with the Pakistani officer corps and intelligence services, which also contained many Pashtuns.[135]

Kashmir also played an increasingly important role in Pakistan's calculations toward Afghanistan. Islamabad sent many Kashmiri fighters to Afghanistan to train and to gain combat experience. As foreign fighters increased their role in Kashmir, Afghanistan became important as a place to house, train, and recruit them. Just as Syria used Lebanon as the location to arm and train its proxies, Afghanistan became a preferred location for Pakistan to conduct such training, as it enabled Islamabad to claim that it was not a state sponsor of terrorism in its own right.[136]

Despite all this support, the Taliban was not Pakistan's puppet. Even before the movement consolidated power, Taliban officials were noting privately that "Afghans are proud people who do not like the Pakistanis always trying to run things and place the Afghans on a lower level."[137] Similarly, a senior al-Qaʿida official warned other Arabs that Pakistan would eventually try to find a substitute for the Taliban that would subordinate itself to Islamabad.[138]

Over time, as the Taliban established itself, it used its ties to Pakistan's government, opposition parties, Islamic societies, and drug networks to ensure its autonomy in the face of any pressure. The Taliban even refused to drop Afghanistan's long-standing claim to parts of Pakistan's Northwest Frontier Province, a remarkable statement of independence given the Taliban's reliance on Pakistan for support.[139]

The United States and al-Qa'ida

The United States also tried limited interventions to fight al-Qa'ida. Before 9/11, the United States sought to work with various groups in Afghanistan as well as with neighboring states in its efforts to capture or kill Bin Laden.[140] If anything, the limited U.S. interventions backfired. The U.S. cruise missile strikes on terrorist training camps in Afghanistan on August 20, 1998— Operation Infinite Reach—in retaliation for his bombing of U.S. embassies in Kenya and Tanzania, appeared to improve the Taliban's relationship with Bin Laden.[141] The strikes were intended to kill Bin Laden and affiliated terrorist leaders and to demonstrate American will.[142] Rather than intimidating the Taliban, the attacks demonstrated to its leaders the West's hostility and placed the movement in the politically difficult position of being asked to make concessions under threat. The Taliban's anger at Bin Laden for conducting the East African attacks that triggered the American assault was more than outweighed by its outrage at the United States for the response. Although in the months before the bombing the Taliban had indicated that it might be willing to surrender Bin Laden or curtail his activities, the day after the bombing, Mullah Omar declared, "Even if all the countries in the world unite, we would defend Osama by our blood."[143] The head of Saudi Intelligence, Prince Turki al-Faysal, met with Mullah Omar after the U.S. bombing and found that previous promises that the Taliban would send Bin Laden back to Saudi Arabia or at least expel him were no longer binding. The U.S. cruise missile strikes on Afghanistan thus solidified a shaky bond, leading Mullah Omar to at first protect and, over time, embrace al-Qa'ida.

Outside Efforts to Limit Spillover

Although a number of regional actors did attempt to mediate the conflict in the 1990s, none of them succeeded in doing so. Under the aegis of the United

Nations, Afghanistan's six neighbors worked with the United States and Russia to find a settlement to the crisis in Afghanistan. The talks failed completely for several reasons. The various external powers had different, and at times conflicting, interests in Afghanistan. Pakistan in particular sought hegemony, which other neighbors resisted. Equally important, the external actors had at best limited influence over the Afghan groups they supported. As the Afghan groups were engaged in a bitter struggle for power and past efforts and power-sharing had failed, they were less than receptive to lukewarm outside mediation efforts. The Taliban representatives regularly rebuffed U.S. and Saudi officials who sought to end the fighting.

Some countries did attempt to limit spillover, either by backing their own Afghan proxies against the Taliban (as Iran did) or by providing aid to the Taliban's victims. Others tried to prevent the Taliban's own proxy groups from gaining ascendancy in Central Asia by offering financial and technical support to their opponents. For example, in response to the Islamic Movement of Uzbekistan's offensives into Uzbekistan and the Kyrgyz Republic in 2000 that killed several dozen Uzbek and Kyrgyz soldiers, the United States, Russia, China, Turkey, France, and Israel flew supplies and counterinsurgency equipment to both countries. The Chinese alone delivered $365,000 in flak jackets, night-vision goggles, and sniper rifles. At the time, the Islamic Movement of Uzbekistan was being supported by the Taliban.[144] By undertaking such operations, these countries hoped to counter the influence of the Taliban and its allies.

The Taliban problem was not "solved" until the United States and its allies overthrew the regime after the 9/11 terrorist attacks. Despite being driven from Afghanistan's cities, the Taliban survived as a fierce guerrilla group. They regularly attack foreign aid workers, U.S. and other Western troops, the security forces of the new regime of Hamid Karzai, and other Afghans perceived as collaborators. They continue to receive financial support from Pakistan's Jamiat-e Ulema Islam, which is part of the governing coalition that runs the Pakistani state of Baluchistan. The country as a whole remains at risk of sliding back into all-out civil war.[145]

Indeed, 2006 was an exceptionally bloody year. Painfully, many of the techniques *jihadists* used in Iraq (such as improved improvised explosive devices and suicide bombing) are now showing up among fighters in Afghanistan.

The United States did not finish the job with the Taliban because it sent far too few troops to ensure a successful occupation and did not make a major investment in Afghanistan's infrastructure. Indeed, Afghanistan was perhaps the most under-resourced nation building effort the United States has undertaken in recent years. Not surprisingly, the former Taliban, foreign *jihadists*, and other fighters are steadily creeping back.

5

DEMOCRATIC REPUBLIC OF THE CONGO
A WAR OF MASSIVE DISPLACEMENT
AND MULTIPLE INTERVENTIONS

The civil war in the Democratic Republic of the Congo,[146] perhaps the most destructive war of the second half of the twentieth century, was itself a case of spillover, and it in turn proved a cauldron of instability that fostered conflicts in neighboring states and led to their intervention in the war. The role of outsiders, particularly Uganda and Rwanda, was tremendous, and as many as ten African countries have been involved in the conflict. It is a prime example of a civil war in one country causing a civil war in another, as well as of a civil war escalating into a regional war because of neighboring state interventions.

The human toll has also been staggering, with well over three million people dying simply in the years 1998–2002. Disease; ongoing violence, including sex crimes (by militias and UN peacekeepers); and the existence of thousands of child soldiers are some of the other low points of the Congolese conflict. Not surprisingly, there has been an exodus of refugees from countries in the Great Lakes region. At the end of 2004, there were more than 400,000 refugees from Congo alone, one of the highest in the world.[147] Overall population displacement is at least in the several hundreds of thousands. In recent years the conflict has diminished considerably, but it remains active, particularly in the eastern part of Congo.

Characterizing this almost decade-long conflict in Central Africa is difficult. Rather than see one long, continuous war, some experts have taken to speaking of three wars.[148] The conflict has been described as a civil war, a regional war, and an ethnic and/or national struggle between several competing groups, involving both state and non-state actors. In truth, it is all of the above.

First Congo War (October 1996–May 1997)

Ironically, the First Congo War, which led to the spillover of violence in the Great Lakes Region of Africa, was in many ways a spillover conflict from the 1994 Rwandan genocide. When the Tutsi-dominated Rwandan Patriotic Front took power, many Hutus, including most of the murderous *interahamwe* ("those who fight together") militia and the Forces Armées Rwandaises (Rwandan Armed Forces), fled to refugee camps in Congo. Congo was a natural refuge, not only because it bordered Rwanda, but also because it was very difficult for the Mobutu government to control its own territory. As a result, a great many groups—both aggressors and victims— were able to hide in corners of Congo.

The resulting influx of almost one million Rwandan Hutus into Congo not only changed the ethnic balance in the eastern provinces of North and South Kivu, it also led to deteriorating relations between the Mobutu government and the new Tutsi government in Rwanda.[149] From 1994 to 1996, the Hutu militias continued to attack Rwandan territory from their bases in Congo. For its part, the Mobutu regime embraced the Hutu militias and even used their presence to launch a campaign against the Banyamulenge, a Congolese Tutsi community living along the Rwandan-Congo border.

The Hutu militias were only the latest band of rebels to operate from Congo. Sudan and Uganda, led by President Yoweri Museveni, have been engaged in a proxy war since the mid-1980s, with each supporting rebel anti-government forces against the other. Sudan's support of the Lord's Resistance Army and other anti-Museveni forces began in 1986. Uganda has provided equipment and a safe haven for the Sudanese People's Liberation

Army since at least 1993.[150] Sudan began using Congo as a base for anti-Ugandan operations in 1994. From 1994 until Mobutu's downfall in 1997, his government granted the Lord's Resistance Army safe passage through Congolese territory to attack Uganda and also gave access to former soldiers of the ousted Ugandan dictator Idi Amin. This move only further strained what were already fragile ties between the two countries.

In addition to support for Sudan and the Lord's Resistance Army, Mobutu's government at the time was supporting other anti-government rebels. The Bakonjo and Baamba tribes situated along the southern Uganda-Congo border had been involved in a century-long on-again, off-again insurgency against, first, the British colonial forces and later the Ugandan government. Starting in the late 1980s, however, both the Kenyan government of Daniel Arap Moi and Mobutu's regime began aiding anti-Museveni insurgents. Mobutu's support for the Bakonjo rebellion, then led by the National Army for the Liberation of Uganda,[151] antagonized Museveni, as did his decision in 1994 to adopt a friendly policy toward Sudan.[152] When Rwanda moved against Hutu militias in Congo in late summer 1996, Museveni decided to take advantage of the situation and joined in supporting Mobutu's overthrow.

In October 1996, Rwandan forces attacked the *interahamwe* and ex-Forces Armées Rwandaises camps, sparking the First Congo War. The Rwandan army was soon joined by Ugandan forces, who were motivated by a similar desire to crush anti-regime insurgents from the Lord's Resistance Army. Angola joined the alliance a few months later, motivated by a desire to destroy its own insurgent opposition group, the União Nacional pela Independência Total de Angola (National Union for the Total Independence of Angola, often known by its acronym UNITA), that, like the Hutu militias and anti-Museveni forces, was operating from bases inside Congo. Thus, in many respects, the anti-Mobutu alliance was formed around a single goal: "to cripple the insurgency movements challenging their governments from bases in the Congo."[153]

It took this regional coalition—now composed of Rwanda, Uganda, Angola, Burundi, and Eritrea—only eight months to defeat Mobutu, who had been in power since 1965. Mobutu's dictatorship was always weak, and the withdrawal of U.S. support at the end of the Cold War had left it increasingly hollow. Government soldiers fled or joined the rebels in large numbers whenever they encountered them. The biggest military challenge was geography: Congo's infrastructure ranged from dilapidated to non-existent, and the expanse of territory is huge. In May 1997, the regional alliance installed Laurent-Désiré Kabila of the Alliance des Forces Démocratiques pour la Libération du Congo-Zaïre as the country's new leader.[154] Kabila's foreign sponsors, however, quickly became dissatisfied with their proxy—in part because he did little to end the attacks on Rwanda, and may even have encouraged them in order to assert his independence. Not surprisingly, hostilities broke out again just 15 months later.

Second Congo War: (1998–2002)

In July 1998, rumors of a coup in Kinshasa supported by Rwandan forces emerged. President Kabila responded by sending home the Rwandan troops stationed in Congo and responsible for training the Congolese army. In early August 1998, as the Rwandan forces began to depart, a military uprising backed by Rwanda erupted in the eastern part of the country. The Ugandans too decided to support the uprising. As the rebels advanced on Kinshasa, however, Zimbabwe and Angola unexpectedly intervened on the side of Kabila. The motives of those intervening were diverse. Uganda, for example, backed the rebels to prevent Sudanese government forces from capturing bases in Eastern Congo which they could use to attack Uganda.[155] Others supported Kabila as a way of diminishing Rwanda's growing influence in Congo and central Africa.

The coup itself began on August 2, 1998, with a mutiny among Congolese troops in the town of Goma. It was led by the Banyamulenge, a group of Tutsi living along the Burundi-Congo-Rwanda border in the eastern province of the country. The mutineers formed a rebel group, backed by Rwanda and Uganda, known as the Rally for Congolese Democracy–Goma. Many in the group had been part of the original campaign to overthrow Mobutu. Kabila responded by encouraging local Hutu militias to fight the Tutsis, and the violence quickly took on an ethnic as well as a national dimension.

The violence intensified further as the alliances formed during the First Congo War began to break apart. Within one year, fighting had spread to 40 percent of Congolese territory and drawn in the armies of seven African countries: Rwanda, Uganda, Zimbabwe, Angola, Namibia, Chad, and Burundi.[156]

At first, the pro-Kabila coalition appeared to be winning. In August 1998, it halted a rebel attempt to capture the capital. Over time, however, it began to weaken. By the fall of 1998, the Angolan government began to withdraw some of its battalions and Zimbabwe started to act more cautiously after higher than anticipated casualty and equipment losses.[157] Rebel forces did achieve a number of significant victories in the fall of 1998, but they were unable to effectively control the territory they captured and a stalemate soon prevailed. Over time, rifts within the rebel forces also emerged.

A number of regional and international organizations, as well as individual nations, attempted to mediate the conflict. These included but were not limited to the Southern African Development Community, the Organization of African Unity, and the international Francophone community. Between August 1998 and January 1999, these groups held more than a dozen summits and ministerial consultations.[158] All told, there were more than 20 failed efforts by the United Nations, the Organization of African Unity (since wound up, now the African Union), and Southern African Development Community.[159]

There were a number of reasons why these negotiation attempts failed, but the most important was the inability of the actors involved to agree on who had a legitimate reason to be at the negotiating table.[160] The undefined status of "non-state" actors was another complicating factor. In addition to external forces, there were a number of guerrilla and militia movements, grouped around political, ethnic, and national lines, each of whom seemed to have their own motives and goals, taking part in the fighting.

Over time, more armed groups developed further complicating negotiations. How to deal with these groups (and, for that matter, determining who spoke for each one) proved to be a major roadblock to resolving the conflict.

Economic factors also came into play. Congo possesses diamonds, gold, timber, and columbite-tantalite ore, which the intervening states greedily looted. Over time, the plunder motive rivaled security concerns for Uganda and other states.[161]

On July 10, 1999, Congo, Angola, Namibia, Zimbabwe, Rwanda, and Uganda signed the Lusaka Ceasefire Agreement. Several militias later signed the Agreement as well. The agreement called for various forces to cooperate in disarming all armed groups in Congo, though it was vague on specifics.

Most of the outside nations saw the conflict as bloody and difficult, draining their weak economies and straining their weak militaries with little progress on the ground to show for it. In addition, pressure from the international community created incentives for neighboring states to at least show some willingness to negotiate.

The Lusaka Ceasefire Agreement paved the way for a UN peacekeeping mission, though at first the number deployed was extremely small. The UN Security Council agreed to the creation of La Mission des Nations Unies en République Démocratique du Congo (United Nations Mission in the Democratic Republic of Congo), Resolution 1279 on September 30, 1999. On February 24, 2000, the UN Security Council approved Resolution 1291, authorizing the deployment of more than 5,000 peacekeepers to monitor the July 10, 1999 Lusaka Ceasefire Agreement.[162] The force was increased to 10,800 in 2004.[163] According to the website of the UN force, there are more than 16,000 peacekeepers stationed in Congo today.[164]

Sporadic fighting continued, however, and little progress was made on disarming the militias. Even removing foreign elements from the conflict also proved to be difficult. In June 2000, UN Security Council Resolution 1304 called for the withdrawal of all foreign forces from Congolese territory. But despite this, most foreign armies did not depart until more than two years later. Many outside regimes still saw a need to be in Congo as long as neighboring rivals were there and as long as rebel groups operated out of Congo—and over time, economic reasons came into play as well. A number of foreign rebel groups are still active in Congo.[165]

On January 16, 2001, President Kabila was assassinated; his son, Joseph, succeeded him as president.[166] Under the younger Kabila, the Congolese participated in new talks in South Africa in February 2001, known as the Sun City Dialogue, after the resort that hosted them. The talks, however, failed to achieve an agreement among the three main players: the new Kabila government, the Rally for Congolese Democracy-Goma, and the Mouvement de Libération du Congo (Congo Liberation Movement), a Ugandan-sponsored group opposed to Kabila. But a separate agreement was signed between Kinshasa and the Mouvement de Libération du Congo, which saw its leader Jean-Pierre Bemba become prime minister while Kabila remained president. The deal, an attempt by Kabila to unify the country, eventually collapsed, however, as he and Bemba could not agree on the specifics of power sharing.

Switching tactics, Kabila's government then entered into talks with the Ugandan and Rwandan governments. On July 30, 2002, a bilateral agreement was signed between Kinshasa and Kigali in Pretoria, South Africa. The deal called for the withdrawal of Rwandan forces in exchange for Kinshasa's promise to dismantle the Hutu militias and hand over *genocidaires* to the International Court to stand trial for war crimes.[167] A similar deal was signed with the government of Uganda on September 6, 2002. However, the withdrawal of foreign troops created another power vacuum that appears to have directly contributed to the Third Congo War.

Many of the proxies for foreign governments proved opportunistic and disloyal. Rwanda has had to deter desertions from its supposed proxies by force, in some cases massacring and interning Tutsi villagers in Congo to stop them from joining deserters.[168]

THIRD CONGO WAR: (2004–PRESENT)

The third war has differed markedly from the previous two. For starters, almost all of the violence has been limited to South and North Kivu provinces and the district of Ituri. Second, for the most part, the fighting has been isolated to only two groups/alliances: Congo Mai Mai groups and Rwandan and Burundian Hutu groups, such as the *interahamwe*/ex-Forces Armées Rwandaises and the Conseil National Pour la Défense de la Démocratie–Forces pour la Défense de la Démocratie (National Council for the Defense of Democracy–Forces for the Defense of Democracy), and the Tutsi-dominated Rally for Congolese Democracy–Goma. Moreover, as Weiss and Carayannis have noted, the conflict is "far less structured and involves many more, though smaller, military actors."[169] Third, unlike during the previous two wars, the countries of the Great Lakes region are working together to fight the rebel and militia groups. Finally, for all of the above reasons, the scale of the carnage is much less than that of the Second Congo War.

SPILLOVER

By far the greatest manifestation of spillover was neighboring interventions. Congo suffered refugee flows and other forms of spillover, but these had at most a limited impact on its neighbors.

Just as there have been a number of phases to the Congo conflict, there have been several phases to its spillover. Identifying these phases, however, is difficult. The removal of Mobutu in 1997 and the First Congo War were themselves examples of spillover from the Rwandan genocide in 1994. Determining the proper sequence of spillovers in the Great Lakes region in the last ten years is difficult. Violence that began in Rwanda quickly spread to the Congo and then boomeranged back to Rwanda, spreading to other countries in the process. It is also worth remembering that the ethnic tension which lies at the root of much of the violence dates back to colonial times.

Although the First Congo War ushered in a period of interstate conflict, *intrastate* conflicts (in the form of guerrilla wars and insurgencies) had been going on for several years prior to the start of the war. After 1997, however, the levels of both inter- and intrastate violence escalated dramatically. At times, Rwandan and Ugandan forces engaged in direct clashes in Congo.[170] Most recently, however, the fighting has been characterized by local militias with at best loose ties to foreign states rather than government proxies or state armies.

Neighboring Interventions

Congo's neighbors have regularly intervened in the conflict for a variety of reasons. Most important, neighboring states intervened to settle scores with domestic foes—militias and terrorist groups—that were using Congolese territory, including refugee camps in Congo, as a base. Some appeared to fear the effect of instability in Congo on their own stability. For several states, plunder was a factor. During the Second Congo War, regional balance of power considerations came into play, with some states "balancing" against Rwanda and otherwise seeking to prevent any country from dominating Congo. With the exception of Rwanda, neighboring states were opportunistic in their approach to the conflict. They intervened to score victories against foes or to loot Congo's resources rather than as part of a grander scheme. In general, the neighboring states did not create new social divisions, but they greatly exacerbated existing ones.

As already discussed, measuring the spillover from Congo into neighboring countries is difficult. This is particularly true in the case of Uganda and Rwanda. Both countries experienced violence and guerrilla warfare before the fall of Mobutu in 1997; moreover, both were involved in planning

Mobutu's overthrow, so it is hard to make the case that they were drawn into the conflict when the conflict was, in part, one of their choosing. This is not to suggest that neither country had grounds to act—they did. Mobutu's support for anti-government rebels was a constant thorn in the sides of both the Rwandan and Ugandan governments, but the outbreak of violence in Congo was sparked by the Rwandan and Ugandan armies' invasion. As such, the two countries bear at least some of the responsibility for the chaos that followed.

RWANDA. Rwanda is perhaps the most important foreign actor in Congo in the last 12 years. Rwandan forces were responsible for toppling Mobutu and installing Kabila and, when he proved unsatisfactory, for sparking a massive conflict when they tried to remove him. Rwanda's initial reason for intervening was the cross-border attacks of Hutus from the Forces Armées Rwandaises. The Forces Armées Rwandaises's depredations against ethnic Tutsi in Congo only added to Rwanda's determination. By intervening, Rwanda hoped to kill or at least disrupt ex-Forces Armées Rwandaises operations and protect ethnic Tutsi.

As efforts to topple Kabila faltered, Rwanda shifted to more limited interventions. This focused on securing eastern Congo near the Rwandan border and ensuring Kigali's control over various militia there. These militia at times fought among themselves and did not always heed Rwanda's wishes. Rwandan leaders apparently thought that removing Kabila would prove as easy as removing Mobutu, but they did not count on neighboring states intervening effectively on behalf of Kabila.

The Rwandan intervention both helped and hurt the Banyamulenge. On the one hand, they became a major player in Congo and were able to defend themselves against Hutu and other marauders because they were armed and supported by Rwanda. On the other hand, that Rwandan support made the Banyamulenge appear to be foreign government agents to their fellow Congolese. Kabila turned them into scapegoats, and their integration into Congo has become increasingly difficult.

The presence of Hutu militias in Congo continues to negatively impact the security situation in the region and destabilize Rwanda. Thousands of Forces Démocratiques de Libération du Rwanda fighters still remain in the country, despite the government's September 30, 2005, deadline for all foreign soldiers to leave Congo. According to Jim Terrie of the International

Crisis Group, this group "is a key source of regional instability . . . [It] gives Kigali justification for continued interference in the Congo . . . remains a menace to Congolese and Rwandan civilians and a potential tool with which hardliners in Kinshasa could sabotage the Congo's fragile peace process."[171] Until the Rwandan and Congolese governments give the Forces Démocratiques de Libération du Rwanda an incentive to do so, Terrie believes the majority of these fighters will not repatriate voluntarily.

UGANDA. Like Rwanda, Uganda intervened against Mobutu because he was tolerating anti-Ugandan rebels to operate against Uganda from Congo's territory. However, as the conflict wore on, Uganda turned against Rwanda. Within Congo itself, the two powers backed competing militias and were at times drawn into conflicts on their behalf. In addition, both sought to loot and exploit the territory they captured, leading them to conflicts over resources.

Today Uganda's government is still fighting the Lord's Resistance Army. The violence is largely confined to the northern part of the country and comes in waves. There are signs that the conflict may finally be winding down, however.

ANGOLA. Angola too helped overthrow Mobutu because he was backing UNITA. Although Angola aligned with Rwanda and Uganda (and against Mobutu) during the First Congo War, it sided with Kabila during the Second Congo War. This occurred in part because Angola had dealt with much of its rebel problem in Congo. Also, Angola sought to "balance" Rwanda, fearing that Kigali would be too powerful if it had a puppet government installed in Kinshasa.

ZIMBABWE. President Robert Mugabe intervened on the side of Kabila in the Second Congo War. Mugabe's motives were primarily economic and commercial in nature. Under Kabila and Mugabe, the two countries undertook a number of joint mining ventures—clearly bribes by Kabila to induce Zimbabwe to support his government. The two also signed a commercial deal worth more than $200 million.[172] At the time, there was also speculation that Mugabe saw the Congo conflict as a welcome diversion from internal problems. At their height, Zimbabwean forces in Congo numbered between 8,000 and 11,000.[173]

NAMIBIA. According to a 1998 International Crisis Group Report, there was relatively little public support for President Sam Nujoma's unilateral decision to enter the conflict. Parliament was not consulted in the decision.

Public opposition increased after UNITA moved troops, tanks, and artillery to the Namibian border and threatened to invade unless Namibian troops withdrew from Congo.[174] Nonetheless, public opposition to the Namibian intervention in Congo did not unseat Nujoma, who remained in power until his retirement in March 2005.

Like Mugabe, his motives appear to have been primarily economic. In 2001, the Namibian government and military admitted to having diamond interests in Congo. According to the BBC, the revelation provided clues to the reason for Namibia's entrance into Congo, a country where Namibia has historically not had any strategic interests.[175] The number of Namibians killed in Congo is unknown.

BURUNDI. In 1998 there were reports that Burundian troops, which according to the International Crisis Group frequently cooperate with the Rwandan army and Hutu forces, had crossed into Congo. Although exact numbers are not known, Burundian forces do not appear to have been a significant outside factor in the Congo conflict.[176]

CHAD. Chad also answered Kabila's call for allies. In October 1998, Chad sent 1,000 troops to Congo.[177] The war in Congo appears to have had a minimal impact on the country, however.

LIBYA. Qaddafi's government provided the aircraft to transport Chaddian troops to Congo.[178]

SUDAN. Sudan played an indirect role in the Second Congo War. In addition to supporting Kabila's government against the Rwandan-Ugandan coalition, Sudan has for years backed anti-government Ugandan rebel groups like the Lord's Resistance Army and National Army for the Liberation of Uganda/Allied Democratic Forces.[179] Indeed, it was Khartoum's support of Lord's Resistance Army bases in Congo that led to Uganda's decision to invade that country in the first place.

International Terrorism

The Congo wars, however horrible, did not produce international terrorism against the United States or against states involved in the conflict.

Refugees

The UNHCR reports that in 2005 the wars generated over 400,000 people who were still refugees, but figures may be much higher as many refugees are not reported. Data are extremely scarce, but the problem of internally displaced persons is probably far more severe, with several million being displaced during the course of the conflict. The UNHCR puts the figure at a shocking 1.7 million for 2005, a year in which the conflict had abated.[180]

The Congo wars began in large part because of the refugee problem from the genocide and war in Rwanda. The camps in Congo were a major base for the Hutu militants who struck back into Congo. In addition, the influx of so many Hutus upset the local communal balance, as they began targeting Tutsi-linked groups, particularly the Banyamulenge, who had long lived in Congo. This in turn led the Banyamulenge to look to Rwanda for protection when the Kinshasha government would not, or could not, do so. Rwanda, seeking to end the problem of Hutu attacks, intervened massively in 1996 to end the problem by toppling the Mobuto government.

The region's ongoing violence, however, has affected refugees. In August 2004, 160 Congolese Tutsi refugees were killed by anti-government Burundian Hutu rebels, known as Forces Nationales de Libération in Gatumba, Burundi.[181]

However, the refugees from the Congo war have not had the same level of massive destabilization. No neighboring governments have fallen due to refugee issues. Nor have refugees proved a major factor in destabilizing or radicalizing neighboring governments. This may be the case because so many regimes were *already* involved in Congo or fighting Congolese-based rebels that the refugees did not appreciably add to the risk.

Economic Costs

Rwanda and Uganda benefited considerably from exploiting Congo's rich natural resources. Estimates are that both countries have gained hundreds of millions of dollars from plunder—a huge sum for such poor countries. At one point Rwandan soldiers made $20 million per month trading columbite-tantalite ore.[182]

Although much is made of the looting of Congo's diamond, columbite-tantalite ore, and other resources by foreign powers, the costs of intervention have proven considerable. Deploying thousands of troops proved incredibly costly for these poor countries. For example, it is estimated that the Congo adventure cost Zimbabwe more than $200 million.[183] For those without massive stakes in the conflict, such costs led them eventually to seek a way to withdraw their forces. In addition, their militaries became involved in business in general and in smuggling, decreasing the professionalism of their forces.

RESOLUTION

Stopping the cycle of violence has been difficult. The Congolese government is exceptionally weak, and as such cannot impose its will on any of the major armed groups. Neighboring states could also easily disrupt any cease-fire by using their proxies to commit attacks. Consequently, the conflict continues to burn today, albeit at a lower level than ten years ago. As noted above, repeated efforts at negotiation failed. Also, neighboring states often saw the conflict in zero-sum terms and opposed agreements that might favor the proxies of other states.

Part of the problem was the sheer number of factions. In addition, it was often not clear who spoke for various non-state groups. Almost all the ethnic and regional factions had numerous internal divisions, which were worsened as outside powers supported different groups.[184] Many of the local fighters knew only plunder and war, and Congo's economic problems meant that peace would leave them with few opportunities.

The United Nations has been active in trying to stop the conflict. As already mentioned, La Mission des Nations Unies en République Démocratique du Congo (the UN military mission) has tripled in size from 5,000 to more than 16,000, with over 49 countries participating. Although its mandate is due to expire next year, it is unlikely that the situation will be stable enough to facilitate the departure of the peacekeepers. UN efforts have suffered from several problems. First, the number of peacekeepers is extremely limited. Congo has a population of over 60 million, and the UN force is a tiny fraction of what would be needed to disarm militias and police Congo. Second, Congo's infrastructure is rudimentary, with vast swathes of the country having no roads or other ways for troops to patrol and ensure order. Third, the mission is extremely limited, with UN forces not authorized to act aggressively. Fourth, the United States has not participated in the UN mission with its own troops, and few NATO countries or other top-quality militaries have sent significant numbers of forces. Instead, most of the troops are from the developing world, and coordination problems among the many contingents are severe.

One of the largest obstacles to solving the conflict has been getting all the parties to withdraw. For years, Congo's neighbors refused to remove their forces. Once they did, however, the situation began to improve. Foreign insurgent groups like the Lord's Resistance Army, however, are still active in the eastern part of Congo. Programs for the disarmament, demobilization, and reintegration of former combatants show some promise, but without enforcement are unlikely to succeed. The Congolese government has been trying to round up militants in the east for more than a year now, but the country is too weak to confront the rebels on its own and needs help in disbanding them.

In 2006, Congo held UN-supervised elections that most observers saw as relatively successful. These elections were held under conditions where much of the country, particularly in the West, saw only limited violence, with the active civil war largely confined to the east. The scale of the strife is difficult to measure in the east, as much of it is related to brigandage and reporting in general is limited.

However, it does seem that the scale of the suffering is considerably reduced from the horrors of years past. This appears due to several reasons. First, outside powers have increasingly seen intervention in Congo as risky rather than as an opportunity. Negotiations that have led to a reduction in the role of all neighboring states have facilitated this. Second, the Joseph Kabila government is more inclusive and more astute than that of his father, allowing him to make peace with several domestic opponents and with neighboring states. Third, there is a general sense of exhaustion with the war, as few actors see it as in their strategic interest to fight—though many fighters now know only war and brigandage, and the state is unable to bring them to heel.

6

LEBANON
WAR AFTER WAR (1975–90)

The Lebanese civil war that broke out in 1975 still plagues
the Middle East today. The violence that broke out again
between Hizballah and Israel in 2006 is just another round in
this seemingly endless conflict. These recurrent cycles of bloodshed demonstrate both the impact that spillover can have on
even strong neighboring states, and the difficulty of containing
spillover. In particular, this case illustrates that once a civil war
has blossomed into a regional war, it is difficult to bring it to an
end because one or another of the neighbors typically has an
incentive to oppose any specific set of peace terms (even if both
agree that the war should be resolved), and it is far easier to play
spoiler than peacemaker.

OUTBREAK

Lebanon is a multi-ethnic state. Over the centuries, numerous
Middle Eastern minorities sought sanctuary in the difficult terrain around Mount Lebanon, where they could resist attack or
persecution. As a result, Lebanon today is home to several Arab
Christian denominations (most prominently, Maronite

Catholic and Greek Orthodox), Sunni and Shi'i Muslims, and a variety of other sects, such as Druze and 'Alawis, as well. Moreover, Lebanon was a recent invention—carved out by France after the First World War from the territory of Ottoman Syria to create a small Levantine state with a Christian majority, which Paris assumed, correctly, would make them more dependent on their new French suzerains. The new state was thus fragmented along a bewildering number of religious lines that made forming a unified state out of this sliver of territory a challenging endeavor.

The Lebanese political system, established first in 1926 under the French but revised after independence in 1943, reflected both the patchwork nature of the state and Paris's interest in having the Christians predominate. Christians were granted a permanent majority in parliament, along with permanent control of the presidency. In return, the prime minister was always to be a Sunni Muslim and the speaker of the parliament a Shi'i Muslim. As Lebanon's changing demographics quickly rendered these arrangements outdated, they became the basis of constant squabbling and unhappiness among the Muslim groups who sought political power commensurate with their share of the population.

Nevertheless, Lebanon's political fragility can also be exaggerated. There was a sense of shared community and nationhood within Lebanon that was not necessarily felt in other recently created Middle Eastern states. Élites from all communities interacted regularly, sharing bonds of education and class. In the early twentieth century, the Christians held a slim majority of the population, but in truth all of the communities were in a sense minorities and that status caused both fractiousness and a sense of a common destiny. Only Lebanon's Sunni Muslims (who probably never represented more than one-quarter of the population) felt truly accepted by the larger Arab world. All of Lebanon's other communities saw themselves as outcasts, and while they squabbled over power and resources, within Lebanon their sense of shared interests was also palpable.

Lebanon's history before 1975 was actually quite pacific by regional standards. The 1926 constitution and 1943 National Pact enshrined a number of important compromises among the key sects that laid the foundation for a functional democracy that was long considered a model for the rest of the Middle East. While there were constant spats among the different groups, these were seen as manageable by all sides well into the 1970s. Lebanon experienced two political "crises" in 1952 and 1958 (the latter prompting President Camille Chamoun to request that U.S. President Dwight D. Eisenhower dispatch U.S. Marines to prevent the fall of the country to Nasserist elements), but what is most noteworthy about those crises is how easily Lebanon overcame them. Indeed, in retrospect, the 1958 crisis was greatly overblown, with Chamoun essentially using the Eisenhower Administration's tendency to overreact to threats even marginally linked to communism to circumvent constitutional limits on his powers and term. The 1952 and 1958 crises actually suggested considerable resiliency in the Lebanese system. Unfortunately, the problems it was forced to confront in the 1970s, principally, the sudden influx of armed Palestinian refugees who fled to Lebanon after they were expelled from Jordan in 1970–71, simply overwhelmed the country.[185]

Indeed, to a great extent, the Lebanese civil war that broke out in 1975 was itself largely a product of spillover from earlier civil wars beginning in Mandatory Palestine. Soon after the end of World War I, Arabs and Jews in the mandate began a civil war that intensified over time. The Second World War, the persecution of the European Jews, and then finally the revelation of the Holocaust convinced the international community, working under the aegis of the new United Nations, to partition that territory between Arabs and Jews. Their intent was both to give the Jews their own homeland and, hopefully, to quell the violence that had gone on between them for the prior two decades. That decision triggered the Israeli War of Independence, which saw the overt military intervention of five of the Arab states. That war proved decisive in some ways, in that it did establish a Jewish state. As a result of the fighting, however, a great many Palestinians fled and/or were expelled from the Jewish-held territory, creating 700,000–850,000 refugees.[186] These numbers were further swollen by another 300,000 who fled after Israel overran the remainder of Mandatory Palestine, along with the Sinai peninsula and the Golan heights, in the 1967 Six Day War.[187]

Of course, the Palestinians did not give up the fight and formed armed groups (the *fedayeen*, "self-sacrificers") to mount terrorist and guerrilla operations against Israel, ultimately forming the Palestine Liberation Organization (PLO) to serve as an umbrella group in 1964. The Palestinians were eager to carry on the civil war from the territory of the neighboring Arab states to which they had fled, although the states themselves were often more ambivalent. Jordan hosted the largest number of Palestinian refugees (roughly one million in 1970)[188] and had the longest border with Israel, making it the principal *fedayeen* staging base against Israel. However, especially after the catastrophic defeat of 1967, the Jordanian government of King Hussein tried to develop a more peaceful relationship with Israel and attempted to rein in his Palestinian guests accordingly. Very quickly, tensions emerged with tens of thousands of full- and part-time *fedayeen* attempting to carve out a state-within-a-state in Jordan to allow them to go about their war with Israel without interference from King Hussein's government.[189] Tensions led to clashes, and by September 1970 ("Black September" to the Palestinians), the king had decided the situation was intolerable. He unleashed his entire defense establishment on the Palestinians and, in seven months of bloody fighting, smashed the PLO's forces and compelled the PLO, and many Palestinian families, to leave Jordan.

Neither of the strong states of Syria and Egypt was willing to accept large numbers of Palestinians, so the vast majority of the *fedayeen* and their families fled to Lebanon where they tripled the number of Palestinian refugees from 100,000 to 300,000 in the years 1970–75.[190] Here the same pattern reemerged. The Palestinians carved out territory in southeastern Lebanon near the border with Israel where they made their own rules and proceeded to conduct attacks on the Israelis without regard for the views of the Lebanese government. Although many Lebanese Muslims opposed the state of Israel and sympathized with the Palestinians—and so ignored or even supported the *fedayeen* attacks on Israel—the Christians did not. The Christians had no hostility to Israel and, as a fellow oppressed minority in the Muslim world, even had some sympathy for the Jewish state. Most important of all, the Christians had no desire to see Palestinian attacks trigger Israeli reprisals against Lebanon, which they invariably did.[191] In December 1974, Israel bombed the Palestinian refugee camps of Sabra and Shatila in West Beirut in retaliation for a PLO terrorist attack, causing the Lebanese government to fall because it had failed to protect the nation.[192] Earlier that same year, Israel had mounted its first military incursion into Lebanon to try to clear out Palestinian targets near the Israeli border.[193] In response, the Christian-dominated Lebanese government sought to curtail Palestinian attacks on Israel. The Palestinian reaction was to try to solidify their state-within-a-state in the so-called Fatahland in southern Lebanon, while simultaneously attempting to encourage Lebanon's Muslims (who by then were believed to be the majority of the population) to agitate for greater power within the government.[194]

Lebanon's military was wary of taking on the numerous and well-armed Palestinians, both because of the PLO's considerable firepower and out of fear that doing so would tear Lebanese military formations apart along sectarian lines.[195] Since they could not look to the Lebanese military to assert the state's sovereignty, many communities instead began to overtly operate their own armed militias. This was easy to accomplish as various Christian groups had created paramilitary organizations as far back as the 1930s, when the Maronite leader Pierre Gemayel established the Phalange in imitation of Mussolini's fascist black shirts (and Hitler's Nazi brownshirts). In the 1960s, these groups had begun to arm themselves as their fear of one another and of radical Muslim groups grew.[196] The tension with the Palestinians, however, proved a far greater impetus to mobilize their communities and arm themselves to resist the Palestinians—just as King Hussein had, but the Lebanese military feared that it could not. With encouragement from the Palestinians, some Muslim groups also began to form their own armed militias to resist the Christian militias (and Israel, ostensibly).[197] The result was an internal arms race that both provoked and was further exacerbated by rising tensions and eventual clashes among the groups.

Not surprisingly, civil war finally erupted on April 13, 1975, when gunmen shot up the motorcade of Pierre Gemayel, killing four Phalangists. Gemayel's sons retaliated with attacks against various Palestinian targets, including a bus on which 27 were killed. Immediately, the other Christian groups rallied around the Phalange (temporarily) and the Muslims took the side of the Palestinians (equally temporarily). As the fighting spread, even some groups that had stayed out of the fray felt compelled to form their own militias for self defense. Musa as-Sadr, the charismatic leader of the Shi'ah, created the *afwaj al-muqawama al-lubnaniya* ("Battalions of the Lebanese Resistance," known by their Arabic acronym Amal, which also means "hope"). The violence of war spawned new groups that later carried the violence to new heights.

SPILLOVER

Both Syria and Israel experienced virtually every manifestation of spillover imaginable during the 15 years that followed the outbreak of civil war in Lebanon, and both are still suffering to this day.

Refugees

The civil war in Lebanon generated huge numbers of internally and externally displaced persons. By 1990 roughly 800,000 people were believed to
have fled the country altogether.[198] Roughly half the population of Beirut
had fled by then.[199] Altogether, Lebanon's population was believed to have
actually declined from 2.767 million in 1975 to 2.712 million in 1990—a net
loss of 55,000 persons[200] at a time when other Middle Eastern populations
were growing rapidly.

The majority of those who left were Christians, who fled principally to
European countries and the United States.[201] This exodus helped contribute
to a further shift in Lebanon's fragile internal demographics. The loss of so
many Christians, coupled with high growth rates among Lebanon's Muslim
population (and particularly the Shi'ah), further disconnected the political
arrangements of the 1943 National Pact from the true demographic balance in the country. By 1990, the Shi'ah probably accounted for about 35
percent of the population, with the Sunnis constituting another 15 percent
or more.

Not surprisingly, few Lebanese fled to Israel, but Syria was a different
story. Only about 6,000 Lebanese associated with the Israeli-backed South
Lebanon Army ever fled to Israel and these did so in 2000, as the Israeli
army was withdrawing from the south.[202] Syria, in contrast, was forced to
absorb a large number of Lebanese refugees. First came roughly a half-
million Syrians who had been living in Lebanon working as businessmen,
doctors, lawyers, construction workers, and the like, and who fled to their
homeland when the fighting began and after Syria invaded. This group was
supplemented by another half-million Lebanese and 150,000 Palestinians.
Asad himself bemoaned the effect of over one million people entering a
country whose inhabitants then numbered less than nine million.[203]

Terrorism

In the age of al-Qa'ida, it is sometimes hard to remember that Lebanon
was once the terrorism capital of the world. Lebanon spawned new terrorist organizations and techniques, and made new countries the target of
terrorist attack. Of course, it was the PLO that ultimately sparked the civil
war, and the principal source of tension was its desire to mount regular terrorist attacks on Israel, which the Maronite-dominated Lebanese

government opposed. Thus, terrorism played a critical role in the Lebanese civil war from the very beginning. Moreover, as the war ground on, ever greater numbers of would-be terrorists found their way to Lebanon as hired guns, and more and more Lebanese became willing to employ horrific acts of violence in pursuit of their cause, making them easy recruits for various terrorist groups.

The terrorist group Hizballah was born in the chaos of the Lebanese war, woven together from a patchwork of smaller Shi'i fundamentalist groups by the Islamic Revolutionary Guard Corps (IRGC). Over time, Hizballah emerged as one of the most powerful militias in Lebanon, but also one of the most dangerous terrorist groups in the world. As recently as September 2002, then-Deputy Secretary of State, Richard Armitage, warned that "Hezbollah may be the A-Team of Terrorists and maybe al-Qaeda is actually the B team."[204] Hizballah's record of attacks on the United States and its allies would make even Bin Laden proud: the bombing of the U.S. Marine barracks in Beirut in 1983 and the U.S. embassy there in 1983 and 1984; the hijacking of TWA flight 847 and murder of U.S. Navy diver Robert Stethem in 1985; a series of lethal attacks on Israeli targets in Lebanon; the bombing of the Israeli embassy in Argentina in 1992 and of a Buenos Aires Jewish community center in 1994. More recently, Hizballah operatives have plotted to blow up the Israeli embassy in Thailand, and a Lebanese member of Hizballah was indicted for helping to design the truck bomb that flattened the Khobar Towers U.S. military base in Saudi Arabia in 1996. Indeed, before 9/11, Hizballah had been responsible for the deaths of more Americans than any other terrorist group.

Another example of the tremendous impetus to international terrorism from the Lebanese civil war came courtesy of Imad Mughniyah, who in 1983 masterminded the simultaneous bombings of the U.S. Marine barracks and the French military compound, as well as the attack on the Israeli military headquarters in Tyre. He murdered Malcolm Kerr, the president of the American University of Beirut, and then took three other Americans hostage in January–March 1984, including the CIA's Lebanon station chief, William Buckley, and CNN's Lebanon Bureau Chief, Jeremy Levin. Several of these hostages also ended up in Tehran, and Buckley was eventually tortured to death.[205] At least five other Americans were taken in the years that followed.[206] However, while Mughniyah often worked in Lebanon, he also conducted attacks on targets outside the country, often with the Iranians. In early 1984, when 17 members of the Iranian-backed Iraqi Shi'i group ad-Da-'wa—one of them Mughniyah's brother—were put on trial for detonating six bombs across Kuwait, Mughniyah first led the hijacking of TWA 847, and then began seizing Americans in Lebanon to try to use them to bargain for the release of the "Da'wa 17."[207]

As many of these examples make clear, Lebanon also brought the world a range of appalling new terrorist tactics. Suicide bombings were not technically invented during the Lebanese civil war, but Lebanon popularized them and brought them global attention. The first was in December 1981 when a member of ad-Da'wa blew himself up at the Iraqi embassy in Beirut. However, it was not until the suicide bombings of the U.S. Marine barracks and the French paratroop headquarters—in which nearly 300 men died altogether—that the international community realized that a new method of terrorist attack had been born. In addition, the PLO and various Lebanese terrorist groups constantly innovated to find new ways to attack Israel and their Lebanese rivals, including by the use of small boats and even hang gliders.

COSTLY INTERVENTIONS

Both of Lebanon's neighbors, Israel and Syria, found it impossible to remain aloof from the fighting. Both intervened early in the conflict and then remained engaged for its duration. Although each intervened for reasons derived from the fighting itself—Syria because of the radicalization of its own population, and Israel because of the spread of terrorism from Lebanon—their interventions escalated and became protracted because of the other's participation. As a result, the Lebanese civil war expanded to a regional war pitting Israel against Syria, which they played out both through proxies and in direct combat inside Lebanon. Ultimately, the involvement of these countries and the vital interests they then saw in prevailing in Lebanon prolonged the war long after most Lebanese were so weary of it that they might have been able to find a solution.

Syria (1975–76)

The Syrians were the first to intervene in a massive way. Although what Hafiz al-Asad believed in his heart about Lebanon has never been revealed, we have enough information—including from interviews with him and Syrian officials close to him—to piece together a reasonable account of his thinking. It appears that from the beginning, during the breakdown of Lebanese communal relations in the early 1970s, Damascus feared that problems next door would breed problems at home. Asad was well aware of the unhappiness of his own majority Sunni population, and feared that Lebanese and Palestinians taking matters into their own hands to oust a minority government that sought to modulate the conflict with Israel would set a very dangerous precedent for his own Sunni population.[208]

As Adeed Dawisha has pointed out, there was an expectation that internecine conflict in Lebanon would inevitably spread to Syria, if only because this had historically been the case:

> Syria's intervention was also deeply rooted in the history of the region. This was so not only because the religious and communal tensions and cleavages which lay at the heart of the Lebanese civil war had been operative for over a hundred years, but also because these tensions in Lebanon invariably induced similar eruptions in other parts of Syria, for until recently that area was perceived to be a single geographical and social entity.[209]

Consequently, when it became clear to Damascus that the situation in Lebanon was unraveling in early 1975, Asad became alarmed. His first reaction was to try to broker a negotiated settlement among the factions to prevent low-level civil strife from growing into a full-scale civil war. In May 1975, Asad sent Foreign Minister Abd al-Halim Khaddam and the Commander of the Air Force and Chief of National Security, Naji Jamil, to talk to Lebanese Brigadier Nur al-Din Rifai's military cabinet (in effect a military coup d'état that had sought to impose order on the growing chaos). The Syrians succeeded in convincing the Rifai military cabinet to resign and allow civilians to resume power. A month later, Khaddam was sent back to Beirut to try to break the factional logjam that was preventing Lebanese Prime Minister Rashid Karami from forming a cabinet, and again he succeeded. Finally, in September 1975 Asad made a last-ditch effort to bring the initial rounds of fighting under control before the slide became irreversible, this time dispatching Khaddam along with Syrian Chief of Staff Hikmat Shihabi.

Khaddam and Shihabi, no doubt threatening Syrian intervention if the Lebanese did not come to their senses, succeeded in arranging a ceasefire and establishing a Committee of National Reconciliation with most of the major figures from the key Lebanese groups represented.[210]

Although all of these Syrian diplomatic efforts succeeded in their immediate goals, none was able to resolve the underlying problems and prevent the descent into all-out civil war in 1975. So in January 1976, Asad raised the stakes. He ordered elements of the Palestine Liberation Army (PLA) into Lebanon. The PLA was composed of Palestinians recruited, indoctrinated, trained, equipped, and advised by the Syrian military. While nominally part of the PLO, this force was actually a Syrian proxy. At that time, it was the Maronites who were on the offensive and had the upper hand in Lebanon, and Asad ordered the PLA to aid the Muslim groups. Nearly simultaneously, however, Damascus also put forward a reform plan for Lebanon that would have largely preserved the balance of power with only cosmetic changes, a proposal acceptable to most of the Maronite leadership. After months of wrangling, it became clear that the Syrian proposals were not acceptable to the PLO and to the more radical Muslim groups, who increasingly pulled the entire Muslim coalition into opposition against Syria and its efforts to end the conflict.[211]

The split between Syria and its erstwhile Palestinian and Lebanese Muslim clients introduced important new motivations into Asad's perception of the Lebanese struggle. Foremost, it created additional risks to Syria. Asad was all in favor of PLO terrorist attacks against Israel, but he wanted a subservient PLO, not the independent organization that Arafat sought. He feared that these Palestinian attacks from Lebanese territory would trigger Israeli military retaliations against Lebanon that would further undermine Lebanon and force Syria to come to its defense. Given that Syrian forces had been routed by the Israelis during the 1973 Yom Kippur (aka October) War, this was not an inviting prospect.[212] Moreover, Asad's fears of "contagion" from Lebanon into Syria, as he described it, led him to staunchly oppose Palestinian leader Yasir Arafat's efforts to purposely destabilize Lebanon to carve out greater autonomy for the Palestinian *fedayeen*. Asad grew increasingly alarmed that a Palestinian/Muslim victory there would "open floodgates of radicalism in Lebanon," in Dilip Hiro's colorful phrase, that would destabilize Syria as well.[213]

Asad's nightmares about the chaos that civil war in Lebanon could create in Syria included fears of Sunni revolts or coups d'état, as well as the potential for secession. Asad explicitly anguished over the possibility that the civil war next door might lead to the partition of Lebanon, which would set a dangerous precedent for Syria. He worried that if groups within Lebanon were able to secede from the state, it would inspire groups within Syria (again, principally the Sunni majority) to agitate for the same, leaving the 'Alawis with nothing but the small coastal enclave around Latakia where they predominate. Indeed, by 1980, various Maronite groups were already demanding secession from Lebanon.[214] This too made the Palestinian efforts to carve out "autonomy" for "Fatahland," and the Muslim efforts to overturn the Lebanese status quo very dangerous in Asad's eyes. Typically, Asad also assumed that Israel was deliberately attempting to foment precisely such an outcome because of the potential problems it could create for him.[215]

Finally, in addition to all of these defensive motives, it does seem highly likely that Asad spotted an opportunity in his decision to invade Lebanon as well. Most Syrians had never accepted the "artificial" division of Lebanon from Syria by the French after the world wars, and throughout the Lebanese civil war Asad made indiscrete remarks indicating his belief that the two countries were effectively indivisible.[216] This dream of a "Greater Syria" encompassing Lebanon—and eventually other territories formerly part of Ottoman Syria—was almost certainly another important motive for Asad in taking the fateful step to escalate his intervention in Lebanon from supporting a proxy force to outright invasion.[217]

Having failed to quell the fighting in Lebanon through diplomacy or proxy intervention, in June 1976 Asad sent the Syrian army into Lebanon to restore order and quash the efforts of the Palestinians and Lebanese Muslims to overturn the political status quo. Consequently, the Syrians intervened not on the side of their longtime Palestinian and Muslim allies, but on the side of the Maronites, who stood for the preservation of the old order. The military details of these interventions are not germane to this study,[218] but it is worth noting that initially, the Syrians sent in a force of only 6,000 men with only 100 to 150 tanks.[219] This force was stopped cold by the larger Muslim forces fighting in Lebanon's daunting mountain passes, which forced Damascus to mount a much larger invasion—25,000 troops with 500 to 600 tanks—in September 1976.[220] The second Syrian invasion made greater progress, but thanks principally to Syrian military incompetence, it proved incapable of defeating the Muslim and Palestinian forces and achieving Asad's objective of snuffing out the Lebanese civil war before it could have an effect on Syrian domestic politics. Fearing a wider war, greater bloodshed, and more instability, the Arab League brokered a ceasefire in October 1976 and gave the Syrian invasion force the imprimatur of legitimacy by creating a 30,000-man "Arab Deterrent Force" with the 25,000-man Syrian invasion force at its core. Small contingents from Saudi Arabia (1,000 men), Sudan (1,000 men), South Yemen (1,000 men), Libya (600 men), and the United Arab Emirates (500 men) were added as political window-dressing, but also to help convince Syria not to widen its involvement.[221] So instead, Syrian forces settled down in those areas of Lebanon they had managed to conquer, particularly the Biqa'a valley of eastern Lebanon, and again attempted to influence events elsewhere in the country by supporting various proxies. The results were just as disappointing for Damascus as they had been after their initial foray with such a strategy.

Israel (1975–81)

Israel too felt itself sucked into the vortex of the Lebanese civil war, although in its case it was not fear of the radicalizing effect of the war on its own population as it was for Syria. For Israel, the goad to intervene came from the attacks it suffered as the breakdown of the Lebanese state allowed terrorist groups to proliferate, while also removing all barriers to their operations against Israel. According to Itamar Rabinovich, "Earlier Palestinian-Israeli violence in Lebanon was dwarfed by the military build-up, raids, counterraids, and preemptive raids of 1977–82."[222] In the latter half of the 1970s, the Palestinians created a new state-within-a-state in southwestern Lebanon from West Beirut down to the Litani river that the Lebanese angrily referred to as *al-watan al-abadil* ("the alternative homeland").[223] From that autonomous base, they conducted constant and ever bolder terrorist operations against Israel.[224]

In addition, Israel grew concerned about potential changes in the Middle Eastern balance of power that could follow from the Lebanese civil war and the subsequent Syrian intervention. Syria worried about the impact that the partition of Lebanon would have on its domestic situation, whereas Israel worried about the impact that unification with Syria would have on its external situation. The Israelis were deeply concerned that Asad would swallow Lebanon whole, whether his goals were offensive or defensive, adding its vibrant economy and well-educated population to Syria's military resource base.[225] A new dimension was added in 1977 when Anwar Sadat led Egypt into peace negotiations with Israel. This triggered an earthquake within the Arab world, prompting the Syrians to paper over their differences with the PLO and Lebanese Muslim groups to form a united front against Egypt.[226]

Israel's initial response was to try to manage spillover from Lebanon. From 1975 (arguably even before then) to 1982, Israel tried to employ limited measures to prevent terrorist attacks and stop Syria from exploiting the chaos in Lebanon to enhance its military potential.

Israel did so both by bolstering its defenses against attack from Lebanon and by pro-actively intervening in Lebanese politics—with influence, arms, money, and limited military operations. In 1974, Israel built the "Good Fence" along its northern frontier to help keep out Palestinian terrorists. It also inaugurated new programs designed to make it attractive for Christian families living in southern Lebanon to work in Israel, and so secure their support against the PLO. Eventually, the Israelis transformed this new relationship into a more formal proxy arrangement. Israel helped a Lebanese Christian named Saad Haddad build his own local militia to fight the Palestinians in southern Lebanon, in return for his agreement to prevent the PLO from conducting attacks on Israel. The new force, the South Lebanon Army (SLA), quickly became embroiled in heavy and protracted combat against the PLO in 1976–77. Israel also began a covert program to arm the Maronites so that they could better resist the Syrian-backed Muslim coalition, while overtly declaring that the Israeli Air Force would intervene on behalf of the Maronites if the Syrian Air Force acted in support of the Lebanese Muslims.[227]

By 1978, Israel had concluded that its reliance on proxies in Lebanon was not achieving its security needs. Syria was actively supporting the Palestinians with its own proxy forces against the South Lebanon Army, and PLO terrorist attacks were escalating in number, creativity, and damage. In March 1978, after a particularly frightening PLO attack that killed 35 Israeli civilians who had been traveling by bus from Tel Aviv to Haifa, Israel mounted its own first direct intervention, called Operation Litani. As the name implied, Operation Litani was designed to try to clear out the PLO and Muslim military presence south of the Litani River, bolster the SLA, and create a buffer zone that the Israeli proxy would defend and that would prevent further terrorist attacks. Israel dispatched 25,000 troops and temporarily occupied 10 percent of Lebanon.[228] What is important to note about Operation Litani is that it was still an effort by Israel to manage spillover from Lebanon by pushing the terrorists back from its border and reversing the local balance of power in the south in favor of its proxy force there.

Operation Litani resulted in 1,000 deaths and caused 160,000 Lebanese to flee, stimulating new international hand-wringing.[229] The UN Security Council passed Resolution 425, which called on Israel to withdraw and created a peacekeeping force called the United Nations Interim Force for southern Lebanon intended to help the government of Lebanon reassert its authority over the south, prevent attacks on Israel, and create a buffer between the two countries. The Israelis had little faith in the ability or even-handedness of the United Nations and so took unilateral steps as well. In particular, Israel increased its economic incentives for Lebanese to work in Israel and stepped up its military support to Haddad's SLA, which in April 1979 proclaimed the "Free State of Lebanon" in the swathe of territory it controlled along the Israeli-Lebanese border.[230]

Operation Litani was Israel's most determined effort to manage the spillover from Lebanon. But neither a temporary incursion by 25,000 troops, nor a new international peacekeeping force, nor any of the other methods Israel had tried—arming proxies, mounting discrete retaliations and preemptive operations, threatening greater violence, providing economic incentives for those who assisted it, and trying to back the side most favorable to its interests in the civil war—had borne any fruit. By the beginning of the 1980s, Israel felt that its security situation was deteriorating rapidly because of the continuing spillover from Lebanon. This was the critical conclusion that laid the groundwork for Prime Minister Menachem Begin and Defense Minister Ariel Sharon's fateful decision to try to end the civil war in Lebanon in 1982.

Iran

Although Israel and Syria had the most eventful and sustained interventions in Lebanon, they were hardly the only states to do so. (The various interventions of Western states are discussed below.) Iran also took a major hand in the Lebanese civil war, and while it did not suffer nearly to the same extent that Israel and Syria did, the results have been mixed.

Iran had several motives for its own lengthy involvement in Lebanon. At the most immediate level, Iran ideologically opposed the state of Israel and bristled when the Israelis invaded in June 1982. Thus, what ultimately triggered Iran's involvement in Lebanon was its desire to wage a proxy war with Israel on the battleground of Lebanon. However, the Islamic Republic had other motives, including its desire to export the "blessings" of its own glorious Islamic revolution to the benighted peoples of the rest of the Muslim world.[231] The chaos of Lebanon and its large, oppressed Shi'i population created an opportunity for Iran. There were strategic advantages to Iran as well. Like the Shah's regime, the Islamic Republic saw Iran as a major regional power, if not a great power, that should have influence throughout the Middle East. As the Lebanese civil war slowly metastasized into a regional war (helped by Iran's role), it became one of the major events in the region, and Iran's involvement in it gave it influence in one of the critical arenas of the Middle East. Thus, Iran saw an interest in getting involved in Lebanon and staying involved there because this gave them a seat at one of the most important tables in town.[232]

In the summer of 1982, Iran dispatched 1,000 Revolutionary Guards to the Biqa'a Valley to help drive the Israelis out of the country.[233] Many of the Iranians already had extensive connections to the more extreme elements of Lebanon's Shi'i community and were able to ingratiate themselves quickly into Lebanese society and attract numerous adherents.[234] Lebanon's Shi'i community was increasingly frustrated by its marginalization within the Muslim coalition, and large numbers of Shi'i extremists had tired of the relatively moderate course being charted out by the main Shi'i militia, Amal. When the Iranians began to knit together more radical militia groups into the new organization Hizballah, angry young Shi'ah flocked to their banner.[235]

Given their initial successes, the IRGC contingent in Lebanon was quickly doubled in size.[236] The Iranians set up an intelligence network; began providing training, money, weapons, and other supplies; reached out to the various radical splinters from Amal; and began to establish a variety of social services that would provide Lebanon's impoverished Shi'ah with the basic support that no one else could or would. Although the relationship between Iran and Hizballah would mature over time, Iran remained Hizballah's principal backer, providing it with an organizational structure, training, material support, moral guidance, and often operational direction. Hizballahis themselves readily acknowledge that "it would have taken an additional 50 years for the movement to score the same achievements in the absence of Iranian backing."[237]

Once in Lebanon, Iran made its presence felt. With Iran's backing, Hizballah quickly became a major player in Lebanese politics, and engaged in a series of vicious battles with Amal in January 1986, February 1987, October 1987, and March 1988, in which Hizballah slowly emerged as the dominant Shi'i militia.[238] Iran was the ultimate instigator (through Hizballah) of the terrorist attacks on the U.S. Marine barracks, the French paratroop headquarters, and both attacks on the U.S. Embassy, though they also had Syrian support.[239] After the resolution of the Lebanese civil war in 1990, Iran helped Hizballah transform itself into a terrorist/guerrilla group to wage a relentless battle against Israeli forces defending the buffer zone they had carved out in southern Lebanon with the SLA, but also to mount attacks on Israeli interests elsewhere, including South America. Even after the Israeli withdrawal in 2000, Iran continued to provide Hizballah with money, weapons, advisors, and other aid both to carry on the war against Israel, but increasingly to allow them to assert themselves within Lebanese politics.[240]

By its own criteria, Iran gained from its intervention in Lebanon. It was able to carry on its fight against Israel through proxies without incurring direct retaliation from the more powerful Jewish state. It achieved a prominent position in Lebanon and was widely acknowledged as one of the major foreign players there. At a more emotional level, it allowed Iran to stake out its position as the leader of the anti-peace process rejectionist front, and as a nation willing and able to support its political and ideological sympathizers.

However, these achievements came with costs as well, although those costs were more often paid by non-Iranians. Iran's backing of Hizballah and involvement in terrorist attacks helped make it an international pariah. Its constant efforts to block any resolution of the Lebanese conflict led other countries to try to exclude it from regional diplomacy and to contain its influence. It was the key element in the U.S. decision to impose comprehensive sanctions on Iran, barring its access to the largest single market on the planet and adding to Iran's many economic problems. Iran's consistent, and at times violent, opposition to Israel has convinced Israel to actively oppose

Iran—an opposition that bore fruit in 2002–03, when Israeli concerns about Iran's nuclear program helped put this issue at the top of the international agenda. Overall, Iran's aggressive and meddlesome behavior in Lebanon alienated many countries. While it is hard to measure, there can be little doubt that whatever Iran achieved in Lebanon carried a significant price.

Iraq (1989–90)

Never one to be left out of a misguided venture, Saddam Hussein also decided that dabbling in Lebanon could help his regime. While Iraq did not suffer badly from its involvement, neither did it benefit. Although Iran's engagement in Lebanon was not irrelevant to Iraqi thinking, Saddam's primary motivation was revenge against his Ba'thist rival, Hafiz al-Asad. During the Iran-Iraq war, Syria had actively sided with Iran, and had closed down an Iraqi oil pipeline that had transported a major share of Iraqi oil across Syria (thereby bypassing the dangerous and mostly Iranian-controlled waters of the Persian Gulf). Saddam never forgave Asad for this, and when the Iran-Iraq war ended, he paid Asad back by supporting Syria's enemies.

Beginning in 1989, Saddam began to provide arms to the major Maronite militias, including both Samir Ga'g'a's Lebanese Forces and Michel 'Aoun's Lebanese Armed Forces. These were not minor supplies: the Iraqis provided tanks, armored personnel carriers, and artillery pieces. There was no love lost between Saddam and the Christians; he simply sought to aid those who were fighting Asad's Syria. Ultimately, Iraq's weapons shipments were not enough to prevent Syria from crushing the Maronite militias—once Saddam's own mistakes in 1990 brought the West around to acquiescing to Syrian hegemony in northern and central Lebanon. However, for nearly two years, these Iraqi arms shipments sustained the Maronites and convinced them to resist Syrian pressure, at a time when even the Israelis seemed to be warming to the idea of allowing Syria to control much of Lebanon if that could finally put an end to the fighting.[241]

RADICALIZATION OF POPULATIONS

Syria (1976–82)

The Asad regime was not insane to believe that chaos in Lebanon would cause turmoil in Syria. However, while such fear of a "contagion effect" led

Asad to intervene in Lebanon in 1975–76, the radicalization of his population and movement toward civil war in Syria actually followed, rather than preceded, his Syrian intervention. This suggests the possibility that the invasion either caused or greatly exacerbated these problems and had Asad shown greater restraint, there might have been less impact on Syrian society.

Having invaded in 1976, Syria saw no reason to leave Lebanon even though its invasion failed to crush the Muslim coalition and end the civil war. Damascus feared that if its troops were to leave after its disruptive invasion, the chaos in Lebanon would get worse, which was probably correct. It also feared that Israel would be able to take advantage of that chaos to dominate the country, a fear that events would prove less compelling. However, it is also clearly the case that the Syrians themselves attempted to dominate Lebanese politics. From 1976 to 1982, the Syrians were not content to try to simply bring the conflict to a rapid close, but they manipulated Lebanese politics to create a political leadership that would end the fighting in ways that served Syria's interests. Thus, many Syrian actions in Lebanon were intended to further Syrian control over the country, not merely to prevent spillover.[242]

By 1979, Syria had achieved a hegemonic position within Lebanon. Its Maronite presidents were forced to go to Damascus to receive Asad's blessing and his agreement for their cabinet choices.[243] However, the Syrians had not achieved stability in Lebanon (arguably, they had exacerbated the conflict by pursuing hegemony), and this proved to be a nearly fatal mistake for the regime.

The Syrian invasion created a perfect conduit for problems in one country to spread to the other. Even Asad's apologist biographer, Patrick Seale, commented:

> As the overspill in both directions was so immediate, each was highly sensitive to developments in the other's country. The mountain frontier was notoriously permeable to smugglers, to political refugees, to troublemakers, and to ideas. A coup in Damascus was always the subject of anxious speculation in Beirut, while Damascus tried to make sure it had a say in the composition of Lebanese governments—and especially in the choice of president as well as of intelligence and security chiefs. The two countries were like connecting vessels: the political temperature of one could not but affect that of the other.[244]

Syria's problems began within the regime itself, where the invasion was divisive. Many Syrian Ba'thists were appalled by Asad's decision to intervene on behalf of the Maronite Christians and against the Palestinians.[245] Naomi Weinberger notes that the invasion "seriously tarnished (Syria's) Arab nationalist image. Some criticized the intervention as a complete betrayal of what the Ba'th stood for."[246]

The most dangerous impact of the Lebanese fighting, however, was not on the regime insiders, but on Syria's disenfranchised Sunni majority. The Sunnis already believed they were underrepresented in the Ba'thist regime and did not care for the 'Alawi clique around Asad. They saw the uprising of Lebanese Muslims against the Maronite-dominated state as a model. Within just a few years of the invasion, ever greater numbers of Syrians were actively or quietly supporting Syria's Muslim Brotherhood, Sunni Islamic fundamentalists who had always opposed the regime for its secularist rhetoric and 'Alawi (who were considered heretics) leadership.

This discontent did not take long to manifest itself in threats to the regime. The first internal crisis came in the form of a coup attempt from within the Ba'th party and military—a bid thwarted by Asad in April 1976 and followed by widespread purges.[247] Then in late 1976, the Muslim Brothers kicked off a campaign of bombings and political assassinations against Ba'thist officials, security agents, and professionals (such as doctors and professors), designed to draw attention to Hafiz al-Asad's minority origins and favoritism toward his Alawi community.[248] "Every Alawi came to feel he was a potential target and the community as a whole trembled," according to Seale.[249] In June 1979, the Brotherhood ratcheted up their rebellion with an attack on the Aleppo artillery officer's school in which over 80 'Alawi cadets were massacred.[250] This attack marked the beginning of an all-out campaign of "urban warfare" against Syria's 'Alawi population, which featured arson and bombing of buildings; anti-government demonstrations; more assassinations; and attacks on Ba'th party offices, police posts, military vehicles, barracks, factories, and a variety of other facilities—including Russian military technicians, ten of whom were killed in January 1980.[251] From 1979 to 1981, the Muslim Brothers killed over 300 people in Aleppo alone, nearly all of them Ba'thist officials or 'Alawis, but also including some clerics who had denounced the killings.[252] The regime tried desperately to suppress the Brotherhood, killing 2,000 and imprisoning thousands more—many of whom ended up dead or maimed as a result.[253]

In March 1980, the Syrian oppositionists ratcheted up their conflict with the regime still further, closing down the business district of Aleppo for two weeks, which triggered sympathetic strikes in other cities like Hama, Homs, Idlib, Dayr al-Zur, and Hasaka. The regime responded ferociously, dispatching the 3rd Armored Division to Aleppo, where they swept through the city causing considerable damage and arresting hundreds of suspected Muslim Brothers. The division commander, General Shafiq Fayadh, "told the towns-people that he was prepared to kill a thousand men a day to rid the city of the vermin of the Muslim Brothers. His division stayed in Aleppo for a whole year, with a tank in almost every street."[254]

On June 26, 1980, Asad himself was nearly killed by Muslim Brothers who threw grenades and sprayed machine gun fire at him as he waited to greet a visiting African dignitary in Damascus. The 'Alawis of the regime were furious and the next day, members of Asad's key regime protection units slaughtered as many as 1,000 captive Brotherhood members imprisoned outside of Palmyra. Two weeks later, the regime made it a capital offense to be a member of the Brotherhood.[255] The next year, the Muslim Brothers were again able to penetrate the regime's security, detonating car bombs outside the prime minister's office in August 1981, and the headquarters of the Syrian Air Force (which Asad had once headed) in September 1981. This forced the regime to turn the capital into an "armed camp" with a pervasive and oppressive security presence to prevent further attacks.[256] But the attacks were unrelenting and grew more frequent and deadlier. In November 1981, the Brotherhood even managed to penetrate Damascus again, killing 64 with a car bomb.[257]

The straw that broke the proverbial camel's back came two months later, in January 1982. That month, Syrian intelligence uncovered a large Muslim Brotherhood coup plot among officers of the Syrian Air Force, Asad's main power base. If the Brotherhood could penetrate the Air Force, they had to be eliminated. So in February 1982, Asad dispatched several élite brigades to the Muslim Brotherhood's main center of resistance at Hama. In their initial probes, one battalion was ambushed and badly mauled, causing the Syrian Army to retreat and the Brotherhood to declare a general uprising. The regime rushed additional military units to Hama, which cordoned off the city center and then spent three weeks raising it to the ground with tank and artillery fire. The best estimates are that 20,000 to 25,000 people were killed in the reduction of Hama, although the regime itself has claimed as many as 38,000 died there.[258] Hama's fate convinced the rest of the Sunni population to end its revolt or face similar punishment.[259]

The six-year conflict that finally ended with the mass slaughter of Hama was no mere opposition movement, but a full-scale civil war that terrified the regime. It should be remembered that when the Lebanese civil war started in April 1975, the Asad regime had been in power barely five years in a country where coups were so common that the tenure of regimes was measured in months, not years. The fact that the regime prevailed should not denigrate the severity of the threat it faced, as attested to by both Israeli and pro-Syrian experts. In Seale's words:

> In Damascus there was a moment of panic when Hama rose. The government faced defeat by a full-scale urban insurrection such as had never before occurred under Asad's rule. The regime itself shook. After battling for five long years, it was obvious that it failed to eliminate the underground. . . . Hama was a last-ditch battle which one side or the other had to win and which, one way or the other, would decide the fate of the country. Some such understanding that that was going to be the final act of a long-drawn-out struggle may serve to explain the terrible savagery of the punishment inflicted on the city.[260]

Likewise, the great Israeli scholar and diplomat Itamar Rabinovich concluded:

> Most significant, though, were the domestic repercussions of Syria's involvement in Lebanon. The regime headed by Hafiz al-Asad, which from 1970 to 1976 had enjoyed domestic and external successes, encountered difficulties in 1977 which developed into a serious crisis that the regime has not yet been able to overcome. Its eruption was to a large extent a side-effect of Syria's 1976 intervention in Lebanon, which fanned Syria's communal tensions, caused friction in the regime's upper echelons, compounded economic difficulties, and embittered the public. It was against this background that radical elements in the Syrian Muslim brotherhood decided to follow Iranian tactics in a renewed attempt to topple the regime. Their successive

challenges—a campaign of personal terror in 1977, the massacre of the
Alawi artillery cadets in 1979, the revolt in Syria's northern cities later
that year, and the attempt on Asad's life in 1980—nearly brought down
the regime.[261]

Moreover, as Rabinovich argues, this internal crisis was sparked and then
exacerbated by the conflict in Lebanon. The leadership of the Muslim Brotherhood itself has acknowledged that it was inspired to active resistance
against the regime by the model of the Lebanese Muslims.[262] However, there
is reason to believe that they received more than just inspiration from parties in Lebanon. Various sources believe that Lebanese groups provided
money, weapons, and other supplies to the Muslim Brotherhood. Initially,
the assistance came mainly from Muslim and Palestinian groups. Seale
observes that anti-Syrian demonstrations in Beirut chanted: "Asad, we can
stomach you as an Alawite but not as Maronite!"[263] In March 1977, the Syrians assassinated the Druze leader Kamal Jumblatt—whose greatest offense
had been to openly attack the Asad regime in the hope that "anti-Asad forces
then believed to be planning a coup against the Syrian president" would be
encouraged to do so.[264] Once Syria shifted its support to the Muslim camp,
of course, the Maronites did the same, although, even then, neither the
Lebanese Muslims nor the Palestinians ever fully abandoned their support
to the Syrian rebels because of their fear of Syrian domination and the dif-
fering agendas among them.[265] Nevertheless, the Maronites arguably made
the most concerted and overt effort to foment sectarian strife among Syrian
soldiers in Lebanon (who came from all of the various Syrian religious
groups), and to play up incidents of internecine conflict of any kind in radio
broadcasts from Lebanon into Syria.[266] In May 1977, the editor of the regime
newspaper, *ath-Thawrah* (The Revolution), claimed that the opponents of
Syria were acting in devious ways "to inject into our country part of what
happened in Lebanon."[267] In early 1982, Damascus accused not only the
Maronite Phalange but Bashir Gemayel personally of aiding the Syrian Muslim Brothers.[268] The fact that the Brotherhood were well supplied and heavily
armed (the regime captured 15,000 automatic weapons in several enormous
arms caches around the country during the height of the insurrection)
added to the weight of evidence that they were receiving considerable foreign assistance.[269] The Syrians claimed that many of these weapons were

American-made, supplied either directly from Lebanese arsenals or by the Israelis, through their Lebanese proxies, like the Guardians of the Cedars, one of the most pro-Israeli of the Lebanese militias.[270]

RESOLUTION

Israel (1982–85)

During the second half of the 1970s Israel had principally sought to *contain* the impact of spillover from the Lebanese civil war on its population. That spillover came primarily in the form of terrorist attacks, almost entirely by Palestinian elements in Lebanon. Consequently, Israel provided economic assistance to the Christians of the south to win their friendship; armed, trained, and otherwise supported a proxy army of Maronites in the south; helped that army to create a buffer zone between Israel and Lebanon; aided other Maronite militias fighting the Palestinians; and mounted periodic incursions into Lebanon to destroy or disrupt Palestinian forces. But none of it worked. The terrorist attacks just kept coming, and the Israeli government grew more and more frustrated.

The failure to manage spillover increasingly led the Israeli government to shift its thinking from containing the problems of Lebanon to solving them. Israeli leaders, particularly in the Israel Defense Forces and including Defense Minister Ariel Sharon, began to despair of ever shutting down the PLO terror attacks using only defensive operations (and the occasional tactical counteroffensive, such as Operation Litani). Instead, they began to hypothesize that a strategic offensive was needed. To some extent they went further and made a virtue out of necessity by arguing that their ties to the various Maronite groups presented Israel with an opportunity to resolve the civil war altogether in favor of the Maronites, who would then sign a peace treaty with Israel. In the wake of the Camp David accords and the Israeli-Egyptian peace treaty, this did not seem so far-fetched to some Israelis who despaired of finding any other solution to the problems of spillover from Lebanon.

This was the genesis of Israel's 1982 invasion of Lebanon. Although it was initially portrayed to the world as nothing but a larger version of Operation Litani, this offensive, called Operation Peace for Galilee but derived from a military plan called Big Pines, had a very different set of objectives. Its goals were to smash the Syrian military and drive them out of Lebanon, thereby removing Damascus as a player on the Lebanese scene; to do the same to the PLO, to eliminate the Palestinians as a disruptive force in Lebanon as well as to eliminate the obvious terrorist threat to Israel; and to enable the Maronites to defeat the more radical Muslim groups and restore the antebellum political system and their privileged position within it. In return for Israel's help, the principal Maronite military leader, Bashir Gemayel, leader of the Phalange, agreed both to provide immediate assistance and to make peace when the Lebanese political clock had been turned back to 1958.

The problem was that Israel and the Maronites lacked the ability to realize these aspirations. Israel was hated by the Lebanese Muslim population, and the Israelis were never going to be seen as anything but occupiers. Israel was liked by the Maronite community, but the Maronites were not strong enough to dominate the country without direct Israeli military support, which could only undermine their ability to forge political compromises with the Muslims. Because so much of the population hated them, Israel was never going to be able to mount a "friendly" occupation—at best, some communities might have tolerated their presence for a few weeks while they extirpated the Palestinians, but they would not accept a full-blown occupation. But maintaining a hostile occupation would have required a larger troop commitment than Israel was willing to make, sustained for much longer than Israel was willing to bear. Moreover, the Israeli government was heavily dependent on the goodwill of others, particularly the United States which, despite all of the freedom of action granted by the Reagan Administration, was never going to support the kind of occupation and brutal repression of the Muslim population that it would have had to employ. Nor was there reason to believe that Israel's own relatively enlightened population would have supported such a policy.

The results were therefore predictable. The Israel Defense Forces juggernaut tore through Lebanon, swept aside the PLO's military units, smashed the Syrian forces in the Biqa'a valley, and rapidly besieged Beirut. A multinational force of Americans, British, French, and Italians helped escort the remnants of the PLO out of the beleaguered city, and the Israelis seemed to be in complete control. Bashir Gemayel, the Israelis' man, was elected president of Lebanon in August, and proceeded to open negotiations with

Jerusalem over a peace deal. But on September 14, 1982, Bashir was assassinated by Muslim forces, almost certainly assisted by the Syrians. That night, the Israel Defense Forces allowed Phalangist militiamen to enter the Sabra and Shatila Palestinian refugee camps, where they slaughtered 2,000 people in revenge for Bashir's death.[271] This appalling incident greatly increased Western pressure on Israel to pull its forces back, if not to leave altogether. Bashir's brother Amin succeeded him to the presidency a week later and agreed to a peace deal with Israel, a draft of which was promulgated on May 4, 1984, but he could not get any of the Muslim groups (or even some of the Maronites) to accept it. Under tremendous international pressure—and believing that they should leave any additional fighting to their Maronite allies—the Israelis had pulled back from their positions around Beirut, and fighting now broke out among the Lebanese factions. The Israelis attempted to support the Maronites, but were unwilling to intervene directly in the fighting, and were already suffering from insurgent attacks.

By mid-1985 Lebanon had effectively returned to its position before the Israeli invasion. Arguably, in many ways it was worse off. The Israeli invasion had sparked the creation of Hizballah, which proved to be a potent new pro-Syrian and pro-Iranian force in Lebanese politics. The West had intervened briefly in 1983–84, only to be driven off by a few Hizballah terrorist attacks in less than a year. The Maronites were even more fragmented and fractious than they had been before the invasion, and in the years to come would do more damage to themselves in intra-sectarian conflict than they ever did to the Muslims. Even the PLO fighters were returning clandestinely. In June 1985, the Israelis retreated to deepest south Lebanon, bolstered the South Lebanon Army (including with a stay-behind force of 1,000 Israeli soldiers), and resumed its previous formula of trying to manage spillover from Lebanon as best it could.[272]

Syria (1982–90)

Syrian intervention followed a similar trajectory to Israel's. Initially, in 1975–76, Asad had feared civil war in Lebanon. He had first attempted to prevent its outbreak and then, when that effort failed, intervened to try to end it in 1976. However, as described above, Syria did not commit the military force necessary to suppress the violence or to compel the warring factions to reach a compromise. Consequently, the civil war spread. Whether

Asad contemplated ratcheting up the level of Syrian involvement in Lebanon to the point where he might have been able to end the conflict at any point between 1976 and 1982 is unknown. It seems clear that either he never did or he chose to refrain from such a course of action out of fear of provoking a wider war with Israel, a country he believed would work to prevent him from dictating terms in Lebanon.

So, instead, during 1976–82 Asad also pursued a policy of trying to manage the Lebanese civil war and contain its spillover to prevent it from affecting Syria. But like the Israelis, he too found that such a strategy was unsustainable. This revelation appears to have dawned on him in 1982 when his regime was rocked by a pair of major threats, one internal and the other external, both of them related to the Lebanon war. The first threat he faced was the internal conflict with the Muslim Brotherhood, which had become a mid-level civil war by 1982. As noted above, this conflict was extraordinarily dangerous to Asad, and required him to raze the city of Hama and kill 25,000 or more of his own people. For all his reputation for ruthlessness, Asad preferred not to show the iron fist hidden in his velvet glove and while Westerners marveled at his ability to crush so dangerous an internal conflict, he appears to have been badly shaken by the need to do so.

The other major threat Asad confronted in 1982 was the Israeli invasion of Lebanon. Syria had actually tried hard to stay out of the Israeli Army's way and avoided combat as best they could until the Israelis purposely attacked them and smashed the Syrian forces. For all their bravado, the Syrian military was overwhelmed relatively easily by the Israelis, who probably would have had little difficulty marching on Damascus had they wanted to. The Syrian losses were humiliating; they diminished Syrian influence in Lebanon and created dissension within the regime.

Thus, in 1982 Asad appears to have concluded that he too could not "manage" the spillover from the Lebanese civil war. The continued fighting there was breeding rebellion within Syria's Sunni majority and provoking the Israelis to more aggressive behavior, both in Lebanon and against Syria. He seemed to recognize that the longer the civil war dragged on, the more he risked additional internal problems and confrontations with Israel—both of which were potentially life-threatening to his regime.

In response, Syria shifted its strategy. First, the Syrians recognized that it was the competing foreign interests in Lebanon that were making peace impossible—any Lebanese spoiler could easily secure massive assistance from an external power. Consequently, the Syrians did everything they could to convince the Israelis (and the Westerners) to leave Lebanon. This included, of course, terrorist attacks on both groups, as well as aid to the Lebanese Muslim militias battling against the Israelis, their Maronite allies, and their Western patrons—although Syria went to great pains to ensure that these operations were calibrated to avoid provoking Israel into a repeat of the 1982 war.[273] Then, having forced the Israelis and the Westerners out, Asad focused on making peace in Lebanon. What was fascinating about this latter effort was that the Syrians largely stopped trying to manipulate Lebanese politics and instead pursued the most pragmatic approaches to resolving the conflict: returning to the status quo ante with only minor revisions.

So starting in 1984, Damascus pushed, prodded, cajoled, and for the most part threatened the various Lebanese factions to strike a compromise that would, effectively return the state to a slightly amended version of the status quo ante:

—In March 1984, Syria brokered the Second National Reconciliation Conference in Lausanne, Switzerland. The Syrians forced the Lebanese leaders present to designate a new constitutional committee. They also compelled all of the Lebanese groups to agree to a ceasefire, which lasted a mere three months before fighting broke out among various Muslim factions (the Druze, Sunni, and Shi'i militias all attacked one another). The peace effort was forgotten, and the Syrians again backed the Maronite-dominated Lebanese Armed Forces to try to calm the situation.[274]

—In July 1985, Damascus tried again, holding a summit that included Amal leader Nabih Berri, Druze/Sunni Coalition leader Walid Jumblatt, and one of the key Maronite leaders, Elie Hobeika. Eventually, this process produced the October 1985 Damascus Agreement, which was a sort of national reconciliation document. Unfortunately, its proclamation immediately caused schisms within both the Maronite and Muslim camps, sparking a new round of bloody intra-sect violence. Damascus forged ahead, nonetheless, essentially forcing Hobeika, Berri, and Jumblatt to sign the "Tripartite Agreement" in Damascus in December 1985. This merely drove the intra-Maronite and intra-Muslim fighting to even more vicious levels. The divisions became so bad that the Syrians decided that they needed to weaken the PLO further—it was a major obstacle to the adoption of the Tripartite

Agreement, and was back in Lebanon in enough force to be a spoiler. Damascus convinced Amal to attack the PLO, which in turn called on the Druze for assistance and together the combined PLO-Druze forces were able to block the Amal-Syrian forces.[275]

—In July 1987, Damascus tried to force the Muslim militias to unite as the "Unification and Liberation Front," but Hizballah refused to participate. Typically, Damascus convinced Amal to attack Hizballah in 1988, sparking horrible battles between these two major groups for control over the Shi'i movement in Lebanon—a contest Hizballah eventually won after terrible bloodshed. Meanwhile, Syrian forces, in concert with a number of pro-Syrian militias, mounted a systematic campaign against the PLO in their refugee camps and again drove them out of Lebanon with considerable slaughter.[276]

—In 1989, severe fighting between the two leading Maronite warlords, G'ag'a of the Lebanese Forces and 'Aoun of the Lebanese Armed Forces, resulted in a significant victory for 'Aoun's forces. Feeling he had momentum behind him, 'Aoun then turned on the Muslims again, which caused them to put aside their differences and unite (including the Syrians) against the Christians. Both sides fought by conducting massive, indiscriminate artillery barrages of Beirut, which devastated the city and caused 1.5 million people to flee. Still, Damascus took advantage of the situation to force the main militias to unite as the Lebanese National Front. However, Syria was prevented from imposing a solution on the Maronites from an unexpected quarter: the French, who dispatched an aircraft carrier task force to prevent a Muslim victory.[277]

—Nevertheless, Asad did not give up, and in late September 1989, the rump of the Lebanese parliament met at Ta'if, Saudi Arabia. With strong Syrian pressure, as well as the encouragement of both the United States and the Soviet Union, all 31 of the Christian members of parliament present and 27 of the 31 Muslim members of parliament signed a Syrian-orchestrated National Reconciliation Charter which basically reaffirmed the original political system with some modest changes. Inevitably, some Muslim groups and 'Aoun's Lebanese Armed Forces (now the strongest of the Maronite militias) rejected it—which again provoked renewed fighting between G'ag'a's forces and 'Aoun's. Asad seemed determined to force the Maronites to accept the Ta'if accords and increased the Syrian military presence to 45,000 to

50,000 troops. But he backed down once again, for fear of Western—and potentially Israeli—intervention on behalf of the Lebanese Christians.[278]

—Finally, in September 1990, Asad received the opportunity that he sought, courtesy of Saddam's foolish invasion of Kuwait. The Americans wanted Syrian participation in the anti-Iraq coalition. Asad shrewdly agreed, sending his 9th Armored Division to Saudi Arabia—where it refused to participate in any meaningful way in combat against the Iraqis, but was important in showing that the war against Saddam was embraced by all Arabs, not just those armed and supported by the Americans. Asad's price, however, was a free hand in Lebanon, which he used to finally smash 'Aoun, the last obstacle to the adoption of the Ta'if accords. On October 13–15, 1990, 50,000 Syrian troops and a dozen or more Lebanese Muslim militias crushed 'Aoun's forces and then looted, raped, burned, and murdered their way through various Christian areas of the country. By 1991, only Hizballah—the proxy of Syria's ally, Iran—remained as an armed militia, and the system devised at Ta'if became the law of the land.[279]

Asad's "victory" in Lebanon did not completely end the fighting, though the violence diminished dramatically. Most important, Syria did not disarm Lebanese Hizballah and used the group as an anti-Israeli proxy. Israel, in turn, regularly attacked Hizballah positions in Lebanon and twice in the 1990s conducted major military operations (Operations Accountability and Grapes of Wrath) that involved massive bombing and limited ground incursions that generated hundreds of thousands of refugees.

Hizballah attacked Israel directly in the southern part of Lebanon, which Israel still occupied. Hizballah also conducted terrorist attacks in Argentina in 1992 and 1994 against Jewish and Israeli targets. With the support of Syria and Iran, Hizballah also became a mini–"state sponsor" of terrorism, training Palestinian groups to act against Israel more effectively.[280]

These attacks continued even after Israel withdrew from Lebanon in 2000. Hizballah continued limited guerrilla actions and, more important, stepped up aid to Palestinian radicals during the second *intifada*. In the summer of 2006, Hizballah kidnapped two Israeli soldiers, sparking a massive clash with Israel that led to over 1,000 Lebanese deaths and perhaps one million displaced, along with over 100 Israeli deaths. Hizballah emerged triumphant—at least from its perspective, as well as that of its Iranian masters and much of the Arab street—when Israel withdrew in the face of growing international pressure and limited progress against the Shi'i movement.

CASUALTIES AND COSTS

In the final reckoning, it is hard to see anyone as a genuine victor in the Lebanese case. By 1990, out of a population of only 2.8 million, over 150,000 Lebanese had been killed in the war, 25 percent of them children. As a measure of the nature of the conflict, 14,000 people had been kidnapped during the fighting, of whom roughly 10,000 were killed. Another 800,000 (mostly Christians) fled the country.[281] To this day, as witnessed by the most recent rounds of fighting, Lebanon remains a weak, divided, and vulnerable country.

Nor did the war benefit Lebanon's neighbors. From 1975 to 2000, nearly 1,500 Israeli soldiers were killed in Lebanon, making it Israel's third deadliest conflict.[282] As every Israeli knows, Israel was attacked by the Arab states in its two deadliest conflicts—the War of Independence (1948–49) and the Yom Kippur (aka October) War of 1973, while Lebanon was seen as more of a war of choice. The expense of Israel's 25-year involvement in Lebanon is ultimately unclear, but the 1982 invasion alone cost it roughly $2.5 billion (at a time when Israel's nominal Gross Domestic Product was only $35 billion) and slowed economic growth to virtually zero while increasing foreign debt and inflation to record levels.[283] By the 1990s, it was widely called "Israel's Vietnam" by Israelis themselves, who were delighted to pull out altogether in October 2000.

Not even Syria emerged as a winner. Although many members of the regime itself made tidy profits from graft in Lebanon, the Syrian economy was badly damaged by the war. In addition to the military costs of maintaining 10 to 20 percent of the Syrian Army in Lebanon for nearly 30 years, and replacing all of the equipment lost (including to the Israelis), fuel burned, and ammunition fired, there were also the costs associated with the Muslim Brotherhood's revolt from 1976 to 1982. This Syrian civil war stripped the Ba'thist regime of its cherished veneer of popularity, cost lives and money, and forced the regime to build draconian security systems to prevent a recurrence. All of this had both political and economic costs. Before 1982, it was estimated that Syria's intervention in Lebanon was costing it $1 million per day—a huge amount for an economy with an annual nominal Gross

Domestic Product of only about $10 billion in the late 1970s.[284] At various points Syrian actions cost them the generous subsidies they received from Saudi Arabia and other oil producers. Syria also absorbed several hundred thousand Lebanese refugees, adding to its unemployment problems. Inflation accelerated over time as the government struggled to pay for the occupation with reduced income. In the end, Syria received nothing for all its troubles. In 2004–05, the Syrians overplayed their hand trying to control Lebanon and were forced to give up the country they had once dreamed of unifying with their own.[285]

7

SOMALIA

Somalia has been plagued by civil war for decades, and for the last 15 years has been a failed state. In addition to horrific levels of suffering in Somalia, this war has at times involved several of Somalia's neighbors and even sucked in the United States and other members of the international community. Over time, international terrorists linked to al-Qa'ida have also become involved in the conflict and Taliban-like actors have become more powerful. Today, the Somali crisis remains unresolved: anarchy reigns, while its neighbors meddle and radicalism grows.

The sad experience of Somalia illustrates many of the problems that may plague Iraq in the future. The conflict produced massive refugee flows and parts of the country in effect seceded. Over time, Somalia became intertwined with international terrorism. Throughout the war, Somalia's neighbors intervened, both because they feared that the Somali conflict was stoking radicalism at home and because they saw opportunities to gain dominance in their once-powerful neighbor—interventions that usually proved disastrous for the states involved. Finally, Somalia also suggests the risks of half-measures for the international community. The United States, working with the United

Nations, tried both pure humanitarian missions and a limited military intervention, both of which faced severe problems.

OVERVIEW

Since 1991, one million people have died and an estimated two million Somalis have been displaced out of a population that is probably just over ten million.[286] Today, perhaps one million Somalis live outside Africa—labor is Somalia's primary export. Some of the deaths occurred directly in clan-on-clan clashes. Many, however, occurred because the civil strife caused the collapse of Somalia's economy and agriculture, resulting in one of the worst famines of the twentieth century.

In contrast to many other cases of civil war, Somalis are united along ethnic and religious lines—85 percent of those living in Somalia identify themselves as Somalis and almost all are Muslims. But this religious and ethnic unity masks deep clan and tribal fissures. Major clans include the Darod, Hawiye, Issaq, Dir, Digil, and Rahawayn, all of which have multiple sublineages.[287]

The chaos that engulfs Somalia to this day became evident to all in 1991. After more than two decades ruling Somalia, the president, General Mohammed Siad Barre, fell from power in January 1991. Siad Barre had been trying to put down clan-based insurgencies that had plagued the country since the late 1980s—these insurgencies had fed off the simmering unrest and violence Somalia had suffered since at least 1977, and the strife in general involved both Cold War superpowers, with Siad Barre switching allegiance from the Soviets to the United States in 1977.[288] Siad Barre's government was brutal, and tens of thousands of Somalis died in the fighting. As clan-related violence surged, Siad Barre became derided as "the mayor of Mogadishu."[289] As the Cold War wound down, and U.S. support for his regime ebbed, Siad Barre's government fell.

A new government, led by Ali Mahdi Muhammed, claimed its place but was not recognized internationally. After Siad Barre's fall, the army quickly dissolved into rival factions loyal to former commanders or clan-tribal leaders.[290] Soon the central government collapsed entirely. General Mohammad Farah Aideed of the United Somali Congress became the de facto ruler of Mogadishu, having dislodged government troops from the capital, while other warlords occupied different parts of the country. The resulting chaos led to an escalation in hostilities among rival clans and warlords and ultimately a civil war. As a result, Somalia has remained "stateless" to this day. It lacks a functioning executive or judicial branch, and its parliament is weak.[291]

The Somali economy collapsed in tandem with the Somali state in 1991. Although Siad Barre's regime was corrupt, brutal, and repressive, it did initiate significant public works programs and dramatically increased public literacy rates. It also drew on superpower aid to keep the economy afloat. Today, the lack of stability has scared away foreign investment and doomed economic growth. Few Somalis enjoy something as basic as safe drinking water, and adult literacy has declined considerably since 1991.

The early 1990s marked the darkest period in Somalia's recent history. A famine killed hundreds of thousands of Somalis and threatened the deaths of over a million more. The famines were caused not only by a bad harvest, but by the deliberate manipulation of food aid by warlords who used it to increase their own power and deny it to those of rival clans. This prompted several international interventions, including an ambitious U.S.-supported UN effort to rebuild the Somali state. The first intervention was an effort that focused on providing humanitarian relief. When warlords threatened the food supply, the United States and its allies tried to go after warlords and otherwise try to build up the Somali state. These efforts led to the "Black Hawk Down" fiasco in which 18 Americans died and subsequently led the United States to abandon peacekeeping efforts in Somalia, interventions discussed in more detail below.

When the United Nations quit Somalia in 1995, the country remained a failed state. Ethiopia conducted occasional cross-border raids against Islamist terrorists in the country whom Addis Ababa blamed for several attacks in Ethiopia itself. Terrorists based in Somalia also helped conduct the al-Qa'ida attack on the U.S. embassies in Kenya and Tanzania in 1998.

A faint ray of hope shined in August 2000, when the Transitional National Government was established. The Transitional National Government marked the completion of a two-month Somali National Peace Conference hosted by the government of Djibouti.[292] The Transitional National Government, however, proved weak and unable to guarantee security, even in the country's capital Mogadishu. The country's police force and judiciary during this period barely functioned, and the Transitional National Government's prime minister was dismissed in October 2001.

In 2004 Somalia's interim parliament selected Abdullahi Yusuf Ahmed, the former leader of Puntland (the easternmost tip of Somalia that declared its temporary separation from the rest of the country in 1998), as president. However, the election had to be held in Kenya because Mogadishu was deemed too dangerous. Yusuf led the Transitional Federal Government. Ethiopia pushed for the Transitional Federal Government in an attempt to sideline its predecessor, the Transitional National Government, because of its ties to various Islamist groups and factions in Somalia deemed hostile to Addas Ababa.

The Transitional Federal Government in theory was an attempt to include all of the main clans in the government and had more than 80 cabinet positions. Despite the Transitional Federal Government's bulk, its leaders deliberately sidelined many key clans.[293] Various factions within the Transitional Federal Government were themselves divided into subfactions, worsening the overall chaos. Yusuf's use of his private militia from Puntland to act independently of other militias also exacerbated problems, as other leaders interpreted this as a power grab rather than an attempt to bring different factions together.

As the violence continued, the Transitional Federal Government split after some parts of it sought to invite in foreign peacekeepers. Somalis were divided over whether there should be any foreign peacekeepers, and, if they were allowed in, whether some states, such as Ethiopia, should be barred from participating in peacekeeping. Ethiopia's effort to weaken the Transitional Federal Government and bolster its allies alienated the key Hawiye clan, among others.

With echoes of Afghanistan, Islamist militias have done well in recent years, with many Somalis supporting their agenda of apparent law and order. Islamic courts often imposed order locally, acting according to the power of individual shaykhs. The movement became broader, and in 1998 the Islamic Courts Union began as a major political movement when a commander of the al-Qa'ida-linked al-Ittihad al-Islamiyya (Islamic Union) linked to the Ayr clan used it to advance Ayr interests and espouse *jihadi* Islamism—the United States has designated the commander as an individual linked to terrorism. The Islamic Courts Union developed in a rather haphazard fashion with different clans taking the initiative in different places, but in 2004 formed an umbrella group that has at times pooled its members.[294] Some, but not all, of the courts are aligned with *jihadist* groups.

The Islamic Courts Union is a dramatic departure from the traditional factions that have fought for power in Somalia. The International Crisis Group contended at the time, "The Islamists are now the most powerful military and political group in the southern part of the country."[295] They are instituting Islamic governance in the parts of Somalia they control. As with the Taliban, much of their support comes from popular anger at the country's chaos, not support for their ideology.

In 2006, violence again swept through Mogadishu. The fighting was mainly between militias loyal to the Islamic Courts Union and those of the U.S.-backed Alliance for the Restoration of Peace and Counter-Terrorism— with the Islamic Courts Union apparently gaining the upper hand. The collapse of the Alliance for the Restoration of Peace and Counter-Terrorism has, in the International Crisis Group's description, left Somalia in a "bipolar" position, with the anti-Ethiopian, Habar Gedir-clan-dominated Islamic Courts Union up against the pro-Ethiopian, Majeerteen and Abgaal dominated Transitional Federal Government, though these coalitions have numerous internal divisions.[296] The transitional government is based in Baidoa and has not collapsed completely largely because of foreign, mostly Ethiopian, support.

In late 2006, Somalia again experienced foreign intervention. The African Union authorized the deployment of a military force to help the interim government. Thousands of Ethiopian troops were already in Somalia, with more along the border. Eritrea was supporting the Islamic Courts Union because they share Ethiopia as an enemy.[297] In December 2006, Ethiopia threatened the country with outright invasion, while the Islamic Courts Union vowed defiance—with the full support of Bin Laden.[298] Ethiopian troops nonetheless intervened and by the beginning of 2007 had successfully pushed the Islamic Courts Union out of Mogadishu. Although they have been beaten on the conventional battlefield, the indications are that the Islamists will now, like the Taliban in Afghanistan, revert to insurgency and terrorism tactics to fight against Ethiopia and its Somali ally, the Transitional Federal Government that is now installed in Mogadishu.

BARRIERS TO SETTLEMENT

In spite of more than a dozen internationally sponsored peace and reconciliation conferences in the past decade, peace in Somalia has remained elusive.
These efforts have often been led by neighbors with support of international
institutions, such as the United Nations, and regional bodies. The Intergov-
ernmental Authority on Development, whose membership comprises the
seven Horn of Africa states (Uganda, Sudan, Eritrea, Ethiopia, Djibouti,
Somalia, and Kenya), has attempted to reconcile the Somali factions, with little success. Saudi Arabia and Libya have provided aid money, much of which
was mishandled or pocketed by corrupt officials. In general, these efforts
have foundered because of the high level of division within Somalia, with
few stable factions. No group could impose its will, and few groups were willing to put aside the pursuit of temporary advantage to work together for
peace. Warlords in particular fear, correctly, that efforts to establish peace
and disarm them would hurt their power.

Militia leaders have usually opposed efforts to stabilize Somalia and disarm the militias. One effort in 2005, the Mogadishu Security and
Stabilisation Plan, led to mobilization by various nongovernmental organizations, business groups, and others, many of which openly opposed militia
groups. But assassinations of civic leaders, and a loss of popular momentum
in general, led to the collapse of these efforts.[299]

As is often the case in Somalia, individuals switched allegiances quickly.
Alliance for the Restoration of Peace and Counter-Terrorism leaders fighting
against Islamists, for example, often defected and joined their supposed
Islamist enemies when the battle seemed to be turning in the Islamists'
favor.[300] This has made it difficult for any one faction to establish dominance.

SPILLOVER

Refugees

Somalia has been the source of a massive refugee problem for decades.
The UNHCR reports that Somalia had approximately 400,000 internally
displaced persons (IDPs) by the end of 2005, with a further 395,000 Somalis refugees abroad, with over a quarter of these refugees in Kenya alone.[301]
By historic standards, this figure is low, and some Somalis are repatriating.

All of Somalia's neighbors are poor, and most have significant internal problems. The refugees often become bandits and contribute to lawlessness in neighboring states.[302]

Many of the refugees are located in camps along or near the Somali border in Ethiopia and Kenya. Some have been in existence over a decade and are semi-permanent in nature. Camp administrators claim that extremist groups—possibly including some that have ties to al-Qaʻida—recruit in the camps.[303]

Secessionism

Secessionism proved a constant challenge for Somalia. After the fall of Siad Barre, Somaliland in the north (which had been ruled by Britain during the colonial era, unlike the rest of the country that had been ruled by Italy) declared its independence, though this was not recognized internationally. In 1998, Puntland in northeastern Somalia declared its temporary independence, claiming it would return to the state if a new central government was formed. In southwestern Somalia, the territory of Jubaland also proclaimed its independence. Until 2001, the two breakaway republics in the north—Somaliland and Puntland—were relatively peaceful. But violence returned to Puntland in late 2001. Puntland's president, Abdullahi Yusuf, called on Ethiopia to back his militia against his rival, Jama Ali Jama. In 2002 the Ethiopian-backed group, the Rahawayn Resistance Army, declared regional autonomy for six provinces in southwestern Somalia.

Some of the secessionist regions of Somalia have proven relatively stable. Somaliland, which declared its separation in 1991, and Puntland both have provided a relatively high degree of physical security and the rule of law. As a result, they have done better economically, and Diaspora support has been relatively high. Both regions, however, are threatened by the destabilizing effects from other regions of Somalia.

Despite their relatively stability so far, these regions are not without problems. Reuben Kyama writes that the al-Qaʻida-linked al-Ittihad al-Islamiyya is active in Puntland.[304] In addition, the UNHCR reports that these two breakaway areas may become embroiled in conflict over the Sool and Sanaag regions, which both these regimes claim.[305]

Neighboring states have also experienced problems with secessionism related to the strife in Somalia. In particular, the Ogaden National Liberation

Front, which drew on ethnic Somalis living in the Ogaden region of Ethiopia, had bases in Somalia. This Ogaden group is also largely Muslim and is opposed to Ethiopia's government, which is Christian-dominated. Ethiopia is particularly sensitive to this, as in the past the Said Barre government had tried to unite the country by invading Ethiopia in support of Ogaden insurgents.

International Terrorism

After 9/11, U.S. attention once again turned to Somalia and the Horn of Africa—this time because of the global war on terror. Al-Qa'ida has used Somalia as a transshipment point and safe haven for planning attacks in neighboring Kenya: the 1998 bombing of the U.S. embassy in Nairobi; the bombing of a hotel in Mombasa in 2002; and, a foiled plan to attack the U.S. embassy in Kenya in June 2003.[306] With alleged links between Somalia Islamist groups like the al-Ittihad al-Islamiyya and al-Qa'ida, U.S. leaders worried that Somalia, already a failed state, could become a major sanctuary for terrorists.[307] Washington now monitors developments in Somalia closely from a nearby Djibouti military base and reportedly has backed various militias fighting the Islamists.[308] The presence of al-Qa'ida operatives has led the United States to directly attack suspected terrorist sites in Somalia in January 2007.[309]

The International Crisis Group reports that al-Ittihad al-Islamiyya in effect ceased to exist by 2005 but that various "alumni" have established new organizations with links to al-Qa'ida.[310] These new *jihadists* are small in number, but ruthless. Since 2003, they have murdered foreign aid workers and Somalis believed to be helping Western counterterrorism efforts. Leaders of the groups, however, have ties to the Islamic Courts Union and to key clans.[311]

Some observers fear that the Islamic Courts Union may be comparable to the Taliban in its early years: radical and strident at home and ripe for becoming a sponsor of terrorism abroad. The ties of leaders of the Islamic Courts Union to individuals with links to al-Qa'ida-related groups reinforce this fear. Others worry that U.S. efforts to help the Islamic Courts Union's enemies may turn the movement against the United States.

As a possible harbinger of such radicalization, Somalia has also become an exporter of fighters for conflicts outside the region. A UN report found that 700 militants went from Somalia to Lebanon in July 2006 to fight with Hizballah against Israel.[312]

Economic Costs

Weapons, crime, and refugees have all spilled across Somalia's border. Many of the refugees from the conflict are involved in banditry, preying on areas in Kenya and Ethiopia where the rule of law is weak. Eastleigh, a district in Nairobi, has been nicknamed "Mogadishu Ndogo" (little Mogadishu) and is viewed as a major source of armed crime in the city.[313] In response to rising crime and banditry in the country (the government blames Somali refugees and the cross-border trafficking in weapons from the Somali conflict), the country has ordered its border with Somalia closed a number of times in recent years.

Radicalization of Neighboring States and Their Interventions

ETHIOPIA. Today, Ethiopia is the most active external power in Somalia. Acting on fears that Islamic militants might destabilize its own government, Ethiopia has backed various groups in Somalia. The Ethiopian government has been fighting an insurgency for more than a decade with Somali (Muslim) rebels in its own country in the Ogaden region. Ethiopia fears that the Islamic Courts Union and other factions in Somalia will aid the Ogaden National Liberation Front because it is composed largely of ethnic Somalis and as a means of weakening Ethiopia. Ethiopia also fears that Somalia will become a base for Islamist radicals operating against it.[314]

In December 1996, Ethiopian troops invaded a town in southeastern Somalia where rebels were seeking an independent Islamic state. The rebels, the Islamic Unity Group, have fought since 1992 to unify the Ogaden region in eastern Ethiopia with Somalia.[315] Starting in the late 1990s, Ethiopian troops began to enter southern Somalia in pursuit of members of al-Ittihad al-Islamiyya. By 2000, Ethiopian forces had established a permanent foothold in the Gedo region of Somalia.[316] (Somalia and Ethiopia have had boundary disputes dating back several decades and fought a number of wars with each other.) The latest Ethiopian government operation against the rebels (now operating under the name "the Ogaden National Liberation Front") occurred in the summer of 2006.[317]

Ethiopia, according to Ken Menkhaus, is "sensitive to the point of para-noia about any development inside Somalia that could allow Somalia to be used as a base of Islamist operations."[318] Ethiopia suffered terrorist attacks from al-Ittihad al-Islamiyya in the mid-1990s and conducted several cross-border raids on the group's bases in Somalia.[319]

Today, Ethiopian leaders believe the Islamic Courts Union backs various *jihadists* and is controlled by them. After rival Somali groups signed a peace deal in November 2002, an Ethiopian foreign ministry statement welcom-ing the development declared: "As the international community is well aware, Ethiopia—as a major neighboring country—has been affected by the spillover of the conflict in Somalia and its national security has been chal-lenged by terrorist elements that flourished in the chaos that prevailed in Somalia for over a decade."[320] Unsurprisingly, this outside influence has at times had a destabilizing effect on Somalia and the region as a whole.

ERITREA. Tension with Eritrea exacerbates Ethiopia's concerns. In the late 1990s, Eritrea and Ethiopia both backed various Somali clients in a proxy war—a conflict that continues today, with Ethiopia aiding the Islamic Courts against Ethiopia's Transitional Federal Government allies. Eritrea backed Oromo insur-gents who operated from bases in Somalia in their struggle against the Ethiopian government, support that has diminished but not ended.[321]

KENYA. Kenya has also suffered from the unrest in Somalia, but it has not intervened directly. As noted above, Kenya has also been the victim of ter-rorist attacks that had assistance from individuals in Somalia and has suffered economically from lost tourism.

ARAB STATES. According to Ken Menkhaus, Ethiopia and the Arab states are waging a "virtual proxy war" in Somalia: "Arab states seek a strong central Somali state to counterbalance and outflank Ethiopia; Ethiopia seeks a weak, decentralized client state, and is willing to settle for ongoing state collapse rather than risk a revived Arab-backed government in Mogadishu. Both have provided military and financial support to their Somali clients. . . . "[322] Arab involvement, however, is more limited, and Ethiopian aid is far greater than that of the Arab states.

FAILED INTERNATIONAL INTERVENTIONS

In the 1990s, the international community attempted several efforts beyond pure diplomacy to help alleviate the suffering in Somalia and bring an end to the conflict. One major effort was the United States' Operation Provide Relief (which was part of a broader UN Unified Task Force), which began in August 1992 and focused on providing humanitarian relief. The operation was the response to a famine caused by drought and the civil war in which hundreds of thousands of Somalis perished, while over one million were threatened by further starvation.[323] Most of the food, perhaps as much as 80 percent, was looted, however, by various warlords. The Unified Task Force (UNITAF) effort saved some lives, but in the end it made only a small difference.[324] In addition, U.S. attempts to work with the leading warlords to distribute the aid alienated Somalis who hoped that international intervention would weaken the power of the warlords.[325]

The failure of the pure humanitarian operation (UNITAF and Provide Relief) led to an attempt at a more muscular intervention, United Nations Operation in Somalia II. The U.S. Army participated from December 1992 to May 1993, naming its part of the mission "Operation Restore Hope." The second United Nations Operation in Somalia II (UNOSOM) sought to build the Somali state by disarming various factions, establishing a democratic government, and building the Somali state. UNOSOM II quickly became embroiled in a clash with Somali warlords, particularly Aideed.

The warlords correctly saw the UN objective as a threat to their power. Aideed's forces killed 24 Pakistani troops, leading to a U.S. hunt for the warlord that culminated in the infamous "Black Hawk Down" episode where 18 American soldiers died and perhaps a thousand Somalis perished. The deaths of the soldiers led the Clinton administration to end its commitment to use the military to nation-build in Somalia. A follow-on operation, "Continue Hope," lasted until March 2004 but did little. The United Nations withdrew in 1995 without accomplishing its mission of bringing order to the country.

The United States has also tried backing various warlords fighting the Islamists in an attempt to manage parts of the conflict related to terrorism. Because U.S. officials believe that elements of the Islamist Courts Union have sheltered al-Qaʻida members involved in the 1998 Embassy bombings,[326] they backed the Alliance for the Restoration of Peace and Counter-Terrorism when it was formed in 2006. The United States has also worked with various local administrations in Puntland and Somaliland, as well as various factions and clan members in order to monitor and disrupt terrorist activity.[327] The Islamists saw the Alliance for the Restoration of Peace and Counter-Terrorism's formation as a direct U.S. provocation and effort to undermine them, though U.S. goals were probably much narrower and focused on a few key individuals.[328]

8

Yugoslavia

Getting It Right—Sort Of (1990–2001)

Many people conceive of the various internecine conflicts within the borders of the former Yugoslavia in the 1990s as a single civil war. While there were certainly aspects that sustain such a conception, it is more accurate and useful to see them as a series of interlocking civil wars, in which spillover was magnified by the uncertainty hanging over all of the countries that emerged from the wreckage of the failed Yugoslav state after 1989, coupled with the pre-existing linkages among them.

It was during this long series of civil wars in the 1990s that the international community came closest to successfully "managing" a civil war. Whether because of Yugoslavia's proximity to Western Europe or the precedent of so many previous failed efforts, the Western powers both recognized the potential for spillover and attempted to prevent it. Eventually, they hit upon workable solutions that minimized spillover beyond the borders of the former Yugoslavia to the level of bearable (albeit hardly pleasant) problems for a number of European states, and headed off large-scale destabilization of the region.

Although this was a critical accomplishment of international intervention in the Balkans, it was hardly a rousing success. The West was slow to move and slow to do what was necessary, with the result that there were repeated humanitarian tragedies. The half-hearted and partial measures employed throughout could not prevent spillover *among* the former Yugoslav republics, although even here there were some successes at mitigating spillover. Finally, the critical lesson of the Yugoslav experience was that, after trying everything else, the West finally learned that only massive military intervention to end a conflict can solve the problem of spillover.

OUTBREAK

The civil war in Yugoslavia followed a similar trajectory to those already described. The critical factor was the breakdown of the Yugoslav state and the fear and lawlessness it created. In Susan L. Woodward's pithy phrase, "There would have been no war in Bosnia and Herzegovina if Yugoslavia had not first collapsed."[329]

In the late 1970s and 1980s economic conditions worsened and élites within the various republics increasingly came to blame members of Yugoslavia's other ethnic groups—whoever the "others" happened to be.[330] This seemed superficially apparent because of the wide disparities among the relatively more advanced economies of Slovenia and Croatia on the one hand, and the less developed economies in the rest of the country on the other, that appeared to suggest that the economic problems were somehow tied to ethnic factors. In Sabrina Ramet's words, "The conclusion is inevitable: economics could not be divorced from nationality policy in multiethnic Yugoslavia. On the contrary, economic problems fuelled interethnic resentments and frictions."[331]

But these resentments did not flare into conflict until Tito's communist autocracy began to fall apart after the dictator's death in 1980. According to Laura Silber and Allan Little, "When Tito's health began to deteriorate, federal institutions deteriorated with him. Yugoslavia became a country composed of little more than eight regionally-based and separate Communist Parties, the secret police and the Army."[332] The first signs of fragmentation were noted by observers as early as 1983, and by the late 1980s the Yugoslav federal government had lost much of its former control over the country. However, the republics that had helped undermine federal Yugoslavia did not create new institutions capable of fully replacing it within their territories.[333] In a further sign of the decay of the Yugoslav state, ethnic chauvinists—such as Slobodan Milosevic for the Serbs and Franjo Tudjman for the Croats—came to power by playing on the base fears and desires of their people at the expense of other ethnic groups, in direct contravention of the rules formerly applied by the Titoist regime.[334]

The breakdown of the Yugoslav state and the inability of most of the republics to replace its authority with their own created a security vacuum that enabled and encouraged the formation of ethnic militias. The inability of the failing state to provide protection for its citizens created fear among many Yugoslavs that violence would be used against them, while the state's inability to provide for the basic needs of its citizens engendered the desire to create (or join) other collectives that could meet those needs. In 1990, Milosevic campaigned on the electoral slogan, "With us there is no insecurity."[335] Misha Glenny notes that before the Croat declaration of independence in 1991, the word "Chetnik" (a reference to World War II Serb nationalists) began appearing on the houses and doors of Serb families in Zagreb, which conjured up fears that they were being marked for violence.[336] It was on these powerful psychological forces that the ethnic chauvinists played, stoking the fears of their co-ethnics that armed members of other ethnic groups would attack them (which suggested the need for militias to defend the members of the group) while claiming that the answer to their needs lay in access to, or ownership of, land and resources (which argued for the need to create militias to secure what "rightfully" belonged to the group). Both sets of motives led to the formation of militias across Yugoslavia, although Slovenia, Croatia, and Bosnia-Herzegovina (hereafter Bosnia) led the way starting in 1990.[337]

Not surprisingly, these militias, inspired if not directly guided by the chauvinists who spawned them, began creating "facts on the ground." In some places, the militias moved to secure the areas inhabited by their co-ethnics. In other places, they moved to drive out the members of other ethnic groups—to seize strategic territory, conquer valuable resources, or merely to pre-empt similar attacks by the militias of the other ethnic group. As could only be expected, many of those who joined these militias were the dregs of society—those most prone to use violence and those most anxious to overturn the current order. Consequently, criminals, thieves, sadists, psychopaths, pyromaniacs, and murderers often dominated the militias, especially in the early phases. Moreover, these actions took on the aspects of a self-fulfilling prophecy: stories of these kinds of activities spread like wildfire across Yugoslavia because they seemed to confirm the rhetorical warnings of the chauvinistic leaders. These widespread (and often exaggerated, at least at first) fears drove others to leave their homes in expectation of attack, to form their own militias, and/or to attack members of other ethnic groups within their own communities to drive them out before they became a threat.[338] Such developments also added revenge as another explosive motivating force for members of the various militias.[339]

John Mueller has described the general process, which came to be known by the euphemism "ethnic cleansing" in this conflict, in this way:

> A group of well-armed thugs and bullies encouraged by, and working under rough constraints set out by official security services would arrive or band together in a community. Sometimes operating with local authorities, they would then take control and persecute members of other ethnic groups, who would usually flee to areas protected by their own ethnic ruffians, sometimes to join them in seeking revenge. Carnivals of often-drunken looting, destruction, and violence would take place, and others—guiltily or not so guiltily—might join in. Gradually, however, many of the people under the thugs' arbitrary and chaotic "protection," especially the more moderate ones and young men unwilling to be pressed into military service, would emigrate to safer places.[340]

By one count, in Bosnia and Croatia alone, 83 such militias eventually emerged—56 Serb, 13 Croat, and 14 Muslim—together numbering 36,000 to 66,000 members.[341]

In Yugoslavia, the existence of the six federal republics, and the many politicians seeking to use them as vehicles to power, added another dimension to this problem. In nearly every case, leaders of the republican governments moved to consolidate these militias and co-opt them into the formal armed forces of their state. For the Serbs, who dominated the Yugoslav Army, this meant incorporating the Serb militias of Croatia and

Bosnia into the remainder of the Army—a process facilitated by the rump Yugoslav Army's supplying, supporting, and often fighting in conjunction with the militias. For Croatia, Bosnia, and Slovenia, it meant organizing these militias into a formal, unitary command and control hierarchy (sometimes against their will), adding to them a leavening of personnel and equipment from the previous, ethnically mixed Yugoslav Army and renaming them as the armed forces of their new states. For the Albanians of Kosovo and Macedonia, it meant the eventual organization of their militias into insurgencies against the Serb and Macedonian states, respectively. These consolidations did not change the motivations or methods of the militias, but merely increased their killing power, especially against civilians.[342]

Another important feature of the outbreak of civil war across Yugoslavia was the pernicious influence of local media. There was no independent, let alone objective, Yugoslav media. Almost uniformly, the various media outlets reflected the worst prejudices of the republic or ethnic group to whom they catered. Warren Zimmerman, a former U.S. ambassador to Yugoslavia, made this point by quoting Milos Vasic, whom he called "one of the best independent journalists in Yugoslavia": "You Americans would become nationalists and racists too if your media were totally in the hands of the Ku Klux Klan."[343] Glenny notes that in Belgrade, before the Slovene and Croat declarations of independence in 1991, "RTV Belgrade had begun the dress rehearsal for its forthcoming performance as a demonic chorus whose chief function was to encourage the audience to bay for blood. Early on in the war, a surprisingly broad spectrum of people in both Croatia and Serbia singled out Croatian Television (HTV) and RTV Belgrade as two of the most culpable war criminals of the Yugoslav tragedy."[344]

It is important to note the scholarly consensus that the outbreak of civil war in Yugoslavia was derived principally from the structural problems of worsening economic conditions that were blamed by ethno-chauvinists on other ethnic groups, coupled with the breakdown of the state that made it impossible to deal effectively with the economic problems or to stem the fear and anger created by the ethno-chauvinists. While the long history of ethnic tensions among Serbs, Croats, Slovenes, Bosnian Muslims, and Albanians may have made it more likely that blame for the economic problems of each area would take on an ethnic hue, it is simply not the case that the Yugoslav civil wars were a recurrence of "ancient hatreds." There is agreement among both scholars and experts on the region that Yugoslavia under Tito had been a functional multi-ethnic society where the vast majority of residents lived in peace, and that ethnicity was no longer an important source of identity. This state of affairs broke down largely because of the failure of the Yugoslav state, which allowed for the rise of ethno-chauvinist politicians and ethnically based militias, which then tore apart Yugoslav society. Without the failure of the Yugoslav state, there was no cause for the fragmentation of Yugoslav society along ethnic lines, let alone the savage civil wars that ensued.[345]

Indeed, today scholars and experts on the Balkans increasingly see the canard of "ancient hatreds" offered up by Americans and Europeans alike as having been little more than an excuse for non-intervention—a position the proponents typically held long before they stumbled upon this argument—because it suggested that the Yugoslav wars were insoluble and therefore that foreign intervention was futile. Ambassador Richard Holbrooke himself has dismissed this red herring, noting that (emphasis in the original):

> Thus arose an idea that "ancient hatreds," a vague but useful term for history too complicated (or trivial) for outsiders to master, made it impossible (or pointless) for anyone outside the region to try to prevent the conflict. This theory trivialized and oversimplified the forces that tore Yugoslavia apart in the early 1990s. It was expressed by many officials and politicians over the course of the war, and is still widely accepted today in parts of Washington and Europe. Those who invoked it were, for the most part, trying to excuse their own reluctance or inability to deal with the problems in the region. . . . It was, of course, undeniable that the ethnic groups within Yugoslavia nursed deep-seated grievances against one another. But in and of itself, ethnic friction, no matter how serious, did not make the tragedy inevitable— or the three ethnic groups equally guilty. Of course, there was friction between ethnic groups in Yugoslavia, but this was true in many other parts of the world where racial hatred had *not* turned into ethnic cleansing and civil war. . . . Serbs, Croats, and Muslims worked together in every walk of life. There was no noticeable physical or ethnic difference between them, and in fact, there was considerable intermarriage.

Many people told me that until the collapse of their country they did not even know which of their friends were Serb and which were Muslim.[346]

The Slovenes were the first to secede, and it was their departure that brought about the final elimination of what had been the Socialist Federal Republic of Yugoslavia. Slovenia was the only Yugoslav republic that was ethnically homogeneous, which meant that other ethnic groups had little direct stake in what it did. It was also the wealthiest, which made its pursuit of independence much easier.[347] After Slovenia declared its independence in June 1991, the Yugoslav Army fought a desultory conflict against the Slovene militias, which Ljubljana quickly knitted together into a formal defense force. However, the war itself caused the Serb leadership in Belgrade, particularly Milosevic, to conclude that their narrow interests were no longer served by preservation of the old Yugoslav federation. Instead, they needed to focus on securing all of the Serbs and ensuring their safety and access to the maximum resources practicable. That made it both unnecessary and a waste of military assets to try to prevent Slovenia's departure, and so after just ten days of combat, Serbia (still masquerading as the Yugoslav government) agreed to an EU-mediated peace.

Croatia was a different story. Serbs made up 12 percent of the population of Croatia in 1991, and many were geographically concentrated in the Krajina region and in the western and eastern extremities of the Slavonia region.[348] Fearing what the majority Croat population would do to them after Croatia declared independence under its new president, the Croat nationalist Franjo Tudjman, and egged on from Serbia by their own nationalists, Serbs throughout Croatia quickly began to arm themselves, seize control of their own villages, and drive out Croats in those villages or neighboring ones. Unlike the Slovenes, the Croats were not prepared to quickly exert control over their own territory when they too declared independence in June 1991. Croat militias began to emerge, but at roughly the same pace (or slower) than the Serb militias, and the Croat government took far longer to weld these militias into a national army. Meanwhile, Belgrade increasingly supported the Serb militias in Croatia with Yugoslav Army units. The result was bloody fighting, horrific ethnic cleansing, and, by 1992, a stalemate that left the Serbs in control of roughly one-quarter of Croatia.

The worst casualty of the Croatian war was Bosnia, an ethnically intermingled state with a population that was 44 percent Bosnian Muslim, 31 percent Serb, and 17 percent Croat.[349] Furthermore, both Serbia and Croatia believed that large parts of Bosnia rightly belonged to them. In 1992, Germany demanded that the European Union states should recognize Slovene and Croat independence in the wrong-headed belief that this would somehow force the Serbs to cease their resistance/aggression.[350] Not only did this not succeed, but it pushed the weak Bosnian president, Alija Izetbegovic, to hold a referendum on independence lest Bosnia be left behind as part of a Serb-dominated rump Yugoslavia. On March 1, 1992, Bosnians voted overwhelmingly for independence, and on March 2, 1992, the barricades went up all across Bosnia as Serb militias, again supported and encouraged by Belgrade, went on the offensive to defend their own lands and to seize as much of the rest of the country as they could. Croat militias (generally encouraged and supported by Zagreb, albeit not as strongly as the better organized and directed Serbs were) did the same, in many cases similarly looking to annex what they believed was rightly theirs. The Bosnian government was even less prepared for the war than the Croat government had been the year before, and so was entirely reliant on local Bosnian militias to hold their own initially. The result was that the Serbs quickly overran about 70 percent of Bosnian territory.[351]

War took a little longer to reach Kosovo, the southwestern part of Serbia. By the 1990s, the ethnic Serb population had dwindled to just 10 percent, with ethnic Albanians overwhelmingly making up the remainder.[352] The economic problems of the 1980s had produced tensions between the Serbs and Albanians, and in response the government in Belgrade began to strip Kosovo of its autonomy in 1989. This merely provoked a secessionist sentiment among the Albanians, which picked up steam with the secessions of Slovenia, then Croatia, then Bosnia from the Yugoslav state, and with the emergence of Albania from its communist isolation. A referendum among Kosovar Albanians in 1995 showed that 43 percent wanted to secede from Serbia to join Albania, while the rest wanted to secede from Serbia and become independent.[353] Further fuel was added to the fire by the ultimate victories of both Bosnians and Croats in their own wars against the Serbs (discussed below), which convinced the Kosovar Albanians that their own dreams could also come true if they too could trigger the same Western intervention against the Serbs that had produced victory for the Bosnians and, to a lesser extent, the Croats. By 1997, the Kosovo Liberation Army (KLA) was waging a full-blown insurgency against the Serbs and by early 1998 had gained control of roughly 40 percent of Kosovo. Although wary of Western intervention, Belgrade struck back hard in the summer of 1998, unleashing Operation Horseshoe, which drove hundreds of thousands of Kosovar Albanians from their homes in a replay of the tragedies in Croatia and Bosnia.[354]

The final act of the Yugoslav wars played out in Macedonia.[355] Roughly 25 percent of Macedonia's population was ethnic Albanian who were inspired by the example (and ultimate success) of their kindred in Kosovo to mount their own secessionist insurgency against the majority ethnic Macedonians. Part of their inspiration came from roughly 400,000 Kosovar Albanian refugees who fled Operation Horseshoe in 1999, bringing KLA fighters and bitterness with them.[356] These sentiments were further exacerbated by Macedonia's initial refusal to accept so many Albanian refugees, and for nearly a week the refugees were forced to remain out in the open along the border without shelter or supplies. After the fighting in Kosovo ended in 1999 and with these injustices fresh in their minds, some Macedonian Albanians began to agitate for greater autonomy along the lines of what their brethren had just won in Kosovo, while some even called for outright secession and a merging with Albania proper. In February-March 2001, Albanian rebels began an insurgency/terrorist campaign, including bomb attacks against a number of Macedonian police stations.[357] This prompted Skopje to deploy the Macedonian Army to Tetovo, the principal Albanian city in Macedonia. The evidence indicated that the Macedonian Albanian rebels were receiving logistical and financial support from Kosovo—a number of the former KLA personnel were among the Albanian insurgents in Macedonia. Whether that assistance was provided by the Kosovar regional government was unclear.[358]

SPILLOVER

The various civil wars in Yugoslavia produced a similar range of spillover effects as other recent ethnically or religiously based internal conflicts. However, what differed in this case is that while these spillover effects had a tremendous impact on the various states within the borders of the former

Yugoslavia, the West enjoyed a fair degree of success in preventing them from having a similar impact on countries outside the borders of the former Yugoslavia. This degree of success was produced by two factors: the West made a greater effort to prevent external spillover than internal spillover and ultimately intervened massively to end several of the Yugoslav civil wars before they could generate dangerous levels of spillover.

Refugees

The Yugoslav civil wars produced more than their fair share of refugees. In large part, this was a result of the fact that dispossessing people from their homes was a key goal of many military operations. Ethnic cleansing was designed to drive out those from a different ethnic or religious group from any given piece of land, and all of the armies—albeit the Serbs most of all—practiced this tactic to secure land they had conquered. Indeed, although a great deal of the killing, butchery, rapes, and other atrocities were the product of soldiers run amok, in many cases these atrocities were deliberately encouraged and employed by Balkan leaders to inspire such fear in enemy populations that they would voluntarily flee before the other side's armies. Roughly 700,000 Croats became refugees, with 300,000 of them driven out of the country.[359] The war with Croatia alone produced 250,000 Serb displaced persons. All told, over 1 million of Croatia's 4.5 million inhabitants became refugees.[360] Of 4.4 million people living in Bosnia in 1991, fully half became displaced persons and roughly 1 million fled the country altogether, most to Western Europe.[361] The fighting in Kosovo caused 1.3 million of the 1.8 million Kosovar Albanians to leave their homes in response to Serbia's ethnic cleansing operations, of whom 600,000 fled the country.[362] Even in Macedonia, the fighting there in 2001 spawned 170,000 internally displaced persons from a population of 2 million.[363]

Inevitably, such massive population flows played havoc with the various states of the region. Part of the reason that Serbia and Croatia ultimately acceded to the 1995 Dayton Accords was that the burden of so many refugees from the fighting in Bosnia was straining their already weak (and in the case of Serbia, heavily sanctioned) economies.[364] Nearly 350,000 Yugoslav refugees fled to Germany, encumbering its famously generous social services and budget. In the immediate aftermath of German re-unification, with all of the massive costs that imposed, this was an added burden that the Germans could not afford and prompted a series of misguided German policies, particularly its early recognition of Croatia, which helped to unleash the civil war in Bosnia.[365] In less developed states, the results were even more devastating. Albania absorbed 365,000 of the 600,000 Kosovar refugees in 1999, which amounted to 13 percent of its population—the equivalent of the United States accepting roughly 38 million people in less than a year. Such a sudden increase in the population within its borders put a huge strain on Albania's economic and social infrastructure (itself still reeling from the collapse of the pyramid schemes that brought down the government in March 1997), as well as on the budget and balance of payments. Outside observers feared that if the war dragged on for much longer, Albania's weak administrative capacity would break down altogether, creating a crisis for law and order there.[366] Macedonia, with barely 2 million people, was overwhelmed by 400,000 Kosovar Albanians, amounting to 20 percent of its population.[367]

The impact of Kosovar refugees in Macedonia is also a good example of the political problems they created. Macedonia was unequipped to help so many people, especially given the rudimentary state of its health care system, and ethnic Macedonians were wary of accepting more ethnic Albanians into their country. Naturally, this triggered splits between various Macedonian politicians and the Democratic Party of Albanians, a key member of the Macedonian government coalition, which nearly brought down the government. Because of Macedonia's political frailty, many Western states feared that a governmental collapse would trigger a larger national collapse. This too was a motive for NATO intervention to end the Kosovo war.[368]

In addition, refugees directly fueled the spread of the fighting. Wherever they fled to, they brought horror stories of ethnic cleansing which helped mobilize additional populations out of fear or revenge. The refugee populations furnished thousands of ready recruits for the militias and armies of the warring parties. In many cases, they brought ethnic cleansing with them—employing the same tactics in their places of refuge that had been used against them in their place of origin. Obviously, this merely perpetuated a cycle of violence, with angry refugees creating more angry refugees. In Bosnia and Macedonia, refugees played an important role in kicking off the internecine conflicts themselves as refugees spread from the fighting in Croatia and Kosovo, respectively, bolstering the militias and radicalizing their populations.

Terrorism

International terrorism was hardly the worst aspect of spillover from the various Yugoslav civil wars, but it was not absent either. In particular, the Bosnian Muslims were extremely weak, having declared their independence (and so ignited the tripartite war for Bosnia) with few if any preparations to defend themselves. The independent militias that formed in March 1992 to defend Muslim territory were hard-pressed to keep the Serbs at bay, or the Croats when they attacked the next year. The Bosnians responded by quietly inviting in significant numbers of *mujahidin* from the Islamic world. As had been the case in Chechnya and Afghanistan before that, fanatical Islamic fundamentalists responded, including both Sunni *salafis* and Shi'i extremists from Iran and Lebanon. Indeed, Bosnia found Iranian Revolutionary Guards fighting alongside elements of al-Qa'ida against their mutual foes: Catholic Croats and Orthodox Serbs. Although the United States and European Union governments struggled to find ways to assist the Bosnians (without actually committing any troops of their own), turning a blind eye to the presence of these unsavory elements during the fighting, after Dayton the extirpation of these foreign fighters from the Balkans became a priority as the West sought to prevent them from gaining an operations base in Europe.[369] There were also reports of *mujahidin* aiding both the KLA during the Kosovo fighting in 1999 and the Albanian National Liberation Army in Macedonia in 2001.

The Balkan struggle was important to the *jihadists* in several ways. First, their propaganda regularly used horrific images of Serbs killing Muslims to radicalize and recruit Muslims around the world. Second, they juxtaposed these horrors with Western inaction, claiming that the United States and other countries deliberately wanted the Serbs to slaughter innocent Muslims. (The *jihadists* later explained the apparent U.S.-led support for Bosnia as a case of the Americans fearing that the *mujahidin* were already turning the tide and wanting to claim the credit for themselves.) For those who fought in the Balkans, it served as an important bond and later source of networking, even though their military impact was at best limited.[370]

Economic Costs

The wars were devastating to the economies of all of the former Yugoslav republics, except for Slovenia, whose early and largely painless secession diminished the impact on its economy. However, one of the most important ways in which the NATO interventions in Yugoslavia were successful was in mitigating the economic costs inflicted on states neighboring the former Yugoslavia. Many neighboring economies suffered some damage, but in no case was it catastrophic:

—In Bulgaria, reduced exports, tourism, and foreign direct investment caused a corresponding slowdown in growth by 2½ percentage points while the current account deficit and inflation rose slightly.[371]

—For Romania, the worst economic hit came during the 1999 NATO air war with Serbia. NATO warplanes took down the bridges over the Danube, blocking both waterborne transport along the river and truck and rail traffic across it. Lost trade and higher transportation cost Bucharest $30 million to $50 million per week at its height, while foreign direct investment dried up.[372]

—Macedonia did not experience a full-blown war like Croatia, Bosnia, or Kosovo, but its economy was hammered, especially by the Kosovo war. The wars deprived Macedonia of many of its most important markets, gutting exports and boosting unemployment to as high as 40–50 percent.[373] The massive influx of Kosovar Albanian refugees inflicted equal damage, swamping both Macedonia's budget and the country's health care system. Eventually, hospitals would only accept emergency cases to keep space open for refugees.[374]

—Austria, Hungary, Italy, Greece, Ukraine, and even Moldova also suffered significant economic costs as a result of the Kosovo conflict from loss of tourism, loss of trade, and refugees.[375]

—An International Monetary Fund study of the impact of the Kosovo war on six regional economies found an average decline in growth of 1 percent, coupled with a decline in output of about 2 percentage points, as well as "significantly" increased budget and current account deficits.[376]

Radicalization of Neighboring Populations

A key problem in the spread of conflict from one former Yugoslav republic to the next was the radicalization of neighboring populations. This was clearly one of the most important reasons for the outbreak of four (five if the Macedonian conflict is included) civil wars in these states. However, of equal significance, while the populations of neighboring states that had not been part of the former Yugoslavia were also radicalized by the civil wars raging there, they were not radicalized to the same extent, and certainly not enough to trigger either independent intervention by their governments or internal problems within their countries before the decisive NATO interventions shut down the different Yugoslav civil wars.

The Kosovo war had an immense impact on the population of Albania, which sympathized with the aspirations of the Kosovar Albanians and was horrified by Serb atrocities committed against them. Albania regularly threatened to go to war with Serbia on behalf of the Kosovar Albanians, and this was an important impetus to the NATO decision to force Serbia to halt Operation Horseshoe.[377] Beforehand, Albanian President Sali Berisha had warned publicly that Albania would not "stand idly by" if fighting broke out in Kosovo. Many other Albanians, in and out of government, wanted "peaceful unification" with Kosovo and western Macedonia—prompting Serbia, Greece, and Macedonia to declare their opposition to such a scheme.[378]

A less obvious manifestation of this problem was the impact of the fighting, particularly the Bosnian civil war, on Turkey. The Ottoman Empire had once ruled the Balkans, and there remained a deep-seated affinity between Turks and Muslim Albanians, Turkish and other Muslims in Macedonia, Kosovars, and Bosnians. The scenes of ethnic cleansing and concentration camps from the Bosnian civil war appalled many Turks, who brought considerable pressure to bear on their government to find ways to support the Muslims there. Many Turks demanded unilateral Turkish military intervention in the conflict, something that Ankara steadfastly but anxiously resisted. In response to these pressures, in August 1992, the Turkish government publicly proposed an "Action Plan" for the UN Security Council calling for a graduated series of steps to compel the Serbs to cease their aggression. These included everything from lifting the UN arms embargo only for the Bosnian Muslims, to establishing a UN military presence in the country (part of the background to the creation of the UN safe havens), to striking Serb military targets.[379] In addition, there is evidence that Turkish sources provided weaponry to Croatia and Bosnia to fight the Serbs in defiance of the UN embargo, although whether Ankara was aware of these sales is unknown.[380]

Secession Breeds Secessionism

Within the borders of the former Yugoslavia, secessionist movements in one republic encouraged secessionist movements in others. A major impetus to this was the German decision to recognize Slovenia and Croatia, thereby raising the prospect in the minds of Bosnian Muslims, Kosovars, and Macedonian Albanians that they might also receive international backing—which made it impossible for moderates to prevail over extremists in debates over whether to push for independence. Similarly, the eventual success of the Bosnian Muslims at Dayton and the somewhat lesser success of the Kosovar Albanians in their wars for national self-determination were major spurs to those Macedonian Albanians who eventually mounted their own insurgency.[381]

The fear of secessionist sentiment was also a powerful motive for other countries. Bulgaria and Greece have sizable Macedonian communities, and both feared that these would attempt to secede to join Macedonia.[382] As a result, Bulgaria refused to recognize Macedonia for fear that doing so would simply encourage its own Macedonian population to agitate for self-determination of their own.[383] Greece, which denied that a Macedonian ethnic identity even existed, claimed that the existence of an independent Macedonia on its borders might constitute a territorial claim upon its own province of Macedonia in northern Greece. As a result, the Greeks successfully forced the Macedonians to change their flag and insisted that the country be referred to as the Former Yugoslav Republic of Macedonia or the acronym FYROM. To make matters worse, Greek animosity simply drove Macedonia to seek Turkish support, further enraging Athens and confirming (in Greek minds) all of their worst fears. Most American officials considered the dispute between Macedonia and Greece over the name of the new country ridiculous, but they also believed that the two sides were serious enough about it to come to blows. In response, from 1992 to 1999, the United States kept 550 soldiers in Macedonia as part of a 1,000-person UN peacekeeping force.[384]

The outcome of the Dayton Accords also inspired Kosovars seeking independence to use violence. Drawing on the earlier conflict, the KLA concluded that the United States and the international community would intervene if the violence reached horrific levels. This led them to attack the Serbs in Kosovo and to try to ratchet up the violence in an attempt to foster international intervention. There was a deliberate desire to provoke mass reprisals and refugee flows, as eventually happened in 1999.

Political Tensions

The Yugoslav civil wars were political nightmares for a great many countries in Europe, as well as the United States and Russia. European Union governments were petrified by the spillover potential of the Yugoslav civil wars, and this fear drove them to intervene (or demand that others intervene—such as the United Nations or NATO). There are certainly those who claimed both at the time and in retrospect that these fears of spillover beyond the borders of the former Yugoslavia were unjustified. Since these fears never materialized (or were prevented from materializing by the ultimately decisive NATO interventions), it is impossible to know for sure. However, there was tremendous spillover *among* the former Yugoslav republics, and the majority of European and American decisionmakers appear to have accepted the threat that other neighboring states could experience similar problems.[385] The result was nine years of crises that precipitated furious rows among the Europeans, between the Europeans and the Americans, and between the West and the Russians.

Indeed, ultimately the United States agreed to lead NATO interventions in Bosnia, Kosovo, and (more peacefully) Macedonia not because Washington believed there was any threat to U.S. security, but because the United States became convinced that if it did not do so the stresses of the arguments about how to deal with the Yugoslav civil wars would tear NATO apart. Again, commentators at the time and since have insisted that the threats to European and transatlantic unity from the Yugoslav civil wars were greatly exaggerated, but the fact is that they were widely believed at the time, and clearly believed by the most senior decisionmakers. Ivo Daalder has written that the debate within NATO over how to deal with the Bosnian Serb attack on the UN-declared "safe area" of Bihac in 1994 created a "transatlantic crisis on a par with the one the Atlantic alliance had last witnessed over the Suez Canal in 1956," and feared "that NATO itself could be torn asunder by disagreement over Bosnia."[386] Michael Kelly likewise quoted a senior Clinton Administration official who said:

> We have been putting straws on the back of NATO solidarity over Bosnia for the last two years. We have been pushing them over and over to use military force, to the point where we have to threaten the destruction of the transatlantic treaty. We decided that we are not going to do that anymore. We are not going to make this a manhood test. We are not going to break NATO over this.[387]

The Clinton Administration's radical change in policy over Bosnia in 1995 was precipitated by the realization that the war there—and the divisions and paralysis it was provoking among the European powers—was jeopardizing Washington's entire vision for Europe, even though American policymakers long resisted the notion that the two were somehow linked.[388] In Daalder's words, "Bosnia proved to be a major stumbling block for realizing the administration's vision for Europe. . . . As long as the war continued, NATO remained divided, further dimming any prospect for using the alliance to help integrate the other parts of Europe."[389]

In both Moscow and Washington there were grave fears that differences over the Yugoslav civil wars would revive the Cold War and destroy the nascent cooperation that both sides were trying to nurture. To illustrate this point, Derek Chollet quotes Deputy Secretary of State Strobe Talbott as remarking "Bosnia is the beast that could eat not only NATO but the Russian-American partnership."[390] Chollet likewise notes that at roughly the same time, Russian Defense Minister Pavel Grachev was threatening his U.S. counterpart, William Perry, that if NATO's bombing of Bosnian Serb forces continued, "we will have to help the Serbs in a unilateral way."[391] In retrospect, it seems absurd to believe that Bosnia could have re-ignited the East-West conflict that had paralyzed Europe for so many decades, but perhaps only because it did not happen; at the time it seemed to be a very real danger to those involved.[392]

Costly Interventions

One of the great success stories of the Yugoslav civil wars is that there were no costly interventions by any of the small neighbors of the former Yugoslavia, despite the fact that Albania, Greece, Turkey, Bulgaria, and Romania all had powerful incentives to intervene. While true, this accomplishment is not much to brag about. Such interventions appear to have been prevented only by the United Nations, European Union, and eventually NATO interventions, which obviated the need for the smaller neighboring states to act on their own. And none of these interventions prevented Croatia and Serbia from intervening in the Bosnian civil war.

There was also considerable involvement by these governments in supporting various groups inside Yugoslavia. Hungary was providing weaponry to Croatia, the Greeks were helping the Serbs, the Albanians were helping the ethnic Albanians in Kosovo and Macedonia, and the Turks were helping the Macedonians.[393] However, another area where the Yugoslav case differs from the others is that this involvement never escalated to proxy wars or outright military intervention. Again, the small powers were precluded from doing so because the major European states and the Americans intervened to secure their interests instead.

RESOLUTION

From the beginning, the members of the European Economic Community (which would become the European Union in 1992) involved themselves in the Yugoslav civil wars to try to bring them to an end. They were motivated largely by fear of spillover in all of its dimensions, although the humanitarian suffering also exerted a powerful influence through the medium of public opinion. In particular, Germany worried that the political and economic aspects of its reunification would be greatly complicated by instability in Central Europe and the Balkans.[394] The Germans, along with many other European governments, also worried about their ability to absorb large numbers of refugees and the potential for secessionist movements and ethnic animosities to spread throughout the ethnic patchwork of the post-Soviet Balkans.

The United States initially did not see any need to involve itself in Balkan affairs. Many Americans bought into the foolish "ancient hatreds" argument of "Kaplanesque all-against-all conflicts, rooted in old hatreds that could hardly be ameliorated by well-meaning, but innocent and naïve, outsiders."[395] Moreover, Washington did not see its interests engaged in the Yugoslav civil wars and so resisted European pleas for American involvement. Although some Americans agreed that there was the potential for spillover from the Yugoslav civil wars, most believed that it would require virtual tidal waves of spillover before American interests would be affected. Consequently, the George H. W. Bush Administration left Yugoslavia to the Europeans.[396] It was only after the Clinton Administration took office and adopted a policy of NATO expansion—and after repeated EU efforts to dampen the conflict had failed miserably—that the United States changed its views. As noted above, that change was prompted by the realization that the European Union was incapable of handling the Yugoslav civil wars and that this inability was tearing the Western Alliance apart, jeopardizing NATO expansion to the east and the potential for the United States to convince

NATO to expand its security horizon to address problems the United States cared about beyond Europe.

Almost immediately after the outbreak of the Slovene war in 1991, the European Economic Community dispatched negotiators to try to bring the fighting to a rapid resolution. Because the Serbs quickly decided not to make a major effort to contest Slovene secession, the European representatives were able to bring that conflict to an end after just ten days of fighting in negotiations on the island of Brioni in July 1991. Unfortunately, the Brioni agreement proved to be a false dawn. It mistakenly convinced the Western Europeans that the Yugoslav civil wars could be easily solved through negotiations and that each could be addressed piecemeal. It likewise convinced the United States that Europe was perfectly capable of dealing with the problems of the former Yugoslavia. Unfortunately, all of these judgments were mistaken, but they set the pattern of behavior for the rest of the decade.[397]

When the fighting shifted to Croatia, both the European states and Americans applied these wrong-headed lessons. The European states appointed their own negotiator, Lord Carrington, a former British foreign secretary, to try to bring the conflict to an end while the Americans did nothing. Because, unlike in Slovenia, the Serbs were determined to fight for the parts of Croatia in which they lived, Lord Carrington's mission accomplished nothing—18 times he tried to secure a ceasefire, only to fail every time.[398] The Europeans then turned to the United Nations, which appointed its own negotiator, former U.S. Secretary of State Cyrus Vance. Vance proposed the creation of three UN-designated "Protected Areas," which would be garrisoned by UN peacekeepers. In February 2002, the UN Security Council approved the Vance plan and peacekeepers from 30 countries began to deploy as the UN Protection Force (UNPROFOR) under the command of an Indian general who bizarrely decided to set up his headquarters not in Zagreb, but in Sarajevo, thereby binding UNPROFOR's fate to the stability of Bosnia.[399] But after a brief respite, the Serbs and Croats resumed their fighting and UNPROFOR proved powerless to stop them or to stop the spread of civil war into Bosnia within weeks of UNPROFOR's arrival. Eventually, in September 1992, the UN presence was expanded with the creation of UNPROFOR II, charged with keeping the peace and defending six more safe areas in Bosnia.[400]

Carrington was replaced by Lord Owen, another former British foreign secretary, who joined forces with Vance to try to broker a truce, but had no more luck than his predecessor. In late 1992, Vance and Owen proposed a peace plan for Bosnia that would have divided it up into ten ethnically controlled cantons. Although there is considerable debate over whether it could ever have worked, what was clear is that it would have effectively rewarded Serb aggression by forcing the Serbs to disgorge only 25 percent of their conquests. This pitted Croats, Bosnians, and humanitarian groups firmly against it. Moreover, it would have required 50,000–70,000 additional troops to enforce it. Since there was no appetite among UN members, and especially the United States, to deploy such a force, the plan withered on the vine.[401]

Overall, the United Nations' performance in Yugoslavia was nothing short of disastrous. Key UN personnel, from commanders on the ground through Secretary General Boutros Boutros Ghali, were so determined to avoid using any force that they ended up doing nothing, thereby allowing the various sides (but particularly the Serbs) to use force whenever they could, including massively against civilians. Between April 1992 and October 1993, the UN Security Council passed 47 resolutions related to the former Yugoslavia and none had any discernible impact on the fighting.[402] Without question, however, the low point in the history of UN involvement in Yugoslavia came in July 1995, when UNPROFOR II stood by helplessly and the UN Security Council did nothing while Serb forces attacked the UN-designated safe area of Srebrenica and slaughtered over 8,000 Bosnian Muslim men, driving the women, children, and elderly from the town.[403]

The one action that the UN Security Council took to try to end the conflict that played an important role eventually, albeit not immediately, was the imposition of sanctions. Early on, the UN Security Council imposed an arms embargo on all the war parties, which mostly aided the Serbs who had plenty of arms and a significant small-arms manufacturing capability. In late May 1992, the sanctions were expanded to include an economic embargo against Serbia in response to revelations of Serb ethnic cleansing. Briefly, this sparked internal demonstrations against Milosevic in Belgrade, although he was able to quickly regain control over the situation.[404] Although these sanctions did begin to erode the strength of the Serb economy, this was a slow process and had no impact on the immediate fighting. Almost a year later, the UN Security Council tried to ratchet up the pressure on Serbia by freezing its assets and forbidding the transshipment of goods through the country—which was an important conduit for trade flowing between the Adriatic and the rest of the Balkans. Together, these economic sanctions against Serbia slowly exerted a powerful effect on Belgrade, to the point that, by 1995, observers described Serbia's economy as "gutted."[405]

The massacre at Srebrenica in 1995, coupled with Serbian moves against another UN-designated safe area at Gorazde, brought about a radical change in U.S. thinking about Yugoslavia. The Clinton Administration concluded that the European Union and the United Nations were simultaneously proving unable to cope with the problems there, while it remained deeply fearful of the consequences of failure. Washington began to conceive of the downward spiral of events in Yugoslavia as one that was directly affecting its interests by threatening to destabilize more and more of Central Europe, and tearing the Western European powers apart as they fought over how to prevent it and kept failing to do so. In the minds of Clinton Administration officials, this argued for a more forceful Western approach to try bringing the civil wars there to a conclusion, and U.S. leadership to provide what had been lacking in the past.[406]

After much debate both within the U.S. government and among the United States and its European allies, a new U.S. approach to ending the Croat and Yugoslav wars emerged that ultimately proved successful. Washington began to press for the partial lifting of the UN arms embargo to allow the West to arm and train the Bosnian Muslim forces so that they could better resist the Serbs. The United States and the European Union pushed for the Bosnian Croats to agree to a federation government with the Bosnian Muslims. The United States took a "don't ask, don't tell" position toward covert assistance to the Croats to allow them to better contest the situation on the ground.[407] Perhaps of greatest consequence, Washington practically forced NATO to agree to mount air strikes against Serb positions in the event that they kept assaulting Gorazde and the Bosnian capital of Sarajevo. At the end of August 1995, this commitment was put into effect with Operation Deliberate Force, during which NATO warplanes flew 3,536 combat sorties against 56 Serb ground targets. These strikes could not cripple the Bosnian Serb army, but did hurt it.[408] Indeed, the Serbs complained incessantly about the bombing, making it seem likely that it did have an impact on their forces.[409]

At roughly the same time, the re-equipped and retrained Croat Army launched a series of offensives against the Serbs, first in Croatia and then in Bosnia. In these latter attacks the Croats were joined by Bosnian formations in joint campaigns. The Croats quickly and dramatically overran the Serb-held areas of the Krajina and Western Slavonia in Croatia itself. With advice from a team of former American military officers, they next moved against Serb forces besieging the Bosnian town of Bihac, relieving it and turning the flank of the Serb position in western Bosnia. Finally, in late September 1995, the Croats and Bosnians assaulted Serb positions in western Bosnia, seizing huge chunks of territory, although they were ultimately checked before they could take the main Serb city of Banja Luka and a number of other key towns.[410]

Although the Croat offensive had largely run out of steam—and was in danger of being rolled back by a Serbian counterattack—it proved to be the final straw for Milosevic.[411] Economic sanctions were crippling Serbia's economy, NATO air strikes were pounding Serb forces in Bosnia, and they now had capable Croat enemies to contend with. He apparently decided that Serbia's interests were no longer served by continued fighting over scraps of land in Croatia and Bosnia.[412] In November 2005, he came to the proximity talks in Dayton, Ohio, presided over by Holbrooke and agreed to arrangements that brought both the wars in Croatia and Bosnia to an end.

The 1995 Dayton Accords created a workable political framework, but they did not actually resolve the conflict with the support of all the parties. Especially for Bosnia, the Dayton Accords were largely an imposed solution, with Milosevic delivering the Bosnian Serbs, Tudjman delivering the Bosnian Croats, and the United States doing the same for the Bosnian Muslims. As Holbrooke himself has pointed out, however, the key to actually ending the conflict would be in seeing the terms of Dayton actually implemented. To make sure that they were, NATO agreed to deploy 60,000 combat troops, including a 20,000-strong American armored division, as the Implementation Force of the Dayton Accords. After the Implementation Force's mandated year, NATO recognized that civil war would re-ignite if all Western troops were removed, and so the Implementation Force was replaced by the 32,000-strong Stabilization Force, which remained in Bosnia until December 2005 (when it was replaced by a European Union force). Thus, in the end, air strikes, economic sanctions, and the Croat ground offensive were not sufficient to resolve the Bosnian civil war. It still required massive Western military intervention and a ten-year occupation of Bosnia to do so.[413]

When the situation in Kosovo began to deteriorate in 1998, the United States and its NATO allies believed that the demonstration effect of their actions in Bosnia would be enough to bring Milosevic to heel. They considered him little more than a bully and did not understand the importance that he and other Serb nationalists attached to Kosovo, and so they believed that if they merely convinced him that they were willing to do to Serbia for Kosovo what they had done to the Serbs on behalf of the Bosnians, Milosevic would back down. The United States and NATO decided not to arm the KLA for fear that this would make a negotiated settlement in which Kosovo remained part of the Serb-dominated Federal Republic of Yugoslavia (which the West wanted) more difficult. Nonetheless, in March 1998 the UN Security Council re-imposed economic sanctions on Serbia because of growing Serb repression of Kosovar Albanians. By October 1998, NATO began to threaten air strikes. This was enough to convince Milosevic to agree to a vague and ineffectual set of compromises, but, in so doing, merely convinced him that NATO was desperate not to use force. The next month he authorized Operation Horseshoe to begin driving the Kosovars out altogether.[414]

Having had its bluff called, NATO was forced to start air strikes against Serbia, but did so from a poor position and in the belief that, as in 1995, a few days would be enough to make the "Bully of Belgrade" back down.[415] Only after 1,200 NATO aircraft had flown 38,000 sorties during the 78 days of Operation Allied Force, including over 5,000 strike sorties against Serb military forces in Kosovo, would Milosevic agree to NATO's terms.[416] Even then, the weight of scholarly argument is that the bombing was only a part of his decision. Another crucial factor was NATO's decision to begin building up forces for a ground invasion and Russia's warning to Belgrade that Moscow could not stop NATO from doing whatever it wanted to Serbia.[417]

The resolution of the Kosovo conflict is still to be determined. The 1999 war resulted in de facto partition, but independence is still elusive. The Serb-populated parts of Kosovo are under pressure from Albanians to leave for greater Serbia, which in turn fears that independence for Kosovo would create political unrest in Serbia proper (in Preševo, Vojvodina, and Novi Pazar where there are Albanian, Hungarian, and Muslim communities, respectively). The Kosovar "state" is plagued by a poor economy, widespread corruption, and at best a limited rule of law. Over 11 years after Dayton, NATO forces are still in the Balkans.[418]

RESOLUTION

The Yugoslav civil wars point to both the difficulty of managing spillover and the one feasible solution that modern nations have found: massive intervention. The Yugoslav wars fit the pattern of other wars in terms of their impact on neighboring states. They produced vast numbers of refugees, radicalized neighboring populations, created a secessionist domino-effect, introduced new elements of terrorism in the region, severely taxed the political and economic systems of their neighbors, and (largely because of these other five problems) prompted repeated interventions by foreign powers.

Interestingly, the international community—particularly the European Union—was so afraid of the impact that spillover was having on the rest of the Balkans that it intervened repeatedly to try to head off regional intervention. This was one of the unique features of the Yugoslav civil wars. The constant international and European interventions precluded or obviated the need for local intervention. The evidence strongly suggests, however, that had the international community, the United Nations, the European Union, and eventually NATO not done so, the fighting would have provoked other countries to intervene. Macedonia, Greece, Turkey, Hungary, Romania, Bulgaria, and possibly others would likely have taken a much more active role aiding proxies and would have felt a tremendous pull to intervene directly on one side or another.

Despite all of this great power attention, the ending of the Yugoslav civil wars can be considered only a partial success. There was tremendous spillover within the former Yugoslavia, largely because of how unsettled the political circumstances were in all of the new states to emerge from the Communist collapse and the psychological presumptions this created. There was considerably less spillover beyond the old borders of Yugoslavia—but only because the great powers took it upon themselves to get involved in the wars and prevent them from spreading, and only then at great cost to themselves. Moreover, in the end, in each of these conflicts except the final Macedonian insurgency, the international community could not prevent spillover, and instead had to end the conflict decisively. The Croat-Serb civil war in Croatia was ended by Croatia's military victory (aided partially by American contractors, although the extent of U.S. support has been exaggerated). Bosnia and Kosovo required massive NATO interventions sized to the canonical 20 security personnel per thousand of the population ratio that history has repeatedly proven necessary for both counterinsurgency and stability operations. Thus, far from showing that civil wars can be successfully "managed" by external powers, the Yugoslav wars suggest that the only way to end the problem of spillover is to end the war by employing massive force.

Notes

1. Dan Ephron, "Iraq: A Growing Body Count," *Newsweek*, October 23, 2006, p. 8; Rebecca Goldin, "The Science of Counting the Dead," STATS at George Mason University, October 17, 2006, available at http://www.stats.org/stories/the_science_ct_dead_oct17_06.htm. In October 2006, an article in *The Lancet* argued that Iraqi deaths greater than the pre-war invasion mortality rates ranged from 393,000 to 943,000, with the most likely estimate 655,000 "excess" deaths as a result of the violence that has prevailed since the fall of Saddam's regime. See Gilbert Burnham, Riyadh Lafta, Shannon Doocy, Les Roberts, "Mortality after the 2003 Invasion of Iraq: A Cross-Sectional Cluster Sample Survey," *The Lancet*, 368/9545, October 21, 2006, pp. 1421–28. However, while irrelevant to our study, we note that the results of this article have been disputed by a number of experts. See John Bohannon, "Iraqi Death Estimates Called Too High; Methods Faulted," *Science*, 314/5798, October 20, 2006, pp. 396–97; Steven E. Moore, "655,000 War Dead?" *Wall Street Journal*, October 18, 2006, p. A.20; Fred Kaplan, "Number Crunching: Taking Another Look at the *Lancet's* Iraq Study," *Slate*, October 20, 2006, available at http://www.slate.com/id/2151926/; Malcom Ritter, "Mixed Reviews of Iraq Death Toll Study," Associated Press, October 11, 2006. Finally, an organization called Iraq Body Count has been critical of the studies in *The Lancet*. See Hamit Dardagan, John Sloboda, and Josh Dougherty, "Reality Checks: Some Responses to the Latest Lancet Estimates," *Iraq Body Count Press Release*, 16 October 2006, available at http://www.iraqbodycount.org/press/pr14.php; and Hamit Dardagan, John Sloboda, and Josh Dougherty,

"Speculation Is No Substitute: A Defence of Iraq Body Count," Iraq Body Count, April 2006, available at http://www.iraqbodycount.org/editorial/defended/.

2. Officially, the UNHCR counted 914,000 displaced Iraqis between April 2003 and October 2006. However, when announcing the latest figures, the chief spokesman for UNHCR also noted "The overall number is likely to be much higher." See "914,000 Fled Homes, U.N. Agency Says," *Washington Times*, October 21, 2006, p. 7; Hassan Fattah, "Uneasy Havens Await Those Who Flee Iraq," *New York Times*, December 8, 2006; UNHCR, "UNHCR Briefing Notes: Iraq Displacement," available at http://www.unhcr.org/news/NEWS/454b1f8f2.html.

3. For a penetrating study of the sectarian violence in Iraq and its impact on the population, including the rise in displaced persons, see Ashraf al-Khalidi and Victor Tanner, "Sectarian Violence: Radical Groups Drive Internal Displacement in Iraq," An Occasional Paper of the Brookings Institution–University of Bern Project on Internal Displacement, October 2006, available at http://brookings.edu/fp/projects/idp/200610_DisplacementinIraq.htm. We note that this study makes no estimate of the total number of displaced Iraqis. It does cite the official Ministry of Trade figures for internally displaced Iraqis as 234,000 in September 2006. Al-Khalidi and Tanner also note on p. 21 "These Ministry of Trade figures, however, may seriously underestimate the overall problem of displacement." The study makes no estimate of the numbers of externally displaced Iraqis. However, the U.S. Committee for Refugees and Immigrants estimated in June 2006 that 889,000 Iraqis had left the country as refugees since 2003. See U.S. Committee for Refugees and Immigrants, "USCRI Releases *World Refugee Survey 2006: Risks and Rights*," June 14, 2006, available at http://www.refugees.org/newsroomsub.aspx?id=1622.

4. Gethin Chamberlain and Aqeel Hussein, "I No Longer Have Power to Save Iraq from Civil War," Warns Shia Leader," *Sunday Telegraph* (London), September 3, 2006.

5. See for instance Anne Garrels, "Violence Plagues Iraq, Despite Constitution Breakthrough," National Public Radio, *Morning Edition*, October 14, 2005; Sabrina Tavernise, "Sectarian Hatred Pulls Apart Iraq's Mixed Towns," *New York Times*, November 20, 2005; Sabrina Tavernise, "Many Iraqis Look To Gunmen As Protectors," *New York Times*, October 21, 2006, p. 1.

6. See Kenneth M. Pollack, "The Right Way: Seven Steps toward a Last Chance in Iraq," *Atlantic Monthly*, March 2006, available at http://www.theatlantic.com/doc/prem/200603/iraq. Also see Kenneth M. Pollack and the Iraq Strategy Working Group of the Saban Center for Middle East Policy, *A Switch in Time: A New Strategy for America in Iraq* (Washington, DC: The Brookings Institution, 2006), available at http://www.brookings.edu/fp/saban/analysis/20060215_iraqreport.htm; and Daniel Byman, "Five Bad Options for Iraq," *Survival* (Spring 2005), available at http://www.brookings.edu/views/articles/byman/20050322.htm.

7. One large comparative study finds that "religious contagion influences the extent of both ethnic protest and rebellion" but nonreligious contagion's influence is limited to ethnic protest. Also violent conflict influences conflict in a neighboring state. Jonathan Fox, "Is Ethnoreligious Conflict a Contagious Disease?" *Studies in Conflict and Terrorism* 27 (2004), pp. 89–106.

8. In the Middle East, problems are compounded because the UNHCR budget has been cut dramatically. See IRIN News Agency, "IRAQ-SYRIA: Three Million Uprooted Iraqis Face 'Bleak Future', UNHCR says," October 22, 2006, available at http://www.irin-news.org/report.asp?ReportID=56036&SelectRegion=Middle_East.

9 . See the sources and discussion in footnote 2, above.

10. Charles Recknagel, "Iraq: Some Arabs Fleeing Northern Iraq as Kurdish Refugees Return," Radio Free Europe/Radio Liberty, February 20, 2004, available at http://www.rferl.org/featuresarticle/2004/2/03BDC7DE-DF7A-4882-A03F-7CA300545F4D.html.

11. International Organization for Migration, "Iraq: IOM Provides Emergency Aid to 216,000 Displaced in Falluja," Press Release, December 21, 2004, available at http://www.reliefweb.int/rw/rwb.nsf/db900SID/JMAN-67VEB3?OpenDocument.

12. Ellen Knickmeyer, "Thousands of Iraqis Flee to Avoid Spread of Violence," *Washington Post*, March 29, 2006; Cal Perry and Arwa Damon (contributors), "Fighting Displaces Tens of Thousands in Iraq," CNN, April 14, 2006, available at http://www.cnn.com/2006/WORLD/meast/04/13/iraq.main/; Edward Wong and Kirk Semple, "Civilians in Iraq Flee Mixed Areas as Attacks Shift," *New York Times*, April 2, 2006; Ahmed Rasheed, "Iraq's Refugee Problem Surges as Violence Rages," *Reuters*, April 13, 2006.

13. Yochi Dreazen, "Iraqi Refugees Seek Safe Harbor—in the U.S.," *Wall Street Journal*, August 9, 2006, p. 6; Refugees International, "Iraqi Refugees in Syria: Silent Exodus Leaves 500,000 in Need of Protection and Aid," November 15, 2005, available at http://www.refugeesinternational.org/content/article/detail/7297/?PHPSESSID=5ce))f92 779c166324e1d.

14. Bradley S. Klapper, "UN Refugee Agency Concerned over Death Threats Against Palestinians in Iraq," *Associated Press*, March 24, 2006; Kirk Semple, Ali Adeeb, and Khalid W. Hassan, "Jordan Blocks Palestinians Fleeing Violence in Iraq," *New York Times*, March 21, 2006, p. A8; Kirk Semple, Hosham Hussein, et al., "As Palestinians Wait at Iraqi Border, Others Get Threats," *New York Times*, March 25, 2006, p. A6.

15. Fattah, "Uneasy Haven," op. cit. See also Dreazen, "Iraqi Refugees Seek Safe Harbor—in The U.S.," op. cit.; Refugees International, op. cit.

16. Sabrina Tavernise, "As Death Stalks Iraq, Middle-Class Exodus Begins," *New York Times*, May 19, 2006, p. A1.

17. U.S. Committee for Refugees and Immigrants, "USCRI Releases *World Refugee Survey 2006: Risks and Rights*," June 14, 2006, available at http://www.refugees.org/news-roomsub.aspx?id=1622.

18. Anonymous (Michael Scheuer), *Imperial Hubris : Why the West Is Losing the War on Terror* (Washington, D.C.: Brassey's, 2004). In addition to numerous outside experts, the U.S. intelligence community apparently shares this assessment. See "Declassified Key Judgments of the National Intelligence Estimate 'Trends in Global Terrorism: Implications for the United States' dated April 2006," available at http://www.dni.gov/press_releases/Declassified_NIE_Key_Judgments.pdf#search='Trends%20in%20Global %20Terrorism%3A%20Implications%20for%20the%20United%20States.

19. Peter Bergen and Alec Reynolds, "Blowback Revisited," *Foreign Affairs*, 84/6 (November–December 2005).

20. See, for instance, Christopher Bodeen, "Up to 150 People Kidnapped in Baghdad," Associated Press, November 14, 2006; Richard Galpin, "Iraq Police Accused of Torture," *BBC News*, July 27, 2005, available at http://news.bbc.co.uk/1/hi/world/ middle_east/4718999.stm; Richard A. Oppel, Jr., "U.N. Finds Baghdad Toll Far Higher Than Cited," *New York Times*, September 21, 2006.

21. Scott Johnson, "A New Enemy Emerges—'The Shiite Zarqawi,'" *Newsweek*, November 13, 2006.

22. International Crisis Group, *In Their Own Words: Reading the Iraqi Insurgency*, Middle East Report 50 (February 15, 2006), p. 10, available at http://www.crisisgroup.org/ home/index.cfm?l=1&id=3953.

23. Reuven Paz, "Arab Volunteers Killed in Iraq: An Analysis," Project for the Research of Islamist Movements Occasional Papers, 3/1 (March 2005), p. 6.

24. International Crisis Group, op. cit., p. 12.

25. Michael Hastings, "Blacksnake's Lair: From Deep in the Hills, Kurdish Rebels Are Stirring Up Turkey and Iran, and Threatening the One Calm Part of Iraq," *Newsweek*, October 9, 2006. See also Louis Meixler, "Iraq's Kurds Face Neighbors' Anger," *Philadelphia Inquirer*, May 12, 2006; Yigal Schleifer, "Turkey Sharpens Response to Upsurge in Kurd Violence," *Christian Science Monitor*, August 29, 2006.

26. Associated Press, "Saudi King Warns Summit of Gulf Leaders Spark Could Ignite Arab World," December 9, 2006, available at http://www.msnbc.msn.com/ id/16128175/.

27. Hassan M. Fattah, "An Island Kingdom Feels the Ripples from Iraq and Iran," *The New York Times*, April 16, 2006.

28. Meixler, "Iraq's Kurds Face Neighbors' Anger," op. cit.

29. Ibid., and Schleifer, "Turkey Sharpens Response to Upsurge in Kurd Violence," op. cit.

30. Megan K. Stack, "Iraqi Strife Seeping into Saudi Kingdom," *Los Angeles Times*, April 26, 2006.

31. Ibid..

32. Jon E. Hilsenrath and Liam Pleven, "Economic Fears after 9-11 Proved Mostly Unfounded," *Wall Street Journal*, September 9–10, 2006, p. A1.

33. Barbara Walter, "Information, Uncertainty and the Decision to Secede," *International Organization*, 60/1 (Winter 2006) pp. 105–36.

34. Meixler, "Iraq's Kurds Face Neighbors' Anger," op. cit.

35. Howard Goller, "Israel Seeks Terms for Pulling out of Lebanon," Reuters, March 2, 1998; Gal Luft, "Israel's Security Zone in Lebanon—A Tragedy?" *Middle East Quarterly*, VII/3 (September 2000).

36. Yair Aharoni, *The Israeli Economy: Dreams and Reality* (New York: Routledge, 1991), p. 85; Yoram Ben-Porath (ed.), *The Israeli Economy*, (Cambridge: Harvard University Press, 1986), pp. 20–21; Gil Merom, *How Democracies Lose Small Wars: State, Society, and the Failures of France in Algeria, Israel in Lebanon, and the United States in Vietnam* (Cambridge: Cambridge University Press, 2003), pp. 164–5.

37. Nawaf Obaid, "Saudi Arabia Will Protect Sunnis If the U.S. Leaves," *Washington Post*, November 29, 2006, p. A23, available at http://www.washingtonpost.com/wp-dyn/content/article/2006/11/28/AR2006112801277.html.

38. Meixler, "Iraq's Kurds Face Neighbors' Anger," op. cit.; Schleifer, "Turkey Sharpens Response to Upsurge in Kurds Violence," op. cit; Hastings, "Blacksnake's Lair," op. cit.

39. Yair Aharoni, *The Israeli Economy: Dreams and Reality* (New York: Routledge, 1991), p. 85; Yoram Ben-Porath (ed.), *The Israeli Economy* (Cambridge: Harvard University Press, 1986), pp. 20–1; Gil Merom, *How Democracies Lose Small Wars: State, Society, and the Failures of France in Algeria, Israel in Lebanon, and the United States in Vietnam*, (Cambridge: Cambridge University Press, 2003), pp. 164–5.

40. Alasdair Drysdale, "The Asad Regime and Its Troubles," *MERIP Reports* 110 (November–December, 1982), p. 5, cited in Naomi Joy Weinberger, *Syrian Intervention in Lebanon: The 1975–76 Civil War* (New York: Oxford University Press, 1986), p. 234.

41. David A. Korn, "Syria and Lebanon: A Fateful Entanglement," *World Today*, 42/8–9, 1986, p. 139; Itamar Rabinovich, *The War for Lebanon* (Ithaca, N.Y.: Cornell University Press, 1984) p. 101; Patrick Seale, *Asad of Syria: The Struggle for the Middle East* (Berkeley: University of California Press, 1988), pp. 286–7, 320–1.

42. Seale, op. cit., pp. 320–1.

43. International Monetary Fund, "The Economic Consequences of the Kosovo Crisis: An Updated Assessment," prepared by the staff of the International Monetary Fund in consultation with the World Bank staff, May 25, 1999, pp. 15–16, available at http://www.imf.org/external/pubs/ft/kosovo/052599.htm.

44. "Romania: Casualty of War," *The Economist*, 351/8123, June 12, 1999, p. 68; Vernon Loeb "War Over Kosovo Turns Balkan Bit Players Into 'Frontline' States," *Washington Post*, April 24, 1999.

45. International Monetary Fund, op. cit., pp. 1–16.

46. International Monetary Fund, "Economic Prospects for the Countries of Southeast Europe in the Aftermath of the Kosovo Crisis," September 22, 1999, p. 9, available at http://www.imf.org/external/pubs/ft/kosovo/092299.htm.

47. Stephen P. Cohen, *The Idea of Pakistan* (Washington, DC: Brookings, 2006), p. 261

48. Ahmed Rashid, *Taliban* (New Haven: Yale University Press, 2001), p. 192.

49. Cohen, p. 261.

50. Rashid, op. cit., p. 183.

51. Ibid., p. 191.

52. Ibid.

53. Timothy J. Burger, "The Great Wall of Arabia," *Time*, August 28, 2006.

54. Ahmed Rashid, "Point of Conflict: Russia and Islamic Militants in Tajik Proxy War," *Far Eastern Economic Review*, 156/2 (June 3, 1993), p. 25.

55. The Croat offensive had run out of steam by the first week in October 2005. A number of Croat attacks had been stopped cold, and even the more successful assaults were being brought to a halt as the Serbs regained their balance and shifted reserves to blunt the Croat thrusts. Indeed, Holbrooke and his team urged the Croat-Muslim Federation to capture Prejidor, Sanski Most, and Bosanski Novi, but Croat and Muslim forces were simply unable to do so. Central Intelligence Agency, Office of Russian and

European Analysis, *Balkan Battlegrounds: A Military History of the Yugoslav Conflict, 1990–1995*, Vol. 1 (Washington, DC: CIA, 2002), pp. 367, 389–92, 393–4, and 425 fn. 821; Derek Chollet, *The Road to the Dayton Accords: A Study of American Statecraft* (New York: Palgrave, 2005), pp. 105–6, 108; Richard Holbrooke, *To End a War* (New York: Random House, 1998), p. 191. On October 4, 1995, Holbrooke had Lt. Gen. Donald Kerrick brief Bosnian President Alija Izetbegovic on the possibility of continuing the offensive, and Kerrick famously told Izetbegovic, "If you continue the war, you will be shooting craps with your nation's destiny." Holbrooke, op. cit., pp. 194–5.

56. Central Intelligence Agency, op. cit., pp. 290–377; Misha Glenny, *The Fall of Yugoslavia: The Third Balkan War*, 3rd rev. ed. (New York: Penguin, 1996), p. 279; Laura Silber and Allan Little, *Yugoslavia: Death of a Nation*, rev. ed. (New York: Penguin, 1997), pp. 357–60.

57. Central Intelligence Agency, op. cit., p. 396; Ivo H. Daalder, *Getting to Dayton: The Making of America's Bosnia Policy* (Washington, DC: Brookings, 2000), pp. 119–29; Alastair Finalan, *The Collapse of Yugoslavia 1991–1999*, Osprey Essential Histories (UK: Osprey, 2004), p. 83; Misha Glenny, op. cit., pp. 168, 270, 277–8, 289; Holbrooke, op. cit., pp. 153–312; Silber and Little, op. cit., pp. 368–9.

58. Richard K. Betts, "The Delusion of Impartial Intervention," *Foreign Affairs*, 73/6 (November/December 1994), pp. 20–33.

59. James D. Fearon, Testimony to the U.S. House of Representatives Committee on Government Reform, "Iraq: Democracy or Civil War," September 15, 2006.

60. Ibid.. Fearon reports that at least 75 percent of civil wars end in a decisive military victory, with successful power sharing arrangements being rare. Decisive military victory often involves foreign assistance.

61. In Afghanistan, a small number of U.S. Special Operations Forces, working with local Afghan allies and air support, managed to topple the Taliban. However, this small number was effective in removing a weak government but has not managed to impose order. Indeed, civil strife has grown considerably in Afghanistan in the last year, despite the presence of around 35,000 U.S. and NATO troops. Many observers believe that far more troops are necessary to prevent the violence from escalating. Seth Jones, "Averting Failure in Afghanistan," *Survival* (Spring 2006), pp. 111–28.

62. See Chaim Kaufmann, "Possible and Impossible Solutions to Ethnic Civil Wars," *International Security*, 20/4 (Spring 1996), pp. 136–75.

63. James Kurth, "Crush the Sunnis," *The New Republic*, November 27, 2006.

64. Fearon argues that a major obstacle to power sharing agreements in a civil war are divisions *within* the communities in the conflict. Fearon, op. cit.

65. On the fighting in al-Amarah, see Christopher Bodeen, "Shiite Militia Takes Over Iraqi City," Associated Press, October 20, 2006; Kirk Semple, "Militias Battle for Iraqi City as Shiite Rivalry Escalates," *New York Times*, October 21, 2006.

66. See, for instance, Peter W. Galbraith, *The End of Iraq: How American Incompetence Created a War without End* (New York: Simon and Schuster, 2006).

67. Nancy A. Youssef and Laith Hammoudi, "Families Swapping Houses to Avoid Sectarian Violence," *San Diego Union-Tribune*, August 28, 2006.

68. Ibon Villelabeitia, "As U.S. Death Toll Spikes, Iraq Asks Troops to Stay," Reuters, October 30, 2006.

69. Associated Press, "Turkish Official Warns Of Chaos If Iraq Is Split Up," November 6, 2006, available at http://www.latimes.com/news/nationworld/world/la-fg-turkey6nov06,1,1399689.story?coll=la-headlines-world.

70. Michael O'Hanlon, "Break Up Iraq to Save It," *Los Angeles Times*, August 27, 2006, available at http://www.brookings.edu/views/op-ed/ohanlon/20060827.htm; Michael E. O'Hanlon and Edward P. Joseph, "A Bosnia Option for Iraq?" *The American Interest*, Winter 2007, available at http://www.brookings.edu/views/articles/ohanlon/20061219.htm.

71. Joshua Partlow and Naseer Nouri, "Neighbors Are Killing Neighbors," *Washington Post*, July 18, 2006.

72. Youssef and Hammoudi, op. cit.

73. With appropriate respects to our friend Fareed Zakaria for misappropriating his terminology.

74. See James D. Fearon and David D. Laitin, "Ethnicity, Insurgency, and Civil War," *American Political Science Review*, 97/1, February 2003, pp. 75–90.

75. Some will doubtless contend that the absence of progress on an Arab-Israeli peace process is just an excuse the Arab states use to not undertake reforms they dislike for other reasons. This may well be true. However, we note that a peace process would be a stabilizing force in a region facing growing instability from Iraq's civil war (and potentially, internal conflicts in Lebanon and the Palestinian territories as well). Moreover, it is still worthwhile as it deprives Arab governments of this excuse so that it will be harder for them to deflect pressure to reform, especially from their own populations.

76. For another account, see George Packer, "Alternative Realities," *The New Yorker*, October 30, 2006. We invited Packer to observe the game, and this article is his write-up and impressions from it. Also see James Kitfield, "U.S. Options to Control Violence in Iraq Narrowing," *The National Journal*, October 30, 2006, which mentions the game. Kitfield was not involved in the simulation, but appears to have spoken to one or more of the participants.

77. For a history, see Mohammed Kakar, *Afghanistan: The Soviet Invasion and the Afghan Response, 1979–1982* (Berkeley: University of California Press, 1995). For a description of the military campaign, see Mohammad Yousaf and Mark Adkin, *Afghanistan the Bear Trap: The Defeat of a Superpower* (Drexel Hill, PA: Casemate, 2001). This case study draws heavily on the Afghanistan chapter in Daniel Byman, *Deadly Connections: States That Sponsor Terrorism* (New York: Cambridge University Press, 2005).

78. It should be noted that the United States, along with its allies Pakistan and Great Britain, deliberately orchestrated spillover into neighboring countries during the Afghan war in the late 1980s. According to Ahmed Rashid, the secret services of these countries encouraged the Afghan *mujahidin* (holy warriors) to cross the Amu Darya River in March 1987 in order to attack villages that were supplying Soviet troops. Ahmed Rashid, *Jihad: The Rise of Militant Islam in Central Asia* (New Haven: Yale University Press, 2002), pp. 43–4.

79. Ahmed Rashid, *Taliban: Militant Islam, Oil, and Fundamentalism in Central Asia* (London: IB Tauris, 2000), p. 97; Michael Griffin, *Reaping the Whirlwind: The Taliban Movement in Afghanistan* (London: Pluto Press, 2001), pp. 30–2. For an overview of Afghanistan after the Soviet withdrawal but before the Taliban's emergence, see Barnett R. Rubin, *The Search for Peace in Afghanistan: From Buffer State to Failed State* (New Haven: Yale University Press, 1995).

80. Rashid, *Taliban*, pp. 82–3.

81. Barnett R. Rubin, *The Fragmentation of Afghanistan: State Formation and Collapse in the International System* (New Haven: Yale University Press, 2002), p. 252.

82. Salamat Ali, "A Peace on Paper," *Far Eastern Economic Review,* 156/11, March 18, 1993, p. 22.

83. Rashid, *Taliban*, pp. 26, 90–7; Larry P. Goodson, *Afghanistan's Endless War: State Failure, Regional Politics, and the Rise of the Taliban* (Seattle: University of Washington Press, 2001), p. 99. Pakistan's Jamaat-e Islami (Islamic Assembly, a political party) worked with Pakistani intelligence to send over 30,000 Muslim radicals to Afghanistan from 1982 to 1992.

84. Omar himself had been a mid-level commander during the anti-Soviet struggle. He was not from a distinguished clan and had not received a comprehensive religious education. U.S. Department of State, "Finally a Talkative Talib: Origins and Membership of the Religious Students' Movement," Cable from Islamabad, 01792, February 20, 1995, available at http://www.gwu.edu/~nsarchiv/NSAEBB/NSAEBB97/tal8.pdf. Journalists have not been able to locate a witness to the tank barrel hanging, and it may be apocryphal. Steve Coll, *Ghost Wars: The Secret History of the CIA, Afghanistan, and bin Laden, From the Soviet Invasion to September 10, 2001* (New York: Penguin Press, 2004), p. 283.

85. Griffin, op. cit, p. 32.

86. Julie Sirrs contends that much of the countryside was not in disorder and that schools and many government offices continued to function in parts of the country. She also notes that while the Taliban brought order to some parts of the country, they also brought war to much of the country that had been relatively peaceful. Julie Sirrs, "Lifting the Veil on Afghanistan," *The National Interest*, 65 (2001).

87. Griffin, op. cit., pp. 34–5 and Goodson, op. cit, pp. 108–11. Coll, op. cit., p. 216–7, notes that the Saudis continued pouring money to various radical Islamists after the Soviet withdrawal, in part due to their geopolitical competition with Iran and in part to appease radicals at home.

88. Rashid, *Taliban*, p. 4.

89. Jason Burke, *Al-Qaeda: The True Story of Radical Islam* (London: I.B.Tauris Publishers, 2004), p. 113 and Griffin, op. cit., p. 36.

90. Rashid, *Taliban*, p. 100; Goodson, op. cit., p. 77; and Peter Bergen, *Holy War, Inc.: Inside the Secret World of Osama Bin Laden* (New York: Free Press, 2001), p. 148.

91. William T. Vollmann, "Across the Divide," *The New Yorker* (May 2005), p. 61.

92. Vollman, op. cit., pp. 63–64. For a review of the Taliban's dismal human rights record, see Mark A. Drumbl, "The Taliban's 'Other' Crimes," *Third World Quarterly*, 23/6 (December 2002).

93. As quoted in Coll, op. cit., p. 289 and fn. 21, p. 611.

94. Peter Marsden, *The Taliban: War, Religion and the New Order in Afghanistan* (London: Zed Books, 1998).

95. U.S. Department of State, "Scenesetter for Your Visit to Islamabad: Afghan Angle," Cable from Islamabad, 000436, January 16, 1997, available at http://www.gwu.edu/~nsarchiv/NSAEBB/NSAEBB97/tal21.pdf.

96. Montasser Al-Zayyat, *The Road to Al-Qaeda: The Story of Bin Laden's Right-Hand Man* (London: Pluto Press, 2004), p. 59.

97. For an excellent review of the military campaign, see Stephen Biddle, *Afghanistan and the Future of Warfare: Implications for Army and Defense Policy* (University Press of the Pacific, 2004).

98. United States of America vs. Enaam M. Arnaout, Government's Evidentiary Proffer Supporting the Admissibility of Coconspirator Statements," 02 CR 892. United States District Court Northern District of Illinois Eastern Division (January 6, 2003), p. 34.

99. Anonymous (Michael Scheuer), *Through Our Enemies' Eyes: Osama Bin Laden, Radical Islam and the Future of America* (Washington, D.C.: Brassey's 2002), pp. 50–3 and Bergen, op. cit., pp. 21–2, 98-101, 208.

100. Anonymous, op. cit., p. 141. National Commission on Terrorist Attacks upon the United States (9/11 Commission), "Overview of the Enemy," Staff Statement 15 (June 16, 2004), p. 7, available at http://www.9-11commission.gov/staff_statements/staff_statement_15.pdf.

101. United States of America v. Usama bin Ladin, May 1, 2001, Exhibit 300B-T. See also United States of America v. Usama Bin Ladin, et al., May 1, 2001 section 5325.

102. 9/11 Commission, op. cit., p. 7.

103. For a broader list, see Anonymous, op. cit., p. 179, 198–204.

104. 9/11 Commission, *The 9/11 Commission Report* (July 22, 2004), p. 67, available at http://www.9-11commission.gov/report/911Report_Ch2.htm> and http://www.9-11commission.gov/report/911Report_Ch2.pdf.

105. David Rohde and C. J. Chivers, "The Jihad Files: Life in Bin Laden's Army," *New York Times,* March 17, 2002.

106. Alan Cullison and Andrew Higgins, "Files Found: A Computer in Kabul Yields a Chilling Array of al Qaeda Memos," *The Wall Street Journal,* December 31, 2001.

107. Thomas Wilshire, Testimony before the Senate Committee on Foreign Relations, Subcommittee on International Operations and Terrorism, December 18, 2001, p. 9.

108. David Rohde and C. J. Chivers, "The Jihad Files: Life in Bin Laden's Army." Anonymous (Michael Scheuer), *Imperial Hubris*, p. 217.

109. Jeffrey Bartholet, "Al Qaeda Runs for the Hills," *Newsweek*, December 17, 2001, pp. 20–26.

110. Chivers and Rohde, "The Jihad Files: Training the Troops."

111. Burke, op. cit., p. 152.

112. A *New York Times* investigation of documents left by al-Qa'ida in Afghanistan indicates that the countries included Algeria, Bangladesh, Bosnia, Britain, Canada, China, Egypt, Iraq, Jordan, Kuwait, Libya, Morocco, Pakistan, the Philippines, Russia, Saudi Arabia, Somalia, Syria, Tajikistan, Turkey, Turkmenistan, Uzbekistan, the United States, and

Yemen. Rohde and Chivers, "The Jihad Files: Life in Bin Laden's Army." See also 9/11 Commission, Staff Statement, op. cit., p. 9.

113. Bergen, op. cit., p. 190. Bartholet , "Al Qaeda Runs for the Hills," pp. 20–6.

114. Rashid, *Taliban*, p. 93.

115. Sirrs, op. cit., p. 47.

116. Phil Zabriskie, "Mullah Omar," *Time Europe*, December 31, 2001, p. 94. The interview occurred before the September 11 attacks. There are many reports that Omar and Bin Laden became linked through marriage, but Omar's driver claims this never occurred. See Scott Johnson, "Mulla Omar Off the Record," *Newsweek*, January 2002, pp. 26–8 and William Maley, *The Afghanistan Wars* (New York: Palgrave Macmillan, 2002), p. 255.

117. Rashid, *Taliban*, pp. 92, 185–8.

118. Vollman, "Across the Divide," p. 60.

119. Ahmed Rashid, "Battle for the North," *Far Eastern Economic Review*, 157/13 (March 31, 1994), pp. 23–4.

120 Rashid, *Jihad*, p. 209.

121. Olivier Roy, "Afghanistan: Back to Tribalism or on to Lebanon," *Third World Quarterly*, 10/4 (October 1989), p. 73.

122. Ibid., p. 76.

123. Barnett R. Rubin, "The Fragmentation of Afghanistan," *Foreign Affairs*, 68/5 (Winter 1989/1990), p. 150.

124. Ahmed Rashid, "A Loss of Trust," *Far Eastern Economic Review*, 157/10 (March 10, 1994), p. 25.

125. Rashid, *Taliban*, p. 5.

126. Paula Newberg, "Pakistan," *The Taliban and Afghanistan: Implications for Regional Security and Options for International Action*, Special Report 39 (Washington, D.C.: United States Institute of Peace, 1998).

127. Martha Brill Olcott, "Central Asian States and Russia," *The Taliban and Afghanistan: Implications for Regional Security and Options for International Action*, Special Report 39 (Washington, D.C.: United States Institute of Peace, 1998).

128. CNN (with contributions from the Associated Press and Reuters), "Iran Reports Clash with Afghan Militia, Taliban Denies Incident," October 8, 1998, available at http://www.cnn.com/WORLD/meast/9810/08/iran.afghan.01/.

129. Maley, op. cit., p. 219.

130. Griffin, op. cit., pp. 33–4; Goodson, op. cit., p. 111; Human Rights Watch, *Afghanistan—Crisis of Impunity: The Role of Pakistan, Russia and Iran in Fuelling the Civil War* (New York: Human Rights Watch, 2001), pp. 23–6. Taliban officials claim that Pakistan only aided them after they had established themselves, but several sources claim that the Taliban were largely the creation of senior Pakistani officials. U.S. Department of State, "Finally a Talkative Talib," op. cit.

131. Burke, op. cit., p. 116; Maley, op. cit., p. 235; and Rashid, *Taliban*, p. 183. Sirrs notes that the anti-Taliban Northern Alliance claimed that as many as 50 percent of the Taliban corpses they see have Pakistani civilian identity cards. Julie Sirrs, "The Taliban's International Ambitions," *Middle East Quarterly* (Summer 2001), pp. 61–3. Given that

many Afghan refugees lived in Pakistan for more than 20 years, however, it is difficult to discern how many are of Afghan origin.

132. Coll, op. cit., p. 548.

133. Goodson, op.cit, p. 118; Bergen, op. cit., p. 148.

134. U.S. Department of State, "Finally a Talkative Talib," op. cit., and Goodson, op. cit., pp. 82–8.

135. Rashid, *Taliban*, pp. 27–8, 98; Burke, op. cit, p. 114; Gilles Kepel and Anthony F. Roberts, *Jihad: The Trail of Political Islam* (Cambridge: Belknap Press, 2002), pp. 227–8; and Sirrs, "The Taliban's International Ambitions," pp. 64–5. The Taliban drew particularly heavily from the Pashtun tribes in southern Afghanistan near Qandahar. Other Pashtuns were better represented within the movement than were non-Pashtuns, but those from Qandahar dominated. The Taliban's leaders were primarily from the Durrani tribal association, which had dominated Afghanistan before the Soviet invasion but had lost out to Ghilzai Pashtuns as well as to other ethnic groups. Goodson, op. cit., p. 107. However, the Taliban's effort to dominate the community involved assassinations of other Pashtun leaders and other brutal measures, which in turn alienated many Pashtun notables. Coll, op. cit., p. 459.

136. Rashid, *Taliban*, p. 186.

137. U.S. Department of State, "Finally a Talkative Talib," op. cit.

138. United States of America v. Usama bin Ladin, May 1, 2001, Exhibit 300B-T.

139. Rashid, *Taliban*, pp. 185–8.

140. For more detail on these efforts, Coll, op. cit., and the 9/11 Commission, *The 9/11 Commission Report*, op. cit.

141. Rashid, *Taliban*, p. 182.

142. Madeleine Albright, *Madame Secretary: A Memoir* (New York: Miramax Books, 2003), pp. 368, 376.

143. As quoted in Griffin, op. cit., p. 174.

144. Rashid, *Jihad*, p. 172.

145. Rashid, "The Mess in Afghanistan," *New York Review of Books* (February 12, 2004), pp. 24–7. For an interesting overview of pro-Taliban parts of Pakistan, see Eliza Griswald, "Where the Taliban Roam," *Harper's* (September 2003). For a broader critique of U.S. policy toward Afghanistan, see the Council on Foreign Relations report "Afghanistan: Are We Losing the Peace?" June 2003, available at http://www.cfr.org/content/publications/attachments/Afghanistan_TF.pdf; and Anonymous, *Imperial Hubris*, op. cit.

146. All mentions in the text to Congo and Congolese are references to the Democratic Republic of the Congo, of which the capital is Kinshasa, as opposed to the Republic of the Congo, of which the capital is Brazzaville. Although the Democratic Republic of the Congo was named Zaire during the rule of President Mobutu Sese Seko, it is referred to as Congo throughout this appendix for ease of reference.

147. United Nations High Commissioner for Refugees, *Global Refugee Trends*, Table. 4, available at http://www.unhcr.org/statistics/STATISTICS/4486ceb12.pdf.

148. For an example, see Herbert F. Weiss and Tatiana Carayannis, "Reconstructing the Congo," *Journal of International Affairs*, 58/1 (Fall 2004), pp. 115–41. Most of the literature, however, refers to only two wars.

149. Weiss and Carayannis, op. cit., pp. 121–2.

150. Gerard Prunier, "Rebel Movements and Proxy Warfare: Uganda, Sudan and the Congo (1986–1999)," *African Affairs*, 103/412 (2004), pp. 359–83.

151. The National Army for the Liberation of Uganda transformed itself into the Allied Democratic Forces in 1996, another rebel movement opposed to Museveni with bases in Congo.

152. Prunier, op. cit., pp. 367–8.

153. Weiss and Carayannis, op. cit., p. 123.

154. International Crisis Group, *Africa's Seven Nation War*, ICG Democratic Republic of Congo Report 4 (May 21, 1999), p. i, available at http://www.crisisgroup.org/home/index.cfm?id=1643&l=1.

155. Ibid., p. 2.

156. Ibid., p. 1.

157. Ibid., p. 2.

158. Ibid., p. 4.

159. Weiss and Carayannis, op. cit., p. 126.

160. International Crisis Group, *Africa's Seven Nation War*, p. 5.

161. Rene Lemarchand, *The Democratic Republic of Congo: From Collapse to Potential Reconstruction*, Occasional Paper, Centre of African Studies, University of Copenhagen (September 2001), p. 47.

162. La Mission des Nations Unies en République Démocratique du Congo (MONUC), UN Mission in DR Congo, Chronology, available at http://www.monuc.org/news.aspx?newsID=884.

163. Weiss and Carayannis, op. cit., p. 126.

164. La Mission des Nations Unies en République Démocratique du Congo (MONUC) official website, available at http://www.monuc.org/ContribMilit.aspx?lang=en.

165. IRIN News Agency, "DRC-Uganda: Foreign Rebel Groups Ignore Deadline to Leave," September 29, 2005, available at http://www.irinnews.org/report.asp?ReportID=49287&SelectRegion=Great_Lakes&SelectCountry=DRC-UGANDA.

166. Kabila was assassinated by one of his own guards.

167. Weiss and Carayannis, op. cit., p. 127.

168. "Africa's Great War," *The Economist*, July 4, 2002.

169. Weiss and Carayannis, op. cit., p. 138.

170. Lemarchand, op. cit., p. 30.

171. IRIN News Agency, op. cit.

172. International Crisis Group, *Congo at War*, ICG Congo Report 2 (November 17, 1998), p. 20, available at http://www.crisisgroup.org/home/index.cfm?l=1&id=1423.

173. BBC News, "Zimbabwe Sends More Troops to DR Congo," June 24, 1999, available at http://news.bbc.co.uk/1/hi/world/africa/377098.stm.

174. International Crisis Group, *Congo at War*, p. 21.

175. *BBC News*, "Namibia Reveals Congo Diamond Role," February 24, 2001, available at http://news.bbc.co.uk/1/hi/world/africa/1187528.stm.

176. International Crisis Group, *Congo at War*, p. 24.

177. Ibid., p. 25.

178. Ibid..

179. International Crisis Group, *Congo at War*, p. 18.

180. United Nations High Commissioner for Refugees, *Measuring Protection by the Numbers 2005* (November 2006), pp. 1–5, available at http://www.unhcr.org/publ/PUBL/4579701b2.pdf.

181. Ruth Gidley, "Why Burundi Massacre Is Fanning Fears of Regional War," Reuters, September 9, 2004, available at http://www.alertnet.org/thefacts/reliefresources/109472481795.htm.

182. Meron Michael, "Congo: The Profits, and Costs, of War," *Worldpress.org*, October 24, 2002, available at http://www.worldpress.org/print_article.cfm?article_id=881&dont=yes.

183. *BBC News*, "Zimbabwe Losses Add Up in Congo," November 25, 1999, available at http://news.bbc.co.uk/1/hi/world/africa/536454.stm.

184. Rene Lemarchand, "Democratic Republic of Congo," in Robert I. Rotberg (ed.), *State Failure and State Weakness in a Time of Terror*, (Cambridge, MA: World Peace Foundation, 2003), p. 30.

185. Faried E. Khazen, *The Breakdown of the State in Lebanon, 1967–1976* (London: I.B. Tauris, 2000), pp. 18–25.

186. The United Nations counted 711,000 Palestinian refugees as of 1950. However, in 1951, the United Nations Relief and Works Agency for Palestine Refugees in the Near East established a list of 860,000 Palestinian displaced persons. Heather Sharp, "Right of Return: Palestinian Dream," *BBC News*, April 15, 2004, available at http://news.bbc.co.uk/2/hi/middle_east/3629923.stm; Steve Sosebee, "How Israel Can Solve the Problem of Palestinian Refugees in Lebanon," *The Washington Report on Middle East Affairs*, XIV/2 (August 1995), p. 16; United Nations Conciliation Commission for Palestine, General Progress Report and Supplementary Report Covering the Period from December 11, 1949 to October 23, 1950, United Nations Conciliation Commission, October 23, 1950 (U.N. General Assembly Official Records, 5th Session, Supplement 18, Document A/1367/Rev. 1).

187. Sharp, op. cit.

188. United States Department of State, "Background Note: Jordan," available at http://www.state.gov/r/pa/ei/bgn/3464.htm.

189. Brigadier Syed Ali El-Edroos, *The Hashemite Arab Army, 1908–1979* (Amman: The Publishing Committee, 1980), p. 449.

190. Robert G. Rabil, *Embattled Neighbors: Syria, Israel, and Lebanon* (Boulder: Lynne Rienner Publishers, 2003), p. 47.

191. Itamar Rabinovich, *The War for Lebanon* (Ithaca, N.Y.: Cornell University Press, 1984), pp. 40–3.

192. Dilip Hiro, *Lebanon, Fire and Embers: A History of the Lebanese Civil War* (New York: St. Martin's Press, 1992), pp. 17–18.

193. Ibid., p. 17.

194. Rabinovich, op. cit., pp. 43–4.

195. Hiro, op. cit., p. 49.

196. Ibid., p. 21.

197. Ibid., p. 16.

198. Ihsan A. Hijazi, "Lebanon War Spurs New Emigration," *New York Times*, April 15, 1990; GlobalSecurity.org, "Lebanon," available at http://www.globalsecurity.org/military/world/war/lebanon.htm.

199. Ihsan A. Hijazi, "Amid an 'Inferno of Bombs,' with Nowhere Safe, 250,000 Flee Beirut in a Week," *New York Times*, August 1, 1989.

200. "Lebanon Demographics: Population," EconStats, available at http://www.econstats.com/IMF/IFS_Leb1_99Z__.htm.

201. Hiro, op. cit., p. 183.

202. Associated Press, "118 Lebanese Refugees Return Home from Israel," CNN, September 22, 2000, available at http://archives.cnn.com/2000/WORLD/meast/09/22/lebanon.israel.ap/.

203. Naomi Joy Weinberger, *Syrian Intervention in Lebanon: The 1975–76 Civil War* (New York: Oxford University Press, 1986), p. 234.

204. PBS Frontline, "Lebanon: Party of God," May 2003, available at http://www.pbs.org/frontlineworld/stories/lebanon/thestory.html.

205. George P. Schultz, *Turmoil and Triumph* (New York: Charles Scribner's Sons, 1993), p. 644; Howard Teicher and Gayle R. Teicher, *Twin Pillars to Desert Storm: America's Flawed Vision in the Middle East from Nixon to Bush* (New York: William Morrow and Co., 1993), pp. 281–2; Robin Wright, *In the Name of God: The Khomeini Decade* (New York: Simon and Schuster, 1989), pp. 121–2.

206. Schultz, op. cit., pp. 651, 653.

207. Daniel Byman, *Deadly Connections: States That Sponsor Terrorism* (Cambridge: Cambridge University Press, 2005), pp. 90–1; Hala Jaber, *Hezbollah* (New York: Columbia University Press, 1997), pp. 105–17.

208. Weinberger, op. cit., p. 236.

209. Adeed I. Dawisha, *Syria and the Lebanese Crisis* (New York: St. Martin's Press, 1980), p. 17.

210. Dawisha, op. cit., p. 69; Patrick Seale, *Asad of Syria: The Struggle for the Middle East* (Berkeley: University of California Press, 1988), p. 277; Weinberger, op. cit., p. 140.

211. Dawisha, op. cit., p. 8; Rabinovich, op. cit., pp. 49–54.

212. Interviews with the late Sa'id Hamami, the Palestine Liberation Organization representative in London, July 5, 1976, cited in Seale, op. cit., pp. 282–3; Seale, op. cit., p. 270; William Harris, "Syria in Lebanon," MERIP Reports, 134, *Assad's Syria* (July/August, 1985), p. 9.

213. Hiro, op. cit., p. 36. Also see Eitan Haber, Ze'ev Schiff, and Ehud Ya'ari, *The Year of the Dove* (Bantam: New York, 1979), pp. 3–4; William B. Quandt, *Camp David: Peacemaking and Politics* (Washington, DC: Brookings Institution, 1986), p. 109; Seale, op. cit., p. 283; Weinberger, op. cit., p. 142.

214. Hiro, op. cit., p. 69.

215. Harris, op. cit., p. 9; Seale, op. cit., pp. 275–6.

216. President Assad's interview with Salim al-Lawzi of *al-Hawadith*, June 22, 1975, cited in Seale, op. cit., p. 270.

217. Even an author as protective of Asad as Patrick Seale acknowledges that Syrian expansionism was part of Asad's thinking, although Seale concocts a defensive rationale to explain even this. Seale, op. cit., p. 268.

218. For a description and analysis of the Syrian invasions, see Kenneth M. Pollack, *Arabs at War: Military Effectiveness, 1948–1991* (Lincoln: University of Nebraska Press, 2002), pp. 514–23.

219. Lt. Col. Daniel Asher (Israel Defense Forces), "The Syrian Invasion of Lebanon: Military Moves as a Political Tool," *Ma'arachot*, June 1977, p. 3; Lt. Col. David Eshel (Israel Defense Forces, ret.), *The Lebanon War, 1982* (Hod Hasharon, Israel: Eshel-Dramit Ltd, 1983), p. 28; Rabinovich, op. cit., p. 55; Weinberger, op. cit., p. 213.

220. Asher, op. cit., pp. 8–9; Eshel, op. cit., pp. 29–30; Lawrence Whetten, "The Military Dimension," in P. Edward Haley and Lewis Snyder (eds.), *Lebanon in Crisis* (Syracuse, NY: Syracuse University Press, 1979), p. 82.

221. Hiro, op. cit., pp. 43–4.

222. Rabinovich, op. cit., p. 95.

223. Ibid., pp. 101–3.

224. Ibid., p. 107.

225. Ibid., pp. 89–90, 101, 105–6.

226. Ibid., pp. 94–95.

227. Hiro, op. cit., pp. 48, 55, 59; Avi Shlaim, "Israeli Interference in Internal Arab Politics: The Case of Lebanon," in Giacomo Luciani and Ghassan Salame (eds.), *The Politics of Arab Integration* (London: Routledge, 1988), pp. 232–5.

228. Hiro, op. cit., p. 51–3.

229. Ibid., p. 52.

230. Ibid., pp. 53, 62.

231. Maziar Behrooz, "Trends in the Foreign Policy of the Islamic Republic of Iran, 1979–1988," in Nikki R. Keddie and Mark J. Gasiorowski, eds., *Neither East nor West: Iran, the Soviet Union, and the United States* (New Haven; London: Yale University Press, 1990), pp. 13–35; Michael Dunn, "In the Name of God: Iran's Shi'ite International," *Defense and Foreign Affairs*, August 1985, p. 34; Kenneth Katzman, *The Warriors of Islam: Iran's Revolutionary Guard* (Boulder, CO: Westview, 1993), pp. 98–9.

232. Kenneth M. Pollack, *The Persian Puzzle: The Conflict Between Iran and America* (New York: Random House, 2004), pp. 254–5.

233. Byman, op. cit., p. 82; Katzman, op. cit., p. 71.

234. Shaul Bakhash, *The Reign of the Ayatollahs: Iran and the Islamic Revolution*, rev.ed. (New York: Basic Books, 1990), p. 63; James A. Bill, *The Eagle and the Lion: The Tragedy of American-Iranian Relations* (New Haven: Yale University Press, 1988), p. 273; Wilfried Buchta, *Who Rules Iran? The Structure of Power in the Islamic Republic* (Washington, DC: The Washington Institute for Near East Policy and the Konrad Adenauer Stiftung, 2000), p. 67; Elton L. Daniel, *The History of Iran* (Westport, CT: Greenwood Press, 2001), pp. 185–86; Katzman, pp. 7–19, 23–37; Wright, op. cit., p. 69.

235. Byman, op. cit.; Judith Palmer Harik, *Hezbollah: The Changing Face of Terrorism* (London: I.B. Tauris, 2004), pp. 22–23; Hiro, op. cit., pp. 109–10; Amal Saad-Ghorayeb, *Hizb'ullah: Politics, Religion* (London: Pluto Press, 2002), pp. 95–97.

236. Hiro, op. cit., 96; Katzman, op. cit., p. 71.

237. Saad-Ghorayeb, op. cit., p. 14.

238. Hiro, op. cit., p. 123–33.

239. Alvin H. Bernstein, "Iran's Low-Intensity War against the United States," *Orbis*, 30/1 (Spring 1986), pp. 149–67; Byman, op. cit.; Magnus Ranstorp, *Hizb'allah in Lebanon: The Politics of the Western Hostage Crisis* (New York: St. Martin's Press, 1997), p. 70; Jaber, op. cit., pp. 82, 105–117; Teicher and Teicher, op. cit., pp. 256–7; Stansfield Turner, *Terrorism and Democracy* (Boston: Houghton Mifflin, 1991), pp. 165–6. Jaber claims that Syria and Iran helped with logistics and planning, but did not specify the target of the attack. Mohsen Rafiq-Dust, the first commander of the IRGC contingent in Lebanon admitted in 1988 that Iran had trained the suicide bombers, but then insisted that they had not ordered the attacks (Wright, op. cit., pp. 119–20). Rafiq-Dust's statements should be taken as a clear sign that at the very least, the Iranians trained the bombers, but given that Rafiq-Dust does have a strong incentive to deny responsibility for the attack itself, we should not assume that this constitutes the sum total of Iran's involvement. Additional information came after the fact. On September 20, 1984, another truck bomb exploded at the new U.S. Embassy in Christian East Beirut. Again, Islamic *Jihad* took credit. Immediately after that attack American photo interpreters realized that a mock-up of the embassy's defenses and obstacle system had been built at the Shaykh Abdallah barracks—the home of the Pasdaran in Lebanon. Thus, whether Islamic *Jihad* was another name for a part of Hizballah or not, they clearly were connected to Hizballah and, more important, to Iran. Turner, op. cit., pp. 170–8, especially p. 177.

240. Byman, op. cit., pp. 87–91.

241. Hiro, op. cit., p. 143.

242. Ibid., p. 46.

243. Ibid., pp. 62–3.

244. Seale, op. cit., p. 269.

245. Hanna Batatu, "Syria's Muslim Brethren," *MERIP Reports* 110, (November/December, 1982), p. 20, cited in Weinberger, op. cit., p. 236; Itamar Rabinovich, "Limits to Military Power: Syria's Role," in P. Edward Haley and Lewis W. Snyder, op. cit., pp. 64–5.

246. Alasdair Drysdale, "The Asad Regime and Its Troubles," *MERIP Reports* 110 (November–December, 1982), p. 4, cited in Weinberger, op. cit.

247. Nikolaos Van Dam, *The Struggle for Power in Syria* (London: Croom Helm, 1981), p. 92.

248. Batatu, op. cit., p. 20; in Weinberger, op. cit., p. 237.

249. Seale, op. cit., pp. 316–7.

250. Ibid., p. 316.

251. Ibid., p. 324.

252. Ibid., p. 325 citing interviews with Muhammad Muwaldi, Governor of Aleppo, April 18, 1985; Nadim Akkash, Governor of Dayr al-Zur, April 23, 1985; Anwar Ahmadov, Soviet Consul in Aleppo, April 20, 1985. Seale, op. cit., p. 325.

253. Ibid., p. 325.

254. Ibid., p. 328.

255. Thomas L. Friedman, *From Beirut to Jerusalem* (New York: Farrar Straus Giroux, 1989), p. 79; Seale, op. cit., p. 329.

256. Seale, op. cit., p. 331.

257. Friedman, op. cit., p. 80.

258. *Egyptian Gazette*, March 23, 1982; *The Observer* (London), May 4, 1982; *al-Dustur* (London), March 19, 1983 cited in Moshe Ma'oz, *Syria and Israel: From War to Peacemaking* (Oxford: Clarendon Press, 1995), p. 176; Friedman, op. cit., p. 90.

259. Drysdale, op. cit., p. 9; Friedman, op. cit., pp. 81–8; Seale, op. cit., pp. 332–3.

260. Seale, op. cit., p. 333.

261. Rabinovich, op. cit., pp. 100–1.

262. Bilal Saab, interview with Ali Bayanouni, leader of the Syrian Muslim Brotherhood in exile in London, May 2006. From correspondence between Kenneth M. Pollack and Bilal Saab, June 1, 2006.

263. Interview with Salim al-Lawzi (London, July 1, 1976), cited in Seale, op. cit., p. 286.

264. Hiro, op. cit., p. 46.

265. Ma'oz, op. cit., p. 176.

266. Drysdale, op. cit., p. 4.

267. Rabinovich, "Limits to Military Power" op. cit., p. 72.

268. Hiro, op. cit., pp. 74–5.

269. Interview with Anwar Ahmadov, Soviet Consul in Aleppo, April 20, 1985. Cited in Seale, op. cit., p. 335.

270. Interview with President Asad, Damascus, May 12, 1985. Cited in Seale, op. cit., p. 336.

271. Hiro, op. cit., pp. 92–3.

272. Ibid., p. 117.

273. Ibid., p. 130.

274. Ibid., p. 111–13.

275. Ibid., p. 118–21.

276. Ibid., p. 129–34.

277. Ibid., p. 145–59.

278. Ibid., p. 159–77.

279. Ibid., p. 180–91.

280. Byman, op. cit., p. 86.

281. Ihsan A. Hijazi, "Lebanon War Spurs New Emigration," op. cit.; Hiro, op. cit., p. 183. From June 4 to August 15, 1982, United Nations Children's Fund counted 29,500 dead and wounded in Beirut alone, 40 percent of whom were children, quoted in Michael Johnson, *Class and Client in Beirut* (London: Ithaca Press, 1986), p. 204.

282. Howard Goller, "Israel Seeks Terms for Pulling out of Lebanon," Reuters, March 2, 1998; Gal Luft, "Israel's Security Zone in Lebanon—A Tragedy?" *Middle East Quarterly*, VII/3 (September 2000).

283. Yair Aharoni, *The Israeli Economy: Dreams and Reality* (New York: Routledge, 1991), p. 85; Yoram Ben-Porath (ed.), *The Israeli Economy* (Cambridge: Harvard University Press, 1986), pp. 20–1; Gil Merom, *How Democracies Lose Small Wars: State, Society, and the Failures of France in Algeria, Israel in Lebanon, and the United States in Vietnam* (Cambridge: Cambridge University Press, 2003), pp. 164–5.

284. Drysdale, op. cit., p. 5, cited in Weinberger, op. cit., p. 234.

285. David A. Korn, "Syria and Lebanon: A Fateful Entanglement," *World Today*, 42/8–9, 1986, p. 139; Rabinovich, op. cit., p. 101; Seale, op. cit., pp. 286–7, 320–31.

286. *BBC News*, "Country Profile: Somalia," available at http://news.bbc.co.uk/2/hi/africa/country_profiles/1072592.stm.

287. For a useful graphic, see The Economist Intelligence Unit, *Country Profile: Eritrea, Somalia, Djibouti (1996–97)*, p. 24.

288. In response to Siad Barre's atrocities, including the open slaughter of young men in Mogadishu, the United States suspended military aid in 1988 and economic aid in 1989. "Unlike other countries in Africa where such stoppages were gradual," notes Godwin Rapando Murunga. Hussein Adam adds, "In Somalia, an abrupt stoppage of all aid followed a history of too much aid." Godwin Rapando Murunga, "Conflict in Somalia and Crime in Kenya: Understanding the Trans-Territoriality of Crime," *African and Asian Studies*, 4/1–2 (2005), p. 143 and citing Hussein M. Adam, "Somalia: A Terrible Beauty Being Born" in I. William Zartman (ed.) *Collapsed States: The Disintegration and Restoration of Legitimate Authority* (Boulder: Lynne Rienner, 1995), p. 75.

289. Walter S. Clarke and Robert Gosend, "Somalia: Can a Collapsed State Reconstitute Itself," in Robert I. Rotberg (ed.), *State Failure and State Weakness in a Time of Terror* (Washington, DC: Brookings Institution Press, 2003), p. 130.

290. In 1990 the International Institute for Strategic Studies estimated that government forces numbered 64,500, including 30,000 conscripts. In 1996, only Somaliland had a national armed force, estimated to number between 5,000 and 15,000 men. Economist Intelligence Unit, op. cit., p. 28.

291. International Crisis Group, *Can the Somali Crisis Be Contained?*, ICG Africa Report 116 (August 10, 2006), p. 8, available at http://www.crisisgroup.org/home/index.cfm?id=4333&l=1.

292. The Arta conference, named after the city it was held in, was deemed a success in part because the organizers invited representatives on the basis of clans, not factions. The resulting interim government accorded its clan a certain number of seats in parliament. Ken Menkhaus, "Somalia: In the Crosshairs of the War on Terrorism," *Current History*, 101/655 (Summer 2002), p. 210.

293. International Crisis Group, op. cit., p. 3.

294. Ibid., pp. 9–10.

295. Ibid., p. 1.

296. Ibid., p. 19.

297. Ibid., p. 1.

298. Karen De Young, "U.S. Sees Growing Threat in Somalia," *Washington Post*, December 18, 2006.

299. International Crisis Group, op. cit., p. 5.

300. International Crisis Group, op. cit., p. 14.

301. See United Nations High Commissioner for Refugees, *2005 Global Refugee Trends*, table 2 available at http://www.unhcr.org/statistics/STATISTICS/4486ceb12.pdf.

302. *BBC News*, "Somali Refugees Face Bleak Future," January 2, 2000.

303. Eric Westervelt, "Somali Refugees Hang on to Hope in Camps," National Public Radio, December 11, 2006.

304. Reuben Kyama, "Ethnic Somalis Threaten to Destabilize Eastern Ethiopia," *Terrorism Focus*, The Jamestown Foundation, November 28, 2006, p. 6, available at http://www.jamestown.org/terrorism/news/uploads/tf_003_046.pdf>.

305. United Nations High Commissioner for Refugees Global Appeal 2006, *Somalia*, available at http://www.unhcr.org/publ/PUBL/4371d1a70.pdf.

306. Ken Menkhaus, "Somalia, Global Security and the War on Terrorism," in *Somalia: State Collapse and the Threat of Terrorism*, Adelphi Paper 364 (March 2004), p. 9.

307. For more on renewed U.S. interest in the Horn of Africa post-9/11, see Menkhaus, *Somalia, Global Security and the War on Terrorism*, pp. 49–75.

308. See for example, "Somalia: US Policy Options," Hearing before the Subcommittee on African Affairs of the Committee on Foreign Relations, U.S. Senate (107th Congress) February 6, 2002, available at http://frwebgate.access.gpo.gov/cgi-bin/getdoc.cgi?dbname=107_senate_hearings&docid=f:78905.pdf; International Crisis group, *Somalia's Islamists*, ICG Africa Report 100 (December 12, 2005), available at http://www.crisisgroup.org/home/index.cfm?id=3830&l=1; International Crisis Group, *Somalia: Countering Terrorism in a Failed State*, ICG Africa Report 45 (May 23, 2002), available at http://www.crisisgroup.org/home/index.cfm?id=1690&l=1.

309. Jamie McIntyre and Barbara Starr (contributors), "Pentagon Official: U.S. Attacks al Qaeda Suspects in Somalia," *CNN*, January 9, 2007, available at http://www.cnn.com/2007/WORLD/africa/01/08/somalia.strike/index.html.

310. International Crisis Group, *Somalia's Islamists*, p. 3.

311. Ibid., p. 11.

312. Robert F. Worth, "U.N. Says Somalis Helped Hezbollah Fighters," *New York Times*, November 15, 2006.

313. See, for example, Murunga, op. cit.

314. See Kyama, op. cit.

315. "Ethiopian Troops Fight Somali Rebels on Border," *The New York Times*, December 22, 1996.

316. The Economist Intelligence Unit, *Country Profile: Somalia (2006)*, p. 12.

317. *BBC Monitoring*, "Ethiopia: Ogaden Rebels Claim Battle Successes Against Government Forces," May 10, 2006.

318. Menkhaus, *Somalia: In the Crosshairs of the War on Terrorism*, p. 211.

319. International Crisis Group, *Somalia's Islamists*, p. 9.

320. "Addis Hails Somali Peace Deal," *Somaliland Times*, November 9, 2002, available at http://www.somalilandtimes.net/Archive/41/4104.htm.

321. International Crisis Group, *Can the Somali Crisis Be Contained?*, p. 20.

322. Menkhaus, *Somalia, Global Security and the War on Terrorism*, p. 9.

323. Stephan John Stedman, "Conflict and Conciliation in Sub-Saharan Africa," in Michael E. Brown (ed.), *The International Dimensions of Internal Conflict* (Cambridge, MA: MIT Press, 1996), p. 254.

324. Some UNITAF supporters claimed that the operation saved as many as 500,000 people, but the reality is probably closer to between 10,000 and 25,000. See Stedman, op. cit., p. 257.

325. Ibid., p. 256.

326. International Crisis Group, *Can the Somali Crisis Be Contained?*, p. i.

327. Ibid., p. 11.

328. Ibid., p. 12.

329. Susan L. Woodward, "Bosnia and Herzegovina: How Not to End Civil War," in Barbara F. Walter and Jack Snyder (eds.), *Civil Wars, Insecurity and Intervention* (New York: Columbia University Press, 1999), p. 75.

330. Misha Glenny, *The Fall of Yugoslavia: The Third Balkan War*, 3rd rev. ed. (New York: Penguin, 1996), pp. 63–4; Sabrina P. Ramet, *Thinking About Yugoslavia* (London: Cambridge, 2005), p. 56; I. William Zartman, *Cowardly Lions: Missed Opportunities to Prevent Deadly Conflict and State Collapse* (Boulder: Lynne Rienner, 2005), pp. 140–1.

331. Ramet, op. cit., p. 56.

332. Laura Silber and Allan Little, *Yugoslavia: Death of a Nation*, rev. ed. (New York: Penguin, 1997), p. 29.

333. Steven L. Burg and Paul S. Shoup, *The War in Bosnia-Herzegovina: Ethnic Conflict and International Intervention* (Armonk, NY: M.E. Sharpe, 1999), p. 17; Ramet, op. cit., p. 71.

334. Central Intelligence Agency, Office of Russian and European Analysis, *Balkan Battlegrounds: A Military History of the Yugoslav Conflict, 1990–1995*, vol. 1 (Washington, D.C.: CIA, 2002), pp. 44–5; Alastair Finalan, *The Collapse of Yugoslavia 1991–1999*, Osprey Essential Histories (United Kingdom: Osprey, 2004), pp. 13–16; Woodward, op. cit., pp. 80–4.

335. Glenny, op. cit., p. 41.

336. Ibid., p. 83.

337. Ibid., pp. 11, 68, 83; John Mueller, "The Banality of 'Ethnic War,'" *International Security*, 25/1 (Summer 2000), pp. 42–50; Silber and Little, op. cit., pp. 35, 97–98, 186, 212–14, 224–46, 293–301; Woodward, op. cit., pp. 80–1; Zartman, op. cit., p. 148.

338. Burg and Shoup, op. cit., pp. 173–7; Finalan, op. cit., pp. 27–8; Glenny, op. cit., p. 123; Mueller, op. cit., pp. 42–50; Silber and Little, op. cit., pp. 35, 134–43, 170–6, 186, 212–14, 224–46, 293–9, 301.

339. As an example, when Croatia and Bosnia went to war in 1994, the Bosnians formed up units of "cleansed" men, who were deeply embittered and treated the Croats and Serbs as they were themselves treated. In addition, the Bosnians created the "Seventh Muslim Brigade," which consisted of Muslim zealots, who wore Islamic insignia and beards, were hostile to Westerners, had their families attend Islamic education classes, and

their women take the veil. In effect, they were people driven to become Islamic fundamentalists as a result of the war. Silber and Little, op. cit., p. 298.

340. Mueller, op. cit., p. 43.

341. Ibid., fn. 15, p. 49.

342. Central Intelligence Agency, op. cit., p. xv; Glenny, op. cit., pp. 77, 94–5, 122–5; Mueller, pp. 42–50, 64; Silber and Little, op. cit., pp. 97–8, 103, 145, 171–8, 222–40, 293.

343. Warren Zimmerman, *Origins of a Catastrophe* (New York: Times Books, 1996), p. 121.

344. Glenny, op. cit., pp. 21, 31, 123; Silber and Little, op. cit., pp. 137–8, 142; Zimmerman, op. cit., pp. 116–23.

345. For authors exploding the myth that "ancient hatreds" were the primary cause of the Yugoslav civil war, and that this therefore made its wars insoluble and external intervention pointless, see Burg and Shoup, op. cit., p. 17; Glenny, op. cit., pp. 19, 142–3; Richard Holbrooke, *To End a War* (New York: Random House, 1998), pp. 22–3, 62; Mueller, op. cit., pp. 65–66; Silber and Little, op. cit., pp. 26, 95–6, 228; Zimmerman, op. cit., p. 120.

346. Holbrooke, op. cit., pp. 22–3.

347. Central Intelligence Agency, op. cit., pp. 49–50.

348. Robert M. Hayden, "Imagined Communities and Real Victims: Self-Determination and Ethnic Cleansing in Yugoslavia," *American Ethnologist*, 23/4 (November 1996), p. 789; and United States Central Intelligence Agency, *Ethnic Composition in the Former Yugoslavia* (map), 1993.

349. Petrovi, Ru_a, "The National Composition of Yugoslavia's Population, 1991," *Yugoslav Survey 1992* (1): pp. 3–24, cited in Robert M. Hayden, op. cit., p. 787.

350. Glenny, op. cit., pp. 111–12, 163, 188–92; Holbrooke, op. cit., pp. 31–2; Silber and Little, op. cit., pp. 198–201, 205.

351. Finalan, op. cit., pp. 37–9; Mueller, op. cit., p. 50; Silber and Little, op. cit., p. 205.

352. Zartman, op. cit., pp. 165.

353. Ivo H. Daalder and Michael E. O'Hanlon, *Winning Ugly: NATO's War to Save Kosovo* (Washington, DC: Brookings, 2000), p. 8. Also see, Glenny, op. cit., p. 69.

354. Daalder and O'Hanlon, op. cit., pp. 10–41; Zartman, op. cit., p. 165.

355. In addition, another group of ethnic Albanians calling themselves the UCPMB (Liberation Army of Preševo, Medvedja, and Bujanovac), mounted a guerrilla war against Serbia in 1991–2001 to try to detach the three areas of Preševo, Medvedja, and Bujanovac and join them to Kosovo.

356. International Crisis Group, *After Milosevic: A Practical Agenda for Lasting Balkans Peace*, Europe Report 108 (April 1, 2001), p. 9, available at http://www.crisisgroup.org/home/index.cfm?id=3186&l=1.

357. Ibid., pp. 8, 189; P. H. Liotta, "Spillover Effect: Aftershocks in Kosovo, Macedonia, and Serbia," *European Security*, 12/1, (Spring 2003), pp. 94–102; Zvonimir Jankuloski, "Why Macedonia Matters: Spill-Over of the Refugee Crisis from Kosovo to Macedonia," in *The Kosovo Crisis: Papers from a Workshop Held on 18 May 1998 at Green College, University of Oxford*, RSP Working Paper 1, Refugee Studies Programme, Queen Elizabeth House, University of Oxford, June 1999, pp. 28–35.

358. International Crisis Group, *After Milosevic*, pp. 190–1; Liotta, op. cit., pp. 94–102.

359. Maja Povrzanovic, "Ethnography of a War: Croatia 1991–92," *Anthropology of East Europe Review*, 11/1–2 (Autumn, 1993), available at http://condor.depaul.edu/~rrotenbe/aeer/aeer11_1/povrzanovic.html.

360. Silber and Little, op. cit., p. 198.

361. Finalan, op. cit., p. 64; Holbrooke, op. cit., p. 309; Silber and Little, op. cit., p. 252; Myron Weiner, "Bad Neighbors, Bad Neighborhoods: An Inquiry into the Causes of Refugee Flows," *International Security*, 21/1 (Summer 1996), p. 8.

362. Associated Press, "Kosovo Refugee Statistics," April 19, 1999; Daalder and O'Hanlon, op. cit., pp. 108–9.

363. United States Department of State, *The Former Yugoslav Republic of Macedonia*, Country Reports on Human Rights Practices—2001, Washington, DC: U.S. Department of State, Bureau of Democracy, Human Rights, and Labor, March 4, 2002, available at http://www.state.gov/g/drl/rls/hrrpt/2001/eur/8293.htm.

364. Glenny, op. cit., p. 168.

365. "General Description of the Situation of Bosnian Refugees in Germany," European Migration Centre (Europäisches Migrationszentrum), available at http://www.emz-berlin.de/projekte_e/pj2/pj2_1.htm; German Federal Ministry of Interior, available at http://www.zuwanderung.de/english/2_neues-gesetz-a-z/fluechtlinge.html; Glenny, op. cit., pp. 188–92; and Holbrooke, op.cit, p. 275.

366. International Monetary Fund, "The Economic Consequences of the Kosovo Crisis: An Updated Assessment," (Prepared by the staff of the International Monetary Fund in consultation with the World Bank staff, May 25, 1999), pp. 13–14, available at http://www.imf.org/external/pubs/ft/kosovo/052599.htm; and Associated Press, "Kosovo Refugee Statistics," op. cit.

367. International Crisis Group, *After Milosevic*, p. 9.

368. International Crisis Group, *Macedonia: Towards Destabilization? The Kosovo Crisis Takes Its Toll on Macedonia*, Europe Report 67 (May 21, 1999), pp. 2–9, available http://www.crisisgroup.org/home/index.cfm?id=1703&l=1; Jankuloski, op. cit., pp. 28–35.

369. Finalan, op. cit., p. 39; and Richard Holbrooke, "Foreword," in Derek Chollet, *The Road to the Dayton Accords: A Study of American Statecraft* (New York: Palgrave, 2005), p. ix.

370. See Evan S. Kohlmann, *Al-Qaida's Jihad in Europe* (New York: Berg, 2004).

371. International Monetary Fund, op. cit., pp. 15–16, available at http://www.imf.org/external/pubs/ft/kosovo/052599.htm.

372. "Romania: Casualty of War," *The Economist*, 351/8123 (London, June 12, 1999), p. 68; Vernon Loeb "War over Kosovo Turns Balkan Bit Players into 'Frontline' States," *Washington Post*, April 24, 1999.

373. International Crisis Group, *Macedonia: Towards Destabilization?*, p. 2.

374. Ibid., p. 8.

375. International Monetary Fund, op. cit., pp. 1–16.

376. International Monetary Fund, "Economic Prospects for the Countries of Southeast Europe in the Aftermath of the Kosovo Crisis," September 22, 1999, available at http://www.imf.org/external/pubs/ft/kosovo/092299.htm.

377. Daalder and O'Hanlon, op. cit., p. 9.

378. Glenny, op. cit., p. 239.

379. Duygu Bazolu Sezer, "Implications for Turkey's Relations with Western Europe," in *The Implications of the Yugoslav Crisis for Western Europe's Foreign Relations*, Chaillot Paper 17, Institute for Security Studies, European Union, October 1994, pp. 35–7.

380. Chollet, op. cit., fn. 19, p. 209.

381. Liotta, op. cit., pp. 82–108.

382. Glenny, op. cit., pp. 71–2.

383. Ibid., p. 255.

384. Ibid., pp. 240–41; Chollet, op. cit., p. 66; Daalder and O'Hanlon, op. cit., pp. 17, 25.

385. Ibid., p. 9; Silber and Little, op. cit., pp. 332–3.

386. Ivo H. Daalder, *Getting to Dayton: The Making of America's Bosnia Policy* (Washington, DC: The Brookings Institution Press, 2000), p. 7.

387. Michael Kelly, "Surrender and Blame," *The New Yorker*, December 19, 1994, p. 51.

388. Daalder, op. cit., 187–8.

389. Ibid.., p. 187. Also see Chollet, op. cit., p. 185.

390. Chollet, op. cit., p. 83; Talbott is now president of the Brookings Institution.

391. Ibid., pp. 83–4.

392. See also Silber and Little, op. cit., pp. 312, 328.

393. International Crisis Group, *After Milosevic*, pp. 190–1; Liotta, op. cit., pp. 94–102; Sezer, op. cit., pp. 35–7; Silber and Little, op. cit., p. 111.

394. Glenny, op. cit., p. 188–92.

395. Mueller, op. cit., pp. 65–6. A reference to Robert Kaplan's book *Balkan Ghosts: A Journey through History* (New York: St. Martin's Press, 1993).

396. Chollet, op. cit., pp. 1, 3–4; Daalder, op. cit., pp. 4–10; Holbrooke, op. cit., pp. 3–32; Silber and Little, op. cit., pp. 198–202.

397. Glenny, op. cit., pp. 100–1; Silber and Little, op. cit., pp. 198–202, 274.

398. Zartman, op. cit., p. 156.

399. Finalan, op. cit., p. 29; Daalder, op. cit., p. 5; Silber and Little, op. cit., pp. 202–4.

400. Silber and Little, op. cit., p. 261.

401. For concurring views see Finalan, op. cit., pp. 40–2; Silber and Little, op. cit., pp. 277–80, 325–8; Zartman, op. cit., p. 162.

402. Finalan, op. cit., p. 29.

403. Silber and Little, op. cit., pp. 269–73.

404. Glenny, op. cit., p. 210; Silber and Little, op. cit., p. 259.

405. Glenny, op. cit., p. 279. Also see Silber and Little, op. cit., p. 276.

406. Chollet, op. cit., p. 185; Daalder, op. cit., pp. 162–4; Silber and Little, op. cit., p. 387.

407. It is widely believed that the United States transformed the Croat Army and made it into the force that ultimately reversed the course of the war in 1995. That view appears greatly exaggerated. The reform of the Croatian Army began in 1993, long before they hired the U.S. firm Military Professional Resources, Inc., in 1995. Central Intelligence Agency, op. cit., pp. 272–6. Also see the points made by Chollet, op. cit., pp. 35–36, fn. 19, p. 209, which indicate a much lesser degree of American awareness of Croat military activities and improvement than is often claimed.

408. Central Intelligence Agency, op. cit., pp. 377–9, 394–5.

409. See, for instance, Chollet, op. cit., p. 87.

410. Central Intelligence Agency, op. cit., pp. 290–377; Glenny, op. cit., p. 279; Silber and Little, op. cit., pp. 357–60.

411. The Croat offensive had run out of steam by the first week in October 1995. A number of Croat attacks had been stopped cold, and even the more successful assaults were being brought to a halt as the Serbs regained their balance and shifted reserves to blunt the Croat thrusts. Indeed, Holbrooke and his team urged the Croat-Muslim Federation forces to capture Prejidor, Sanski Most, and Bosanski Novi, but Croat and Muslim forces were simply unable to do so. Central Intelligence Agency, op. cit., pp. 367–77, 389–92, 393–4, and fn. 821, p. 425; Chollet, op. cit., pp. 105–6, 108; Holbrooke, op. cit., p. 191. On October 4, 1995, Holbrooke had Lt. Gen. Donald Kerrick brief Bosnian President Alija Izetbegovic on the possibility of continuing the offensive, and Kerrick famously told Izetbegovic, "If you continue the war, you will be shooting craps with your nation's destiny." Holbrooke, op. cit., pp. 194–5.

412. Central Intelligence Agency, op. cit., p. 396; Daalder, op. cit., pp. 119–29; Finalan, op. cit., p. 83; Glenny, op. cit., pp. 270, 277–8, 289; Holbrooke, op. cit., pp. 153–312; Silber and Little, op. cit., pp. 368–9.

413. Daalder, op. cit., p. 180; Finalan, op. cit., pp. 315–19; Silber and Little, op. cit., p. 379.

414. Daalder and O'Hanlon, op. cit., pp. 28–9, 45–62, 135.

415. Ibid., pp. 63–100, especially pp. 91–6.

416. Benjamin S. Lambeth, *NATO's Air War for Kosovo* (Santa Monica: RAND, 2001), p. 62.

417. Daalder and O'Hanlon, op. cit., pp. 4–5; Stephen T. Hosmer, *Why Milosevic Decided to Settle When He Did* (Santa Monica: RAND, 2001), available at http://www.rand.org/pubs/monograph_reports/MR1351/.

418. International Crisis Group, *Kosovo: The Challenge of Transition*, Europe Report 170 (February 17, 2006), available at http://www.crisisgroup.org/home/index.cfm?l=1&id=3955.

About the Authors

Daniel L. Byman is a Nonresident Senior Fellow at the Saban Center for Middle East Policy at the Brookings Institution. He is also the Director of the Security Studies Program and the Center for Peace and Security Studies as well as an Associate Professor in the School of Foreign Service at Georgetown University. Byman has served as a Professional Staff Member with the 9/11 Commission and with the Joint 9/11 Inquiry Staff of the House and Senate Intelligence Committees. Before joining the Inquiry Staff he was the Research Director of the Center for Middle East Public Policy at the RAND Corporation. Byman has also served as a Middle East analyst for the U.S. government. He has written widely on a range of topics related to terrorism, international security, and the Middle East. He is the author of *Keeping the Peace: Lasting Solutions to Ethnic Conflict* and coauthor of *The Dynamics of Coercion: American Foreign Policy and the Limits of Military Might.* He recently published *Deadly Connections: States That Sponsor Terrorism* (2005). He received a B.A. from Amherst and a Ph.D. from the Massachusetts Institute of Technology.

KENNETH M. POLLACK is the Director of Research at the Saban Center for Middle East Policy and a Brookings Senior Fellow. He has served as Director of Persian Gulf Affairs and Near East and South Asian Affairs at the National Security Council, Senior Research Professor at the National Defense University, and Persian Gulf military analyst for the Central Intelligence Agency. Pollack's most recent book, *The Persian Puzzle: The Conflict between Iran and America,* was published in 2004. He is also the principal author of *A Switch in Time: A New Strategy for America in Iraq* (2006) and the author of *The Threatening Storm: The Case for Invading Iraq* (2002) and *Arabs at War: Military Effectiveness, 1948–1991* (2002). Pollack received a B.A. from Yale University and a Ph.D. from the Massachusetts Institute of Technology.

Index